LEGALIZE IT?

THE AMERICAN UNIVERSITY PRESS PUBLIC POLICY SERIES

LEGALIZE IT?

Debating American Drug Policy

Arnold S. Trebach

and

James A. Inciardi

The American University Press

Copyright © 1993 by
The American University Press
4400 Massachusetts Avenue, N.W.
McDowell Room 117
Washington, D.C. 20016

Distributed by arrangement with
National Book Network
4720 Boston Way
Lanham, MD 20706

3 Henrietta Street
London WC2E 8LU England

Library of Congress Cataloging-in-Publication Data

Trebach, Arnold S.
Legalize it? : debating American drug policy / Arnold S. Trebach,
James A. Inciardi.
p.   cm.
Includes bibliographical references and index.
1. Drug legalization—United States. I. Inciardi, James A. II. Title.
HV5825.T745   1993   363.4'5'0973—dc20   93–7639 CIP

ISBN 1–879383–13–6 (cloth : alk. paper)
ISBN 1–879383–14–4 (pbk. : alk. paper)

 The paper used in this publication meets the minimum requirements of
American National Standard for Information Sciences—Permanence
of Paper for Printed Library Materials, ANSI Z39.48–1984.

Contents

Part Two: Against Legalization of Drugs
James A. Inciardi

Preface

Legalize It? Debating American Drug Policy is the second volume in
The American University Press Public Policy Series, which is dedi-
cated to presenting important, controversial issues using a two-author
debate format. The authors of this volume opted not to read and rebut
each other's manuscripts, although future volumes in this series—on
affirmative action, immigration policy, and children's television—may
include such rebuttals.

Arnold S. Trebach and James A. Inciardi stand at opposite ends of
the drug debate. Professor Trebach's views have evolved from selective
decriminalization to a pro-legalization position for all drugs; Professor
Inciardi has consistently advocated a strong anti-legalization position.

As president of the Drug Policy Foundation, Arnold Trebach is an
active and passionate spokesperson for the legalization movement. He
argues essentially that legalization would reduce drug-related crime,
would help persons addicted to drugs, and is consistent with main-
stream American values that grant Americans liberty and freedom of
choice on a wide range of issues involving personal behavior. Professor
Trebach's initial forays into the drug debate focused on the medical
uses of heroin and marijuana: to relieve the pain of cancer patients and
to help treat glaucoma. Over the years, as a function of his contacts
with drug users, his study of U.S. laws and policies vis-à-vis drugs and
their effects, and his exposure to the free-market orientation of Nobel
Prize-winning economist Milton Friedman and psychiatrist Thomas
Szasz, Trebach's position has evolved to that espoused in this book:
legalization of all currently illegal drugs.

James Inciardi adheres to and defends his position as ardently as
Professor Trebach. Inciardi believes the road to legalization is the road

to social disorder: it would be socially and economically detrimental for American society to adopt a legalization policy for any currently illegal drugs, from marijuana to crack cocaine. He demonstrates that illicit drugs now are used by less than eight percent of Americans and that these numbers are decreasing under current policy. Essentially, he says, we are winning the war against drugs, and legalization would mean surrender and, more important, would likely mean a rapid and dramatic increase in drug use. Legalization would legitimate a dangerous activity and would entail enormous costs in health and safety. Inciardi argues that drugs do not necessarily cause crime; instead, the people who engage in criminal activities are often the same people who consume and distribute drugs. The consumption would increase rather than decrease with legalization.

Few scholars could pose the issues in the debate over drug legalization more sharply than Arnold Trebach and James Inciardi. Some readers may find that these passionate arguments on each side have changed their minds about legalization. Others may draw from them support and evidence to strengthen their current views. All of us will come away more enlightened about the drug debate.

Rita J. Simon
Series Editor

About the Authors

Arnold S. Trebach is a professor in the Department of Justice, Law, and Society at the School of Public Affairs at The American University, Washington, D.C. He is also president of the Drug Policy Foundation. His books include *The Rationing of Justice* (1964), *The Heroin Solution* (1982), and *The Great Drug War* (1987). With Kevin B. Zeese, he has served as editor of *A Reformer's Catalogue* (1989), *The Great Issues of Drug Policy* (1990), *Drug Prohibition and the Conscience of Nations* (1990), *New Frontiers of Drug Policy* (1991), and *Strategies for Change* (1992). He holds a J.D. degree from the New England School of Law (1951), and an M.A. (1957) and a Ph.D. in politics from Princeton University (1958). He was admitted to practice before the Massachusetts Bar in 1951. From 1986 to 1988 he served on the Working Group on Substance Abuse and Criminality of the National Academy of Sciences. In 1986, Dr. Trebach founded the Drug Policy Foundation, an independent think tank devoted to promoting peaceful and effective drug policy reform, including legalization and medicalization of some drugs.

Among his previous positions are: chief, Administration of Justice Section, U.S. Commission on Civil Rights (1960–63); administrator, National Defender Project, National Legal Aid and Defender Association (1963–64); chief consultant on the Administration of Justice, White House Conference on Civil Rights (1965–66); founder and president, University Research Corporation (1965–69); co-founder and chairman, National Committee on the Treatment of Intractable Pain (1977–78). He has also served as a consultant to the U.S. Department of Justice, the U.S. Congress, and other governmental agencies.

The American University has twice selected him as its outstanding scholar for the year, in 1978–79 and in 1987–88.

James A. Inciardi is director of the Center for Drug and Alcohol Studies at the University of Delaware; professor in the Department of Sociology and Criminal Justice at Delaware; adjunct professor in the Department of Epidemiology and Public Health at the University of Miami School of Medicine; Distinguished Professor at the State University of Rio de Janeiro, Brazil; and a member of the South Florida AIDS Research Consortium. Dr. Inciardi received his Ph.D. in sociology at New York University and has extensive research, clinical, field, teaching, and law enforcement experience in substance abuse and criminal justice. He has been director of the National Center for the Study of Acute Drug Reactions at the University of Miami School of Medicine, vice president of the Washington, D.C.-based Resource Planning Corporation, associate director of research for the New York State Narcotic Addiction Control Commission, and director of the Division of Criminal Justice at the University of Delaware. He has done extensive consulting work, both nationally and internationally, and has published some 30 books and more than 140 articles and chapters in the areas of substance abuse, criminology, criminal justice, history, folklore, social policy, HIV/AIDS, medicine, and law.

Part One

For Legalization of Drugs

Arnold S. Trebach

For my children and grandchildren
David, Paul, Adam, Jacob, Daniel, and Joshua

Acknowledgments

The idea for this book came from Rita J. Simon, my colleague at The American University, who showed her usual resourcefulness in convincing me of its worth and her patience as I took too long to write my part of it. She showed how intellectual leadership can be combined with the gentle application of guilt in the cause of achieving good works.

The energetic young staff at the independent Drug Policy Foundation provided much assistance on short notice, as they often do on a variety of projects. Dave Fratello was particularly helpful as editor, critic, and utility outfielder. He suffered graciously the grievous deprivation of being taken away from the more exciting daily combat with leading drug warriors in which the DPF public information gang is so often engaged. The exacting Rob Stewart, also from the public information shop, was instrumental in bringing the manuscript into compliance with style requirements, a task for which some of us are ill-equipped and for which he displayed the utmost professionalism. Rob also checked, double-checked, and triple-checked the numbers in this text with tenacity, preventing some potentially disastrous mistakes from making it into print. Meredith Feldman, a summer intern, was energetic in finding arcane bits of data from the past and in checking out a large number of nettlesome details. Mike Winnick, another summer intern, assisted in the process of data gathering and source checking. Staff member Stacie Norton helped locate material and reviewed much of it for useful pieces of information. Stuart Sugg provided frequent guidance on the intricacies and peculiarities of our wordprocessing system. Kevin Zeese, Pam Griffin, and the entire DPF staff were helpful and patient with a president whose eyes were glued for too long on the screen of a wordprocessor. They are all glad it's over, but none more than my wife, Marjorie Rosner, and my new son, Adam, my latest and currently most enjoyable publication.

1. On Becoming Radicalized

This is an argument for the full legalization of currently illegal drugs for sale to adults within regulations similar to those for alcohol. Only in recent years have I become an advocate of such a radical position. The process of my radicalization is, I submit, worth telling—for I suspect many millions of people are now going through that same process.

To explain this process of radicalization, I must tell of personal experiences, thoughts, and even passions, most of which are discussed in this introductory chapter. For those who find talk of such matters inappropriate or even unscholarly in books of this nature, I beg forgiveness.

I view data and statistics as important. Yet I do not believe that the most important elements of the case for any new public policy are based upon statistics but rather upon moral philosophy. Thus, while there are ample data in my section of this book, I have no illusions that the case for legalization can be won or lost on the basis of the amount of cold data I or my opponents present. No major ideological battle has been won in this country solely because the victors had the best data sets. In the end, the case for radical change in the matter of drugs will stand or fall on the extent to which the people of this country and of other civilized nations come to believe that drug prohibition and the drug war[1] are simply inconsistent with the moral heart of a democratic society.

1. By "drug prohibition" I mean the situation created when the government has passed laws making the production, manufacture, sale, and possession of certain chemicals and plants criminal offenses punishable by fines, prison terms, or both—even when, indeed especially when, the people involved are willing, voluntary, and eager participants.

7

A Personal Odyssey

In 1972, during my first year teaching at The American University, I wandered by accident into the study of drugs. My assumption at the time was that the basic rationale underlying the drug laws was rooted in science, compassion, and democratic principles. But very soon, as I became familiar with the story of how drug policy, especially in America, has been developed, that innocent assumption was shattered. I came to see that while there were elements of rationality, planning, and good intentions in the creation of drug laws and the escalation of enforcement tactics, the dominant features were hysteria, demagoguery, racial bias, political opportunism, disregard for the weight of scientific evidence, and ignorance of the unintended effects of the policies. Moreover, I found that U.S. drug laws were unquestioned by the vast majority of people. Prohibition of certain drugs was accepted as an immutable fact of American life.

I became deeply disturbed by the inhumane treatment that the most powerful members of society saw appropriate to unleash against drug users, especially addicts. I learned that during the 1920s, when legal condemnations were in force against both alcohol and narcotics, the pursuit of those who used these disapproved chemicals was particularly harsh. One narcotics enforcement official during that time boasted proudly that he sought "to trap addicts like animals" (Trebach 1982, 88). American excesses in this regard offended the sensibilities of those in more gentle societies, such as the United Kindom, where in a parliamentary debate in 1920, Captain Walter Elliot, M.P., called Americans "the barbarians of the West" because of their "extraordinary savage idea of stamping out all people who happen to disagree . . . with their social theories" regarding narcotics and alcohol (quoted in Judson 1974, 17–18).

While the prohibition on alcohol soon disappeared, the demonization of other drug use and drug users was widened after 1933. In addition to nonmedical drug users, this affected millions of sick people in pain and their doctors who ran afoul of bizarre enforcement practices that invaded the normal compassionate practice of the healing arts.

It continues to be American drug-control doctrine that people who use drugs disapproved by the majority in power have lost their status

---

By "drug war" I mean the situation created when the government puts its awesome power behind the drug laws, enforces them with zeal, and actually imprisons large numbers of drug offenders as if they were enemies in a real war.

as citizens and as decent human beings and deserve the most severe forms of social sanctions—in part to save their own souls. More onerous sanctions are reserved for those who sell illegal drugs.

Those intellectuals and professionals who protest the allegedly just and proper punishment of these heretics are subjected to similar treatment, being deemed traitors, subversives, or fifth columnists in the war on drugs.

Within a short time of learning of the destructive results of our drug policies, I became a vocal critic of our basic attitudes toward drugs and drug users, and an advocate of fundamental reform of our drug laws and uncivilized enforcement tactics. The reforms I advocated for years could best be described now as moderate compromises, involving decriminalization and medicalization. For example, I argued for the decriminalization of marijuana, in this context meaning treating possession of marijuana for personal use as a noncriminal act or a minor violation, akin to a traffic offense.

However, my major concern of this time was not marijuana but the more powerful drugs, especially heroin and other narcotics. This was territory largely unvisited by drug policy reformers of the 1970s and early 1980s. Most prominently, I pleaded for a new, compassionate attitude toward all narcotic addicts and for allowing doctors to decide how to treat their addict patients.

Much of this advocacy was informed by my exposure to the British system for dealing with narcotics addiction, which I examined firsthand almost every year for more than a decade while leading the American University Institute on Drugs, Crime, and Justice in England.[2] These long study trips to England, and later to Holland and Australia, created repeated shocks to my system, almost as if I had taken periodic trips on a spaceship to other planets. I would leave Washington, which was awash with murder on the streets and embroiled in a drug war, and enter the calm and peace of the United Kingdom. Few American, or for that matter British, experts seem to appreciate the dramatic differences between the two countries in terms of drugs and crime. I have explained these differences in detail in works cited herein, but a few summary facts may be helpful.

Even though hard-drug addicts are not honored in the United King-

2. In 1974 I founded the Institute on Drugs, Crime, and Justice in England, which originally was offered every summer through The American University. Both students and professionals had the opportunity to observe British approaches to narcotics and justice firsthand. While not intended, over the years I received as much education as any participant.

dom, they are not considered a major threat to society and are often treated with compassion and understanding. This is so fundamentally different than the harsh American approach that it creates dramatically different expectations and practices. American writer Horace Freeland Judson expressed similar sentiments in a brilliantly perceptive book, *Heroin Addiction in Britain: What Americans Can Learn From the English Experience.* The last sentences of his book are:

> In the course of a conversation I had at yet another English drug-dependence clinic, a doctor said something in passing that seemed so natural that it was an hour later . . . that I woke to what he had said, and to what an overturning of my American expectations it represented. The doctor told me, "We have made it possible in this city for the addict to live without fear" (Judson 1974, 156).

For the most part that lack of fear is mutual: addicts may be pitied or even scorned, but they are rarely feared.

The British have somehow managed to create a society and a system of drug control where, unlike in the United States, there is very little connection between being a hard-drug addict and being a predatory criminal. Crime in general is low in the United Kingdom, and the police do not view most addicts as special criminal threats. While many of those involved in the drug scene are certainly seen as criminal, few are violent or engage in predatory crime.

On one occasion several years ago, I was a guest lecturer at an FBI-sponsored seminar in Quantico, Virginia. There I was confronted by a group of American police chiefs with the claim that my glowing description of the effectiveness of the British system was not supported by the British chief constable sitting at the table. The British chief, the top enforcement official in an urban county just north of London, did indeed proceed to complain about the tolerant methods of his nation. With trepidation, I asked how many addict armed robbers had been arrested in his county the previous year. He replied that none had been arrested during that year, or indeed during any year, a thought that seemed completely alien to the American chiefs in attendance.

A few years later, I recall casually asking a panel of leading British enforcement officials speaking to one of my American University seminars in London how many drug-trade murders there had been the year before. To the amazement of all the Americans listening, none of the officials could recall a single drug-trade murder in the entire country during the previous several years.

Many British doctors have the option of providing a wide array of treatments to addicts, including in some cases prescribing heroin, morphine, and methadone. They also may provide these drugs in injectable form along with clean needles. This flexible system, operating within a compassionate society, creates a situation where calm and toleration dominate a sometimes chaotic drug scene. People still get in trouble with drugs, but such personal tragedies do not translate into major threats to society. The rates of crime and addiction are, by my calculations, a small fraction of those in the United States.

For example, I found that during 1977 there were a total of 432 homicides in England or a rate of 8.8 per million of population, while in the United States there were 19,120, or a rate of 8.8 per one hundred thousand of population (Trebach 1982, 213). Thus, Americans were killing each other at a rate precisely ten times that of their British cousins.

I discovered other dramatic comparisons in regard to rates of addiction and the impact of treatment methods in England. While I do not trust the veracity of many comparative addiction figures, as will be explained later, I calculated that in 1985 the rate of hard-drug addiction in the United States was at least three times as great as that in England (Trebach 1987, 306). I have found that the situations in Holland and Australia are roughly similar, not so much in terms of the precise ratios but in comparison to the general harshness of the situation in the United States. Even though none of those countries had legalized drugs, all demonstrated that peaceful options in drug control were not pie in the sky, that even within a system of limited prohibition or partial legalization there were more effective and more humane approaches readily available to American policymakers. When I visited Liverpool in 1989 I found that enlightened medical treatment practices—which I have termed medicalization—including prescribing heroin and supplying clean needles, have helped produce a relatively healthy group of addicts. In the entire Merseyside Health Region around Liverpool, which contains 2.5 million people and many thousands of injecting addicts, authorities were aware of five addicts with AIDS and nine who were HIV-positive. Tests of approximately 3,000 other addicts had negative results (Trebach and Zeese 1990a, 148). The situation today in Liverpool does not appear to have deteriorated, as it has in so many major cities in the world. For example, it has been estimated that at least half of the 200,000 injecting addicts in New York City today have AIDS or are HIV-positive.

I therefore have long seen medicalization as one important compromise for the United States. Under the medicalization approach, American physicians would be given great freedom to choose the appropriate medicine for their addict patients, including the option of potent narcotics such as injectable heroin, morphine, and methadone, to legally maintain their addictions. The philosophy is quite similar to that which underpins current American oral methadone programs, with one important difference: the medicalization approach to addiction recognizes first and foremost that getting the patient off drugs is the preferred option, but it also acknowledges that some patients may not be able to quit due to the enduring nature of their addiction. These patients are given the promise of indefinite maintenance (see Trebach 1982, esp. chapter 5).

Through several books and dozens of articles over the years, I made clear that I was advocating compromise solutions, a middle ground between harsh prohibition and the other extreme of complete legalization. For example, on the very first pages of *The Heroin Solution* I wrote, "We must fashion middle-level solutions aimed at creating a social balance between complete repression of this drug and allowance of its use in certain circumstances. . . . Total decriminalization of heroin use would be as destructive as the present condition of almost total prohibition" (Trebach 1982, ix–x). These were words of moderation, I thought.

Despite repeated statements of this nature, journalists often referred to me as an advocate of complete legalization of drugs. To my amazement, many scholars did also. For example, reporter Joel Brinkley wrote in the *New York Times*, "In the late 1970s particularly, many people said the United States should simply give up on drug control and legalize some or all illicit drugs. That idea appears to be less popular now, but it still has its proponents, notably Arnold S. Trebach . . . at American University in Washington" (*New York Times*, 14 September 1984, A12).

While the remainder of the thoughts attributed to me in that story were largely correct, I never told Mr. Brinkley that I advocated "simply giving up on drug control" (I still do not), nor had I then said we should legalize some or all illegal drugs. Certainly, I had uttered no such thoughts in *The Heroin Solution*.

Yet, in apparent reliance on the *Times* report, which he cited in a footnote, distinguished scholar James A. Inciardi,[3] director of the

---

3. Professor Inciardi comes in for a great deal of critical attention here because, first, he is a prominent and outspoken prohibitionist scholar, and second, this book is meant to contain a spirited debate and he is my worthy opponent.

University of Delaware's Center for Drug and Alcohol Studies, wrote in *The War on Drugs,* "Finally, there is legalization, or what might be called the Trebach model." He implied that I argued for legalization in *The Heroin Solution* and that legalization had been tried in England and had failed (Inciardi 1986, 210). Inciardi was wrong about my position, about the British system, and I would find later, about much else.

I responded to these distortions in *The Great Drug War:*

> Up to now in this book, I have not argued that we should legalize all drugs or that we should give heroin addicts all the heroin they want. . . . Allow me to state again that I have never taken that position and I do not now. . . . The British have never legalized heroin nor have I, for the umpteenth time, recommended it. The Trebach model of legalization exists only in the imagination of some misguided reporters, scholars, and officials (Trebach 1987, 368–69).

Within a few short years of writing those indignant words, however, I had changed my mind on one important detail. I had become an advocate of full legalization of drugs along the alcohol model: currently illegal drugs would be available with modest government regulation over-the-counter to adults. During recent months, moreover, I have come to believe that the urban situation in America is so desperate as to demand the nearly immediate dismantling of drug prohibition.

The change in my thinking occurred because of the excesses of the American war on drugs, some of which I saw close up in my travels throughout this country in the course of research. I observed that in the relentless and impossible pursuit of a "drug-free society," the drug warriors were filling the jails and prisons with petty drug offenders, invading personal privacy and violating constitutional rights, provoking hatred of racial minorities, wasting billions of dollars, facilitating violent drug traffickers and police corruption, and diverting resources and attention from other pressing social problems. This endless holy war has had no demonstrable effect on drug abuse but has appeared to spur record-level American crime and violence to even greater heights.

Over the years, official government intelligence reports added to my evaluation of the ineffectiveness of prohibition. The latest government estimates continue to show the futility of this destructive effort. In July 1992, the National Narcotics Intelligence Consumers Committee reported that there was no evidence of any drop in production or availability of most illicit drugs. For example, "cocaine . . . was readily available in all major U.S. metropolitan areas during 1991'' (National Narcotics Intelligence Consumers Committee 1992, 1). Cocaine prices were generally down and average purity was up. Cocaine, it must be emphasized, has been the major target of recent drug-war activity. Yet, here we have the government's top intelligence agencies reporting on wide availability, lower prices, and high purity—all signs of a public policy disaster.

Such distressing facts eventually convinced me that any significant government involvement in controlling the right of the people to choose the drugs they want to ingest is fraught with potential disaster, in much the same way that the founders of the Republic concluded that disaster almost always ensues when the state prevents the people from freely choosing the gods they wish to worship. Just as a wall of separation has been built between the freedom to choose a church and the state, I now believe that a wall of separation must be built between the freedom of citizens to choose a drug and the state.

Legalizers versus Drug Warriors

When I started openly advocating even moderate reforms back in the early 1970s, I found my position a lonely one. By the late 1980s, I had a lot of welcome company.[4] As the reform movement gained in power and prestige, spurred and coordinated in part by the activities of the Drug Policy Foundation, which I founded in 1986, the guardians of prohibition and of the drug war brought forth a familiar myth in its defense. They claimed that the current system was from its inception carefully planned, inherently compassionate, and ultimately rational. Change the drug laws, ease up on enforcement even a little bit, and we will become a nation of drugged zombies, they declared. Besides, some added, this country had tried legalization earlier in its history and found it unworkable.

This was followed by the charge that proponents of change were utterly irresponsible in that they had never once laid out concrete, rationally planned proposals for reform. These charges were put forth by a variety of leading authorities in several ingenious ways.

---

4. Among the people who had joined me publicly by the late 1980s, to name only a few, were Baltimore Mayor Kurt Schmoke, Ethan Nadelmann, assistant professor of politics at Princeton University, and former Secretary of State George P. Shultz. Also prominent were those who restated previous legalization positions, including Nobel laureate Milton Friedman and columnist William F. Buckley, Jr.

A majority of the United States Congress was so concerned by the legalization movement that it took the extraordinary step of issuing a blanket legislative condemnation of the entire idea in the Anti-Drug Abuse Act of 1988. The bill declared:

> The Congress finds that legalization of illegal drugs, on the Federal or state level, is an unconscionable surrender in a war in which, for the future of our country and the lives of our children, there can be no substitute for total victory (The Anti-Drug Abuse Act, P.L. 100-690, Section 5011).[5]

Congressman Charles Rangel (D-NY), head of the House Select Committee on Narcotics Abuse and Control, derided the proponents of reform at a 1988 hearing he chaired on legalization by declaring, "Press them, the advocates of change . . . and they never seem to have answers." He then put forth a series of questions, some serious, most loaded. For example: "Would we get the supply from the same foreign countries that support our habit now, or would we create our own internal sources and dope factories, paying people the minimum wage to churn out mounds of cocaine and bales of marijuana?" (Trebach and Zeese 1990a, 207).

In December 1989, then head of the White House Office of National Drug Control Policy, "drug czar" William Bennett, gave a fiery speech at Harvard University's John F. Kennedy School of Government, castigating those naive souls who believed "that the arguments in favor of drug legalization are rigorous, substantial, and serious." He then explained, "They are not. They are, at bottom, a series of superficial and even disingenuous ideas that more sober minds recognize as a recipe for a public policy disaster" (Trebach and Zeese 1990a, 15–16).[6]

Not surprisingly, the national drug strategy documents that issued from Bennett's office contained the same thoughts. In the very first *National Drug Control Strategy* Bennett declared:

5. Such unrealistic, extremist language was scattered throughout the bill. Section 5251-B proclaimed, "It is the declared policy of the United States to create a Drug-Free America by 1995." The first National Drug Control Strategy, issued in 1989, appeared to break with this goal by seeking a 50 percent reduction in drug use over ten years, but no member of Congress to my knowledge mentioned a word about this apparent violation of the will of Congress.

6. The drug czar's not-too-subtle suggestion here that legalization supporters are primarily disoriented drug users ("more sober minds") was consistent with much prohibitionist rhetoric of the past century. Sadly, it has too often helped to cut off rational debate about the facts.

Legalizing drugs would be an unqualified national disaster. In fact, any significant relaxation of drug enforcement—for whatever reason, however well-intentioned—would promise more use, more crime, and more trouble for desparately [*sic*] needed treatment and education efforts (White House Office of National Drug Control Policy 1989, 7).

James Inciardi has been one of the most prominent scholarly proponents of the Bennett-Rangel approach to dealing with drug policy critics. In his book, *The War on Drugs* (1986), Inciardi made scathing attacks on those experts who disagreed with accepted American drug-control doctrine. For example, he wrote that Thomas Szasz's classic dissenting book, *Ceremonial Chemistry* (1974), suffered from "numerous errors of fact, poor scholarship, and his caustic abuse of the English language" (Inciardi 1986, 203).[7] After treating most of the drug dissenters of the past forty years, including this writer, to such assaults, Inciardi then issued this broadside:

Although one runs the risk of being ignored, or being called "fascist" or "arch-conservative" by atavistic liberal thinkers, *it would appear that contemporary American drug-control policies, with some very needed additions and changes, would be the most appropriate approach* (Inciardi 1986, 211; italics in original).

Inciardi took a roughly similar approach in the sequel to the 1986 book (Inciardi 1992), although the broadside above was mercifully deleted and the new book did take pains to suggest some compassionate and sensible improvements in the American war on drugs. A prominent addition also was more detailed criticism of the growing army of reformers:

Although legalizing drugs has been debated since the passage of the Harrison Act in 1914, never has an advocate of the position structured a concrete proposal. Any attempt to legalize drugs would be extremely complex, but all proponents tend to proceed from simplistic shoot-from-the-hip positions without first developing any sophisticated proposals (Inciardi 1992, 240–41).

7. Apparently Inciardi did not wish to get into a discussion of what "errors of fact" Szasz had relied on, nor did he wish to explain his charge of "poor scholarship." The remark that Szasz's writing suffers from "caustic abuse of the English language" is even more mystifying than the other charges. I and many others believe that Szasz writes more colorfully, pleasantly, and understandably than many people who were born and raised in the United States (Szasz emigrated to the United States during World War II). By any standard, he is a great writer.

Also in this harsh vein was the following additional passage:

> In all likelihood [the legalizers'] arguments are born of frustration—
> frustration with the lack of immediate major successes in the prevention
> and control of drug use. Part of the problem is reflected in the old saying
> about a little bit of knowledge being dangerous. As academics, econo-
> mists, and civil libertarians from outside the drug field, their experiences
> have rarely, if at all, exposed them to the full dynamics of addiction, drug
> craving, and drug-taking and drug-seeking behaviors. It should be noticed
> as well that those who have spent their lives and careers in the trenches
> researching the drug problem, treating the drug problem, or otherwise
> coping with the drug problem feel that legalization would initiate a public
> health problem of unrestrained proportions (Inciardi 1992, 255).

The test of an idea should be its ability to help deal with a specific
problem, whether it comes from the mouth of a policy analyst or an
innocent schoolchild. Even so, Inciardi is wrong again in this personal
attack. The power of the drug policy reform movement—not all of
whose members favor complete legalization, as do I—is in the breadth
of its support across all walks of life and professions. Included as
supporters of the Drug Policy Foundation, for example, are many
experts who have seen the horrors of drug abuse from the trenches,
including doctors, psychiatrists, nurses, pharmacologists, and other
treatment specialists. Some of our strongest supporters recently have
been those doctors involved in the treatment of AIDS, who are joining
the foundation in fighting the government ban on marijuana in medicine. That ban is viewed as a major weapon in the war on drugs, but it
is contributing to the public health disaster of the AIDS epidemic.

Other supporters of reform who have seen the misery of addiction
close up are priests, ministers, and rabbis. Through the organizational
efforts of the Reverend Robert Sirico, a Roman Catholic priest, they
have formed the Religious Coalition for a Moral Drug Policy, which
advocates full legalization of drugs. The current president is another
Roman Catholic priest, the Reverend Joseph Ganssle, who specializes
in addiction counseling and is actively involved in Narcotics Anonymous. Contrary to what Inciardi says, these treatment experts and
religious counselors view the war on drugs as harming the very people
it is supposed to help the most, the addicts and the abusers—and they
have very direct knowledge of that harm. These religious leaders see
the issue of drug use primarily as a moral one, not at all the business
of Caesars or czars, or police officers, prosecutors, judges, or prison
guards.

Many of these latter officials, who are drug warriors in the front lines, are also among the strongest supporters of radical reform. Precisely because they see and feel the problem so directly, such officials make powerful advocates. For example, few reformers have had the impact of Kurt Schmoke, mayor of Baltimore, who had previously been the chief prosecutor in that city for seven years and oversaw the prosecution and jailing of thousands of drug offenders. One day a good friend and a police officer, Marcellus Ward, was murdered by drug dealers while taking part in an undercover drug deal. Officer Ward was wearing a tape and prosecutor Schmoke had to listen to that tape over and over, experiencing the death of his friend over and over. Schmoke later wrote,

> However, I didn't need to hear the sound of Marcellus Ward being shot to know that there was something terribly misguided about expecting law enforcement officers to stop drug abuse and drug trafficking. Rather than convince me of our need for a new national drug policy, Officer Ward's murder simply confirmed it (Trebach and Zeese 1990, 200).

It is difficult to see how anyone could say that Schmoke, and many other reformers like him, was not speaking from the trenches rather than an ivory tower.

In another attack that was both personal and factually inaccurate, Inciardi indicted by implication one of the most prominent conservative supporters of drug legalization, Nobel Prize-winning economist Milton Friedman, as well as other distinguished free-market experts:

> . . . the fact that a few free market economists support legalization should be seen for the purely material, or at least intellectual, self-interest that it is. . . . From a free-market perspective, producing, distributing, and expanding the market for a product that is immediately consumed and readily addictive would appear to be a fantasy come true (Inciardi 1992, 254).

I have heard of nobody who supports legalization because it would allow an unfettered, expanding market for drugs and would thereby represent fulfillment of the free-market model. To even suggest that is genuinely insulting. Most of the economists who support legalization simply take their understanding of black markets to the drug field and recognize that suppressing drugs people want is an ultimately impossible mission, thanks to the magic of the profit motive. But Friedman does not even consider the drug issue in primarily economic terms, as he said in an interview with the Drug Policy Foundation's television show, "America's Drug Forum":

> I'm an economist, but the economics problem is strictly tertiary. It's a moral problem. . . . What scares me is the notion of continuing on the path we're on now, which will destroy our free society (Drug Policy Foundation 1992b, 4).

Thus, this free-market economist sees the issue very much like the clergy mentioned above. Certainly, this has little to do with the potential profits to be made from legal drug sales.

Another example of Inciardi's inflammatory rhetoric regarding drug legalization plays on fears that legalization would dramatically increase drug use, especially in minority communities in the nation's inner cities:

> . . . in large part the legalization of drugs would function as a program of social management and control that would serve to legitimate the chemical destruction of an urban generation and culture. As such, legalization would be an elitist and racist policy supporting the old neocolonialist views of under-class population control (Inciardi 1992, 255).

Apart from the inflammatory rhetoric, this statement suffers from numerous false assumptions, many of which are answered here in subsequent pages. Suffice it to say here that the leading victims of current prohibitionist policies are minority citizens of large cities. Their infants often die from the bullets of feuding drug dealers. Their young men are pulled to the lure of profits, whether large or small, from illegal drugs and often end up in prison or dead from turf battles (the leading cause of death among young black males is homicide). Hard-core addiction to powerful drugs has risen in ghetto neighborhoods recently while middle-class drug use has declined. It is difficult to see how any drug policy could be worse for our minority citizens than prohibition.

Inciardi (1992) also lays out an expanded Rangel-type list of complex and often loaded questions that he felt had to be answered before serious consideration could be given to legalization proposals. Inciardi concludes this section of his book by declaring that there is little support for legalization

> in either published research data or clinical experience. By contrast, there are numerous legitimate arguments against the legalization of drugs, all

of which have considerable empirical, historical, pharmacological, and/or
clinical support (Inciardi 1992, 243).

At this point, the saga of my involvement in this field was brought
full circle. I was hooked into it by the realization that there was very
little empirical, historical, pharmacological, and/or clinical support for
continued criminal law prohibition or, more to the point, for an intense
war on drugs. Today, the major supporters of the current system claim
that the exact opposite is true.

I believe they are wrong for many reasons, one of them being that
the history typically cited to support the modern drug war fails to take
account of how mild the drug problem really was before prohibition,
as I will explain in section 3. Legislators earlier in this century
overreacted by making sweeping national laws to try to contain the use
of drugs. Today's legislators and their supporting intellectuals have
compounded the original mistake by following blindly down the prohibitionist path.

Inciardi and other anti-legalizers are also wrong in asserting that
legalization "proponents tend to proceed from simplistic shoot-from-
the-hip positions" (Inciardi 1992, 241). Responsible drug reform experts *have* answered many of the anti-legalizers' loaded questions and
have also produced a wide array of detailed, concrete legalization
proposals. Those proposals will be discussed in section 4.

To me the fact that the millions of people who sense that drugs could
be distributed differently, with a better balance of societal costs and
benefits, have not agreed on a particular system is irrelevant to whether
any one potential system would be viable. I join many of my colleagues
in believing that once the realization strikes state or federal legislators
that some form of legalization must be implemented, the political
process will work to devise a system based on selected aspects of the
many models available. Even if no ideas for legalization systems were
now available, I would hold this faith. The way our political system
works is that the people's representatives agree on a problem and then
compete to get their solutions approved. Elements of everyone's
solutions usually become part of the final product.

It would certainly be advantageous to have a self-contained legalization policy at hand that could be instituted without being watered
down or undermined by contradictory proposals and amendments, but
to imagine such a thing possible is to ignore political reality. So, too, it
would be ignorant to believe that the most important thing legalization

advocates could do now would be to fight amongst themselves over the details of a legalization plan.

In section 4, I lay out some of the vital principles that must be adhered to in any serious effort at legalization, and these are, I submit, more important than most specifics, such as the source of newly legal drugs or the hours of operation of the new stores. The evidence is overwhelming, except to those who refuse to see it, that we must repeal drug prohibition as soon as we can summon up the national will to do so, even though we have not worked out all of the details of legalization.

2. The Case for a Soviet Solution

It may be useful at the outset of this section to coin a phrase to describe the radical action that civilized societies must now take in the drug arena because of the growing disaster created by extreme prohibitionist policies. I suggest a "Soviet solution," in respect for the citizens of the former Soviet Union, who realized that they had to slay communism before they had worked out all of the details of the future order of their society.[8] Likewise, Americans need to come together to reject the drug war and dismantle its vast infrastructure, which as it happens is the most communistic, here meaning totalitarian and personally intrusive, of all U.S. government policies.

Over the past several years, numerous reformist researchers and commentators, including me, have developed the basic themes that show the flaws of drug prohibition and the horrors of the drug war. In this chapter I summarize some of the main current horrors as a means of making the case for the immediate repeal of prohibition, that is, for the Soviet solution. Many more could have been included, which I have discussed in other writings.

The Illusory Line between Legal and Illegal Drugs

It was a surprise to me and I suspect it will be to many people that there is no scientific basis for the line between legal and illegal drugs. All of the popular drugs in use today—from alcohol to heroin to

8. In a speech at the 1991 Drug Policy Foundation International Conference on Drug Policy Reform, Milton Friedman argued from a similar perspective, saying that the drug war is failing because it is a socialist enterprise premised on statist ideas.

marijuana to cocaine to crack to caffeine—pose threats to many users. Yet, all of them, including crack, are used without material harm by the great majority of users.

Dr. Andrew Weil summarized the little-known reality of the drug-human condition best when he observed: *"Any drug can be used successfully, no matter how bad its reputation, and any drug can be abused, no matter how accepted it is.* There are no good or bad drugs; there are only good and bad relationships with drugs" (Weil 1983, 27; italics in original). I recognize that this view strikes many good people as an outrage, but it is irrefutably true. Drugs are not like environmental problems such as acid rain or radioactivity, where everyone is at risk merely because the condition exists. Drugs only affect people in the context of how an individual uses them, and once that human element is brought into the equation, all our well-documented foibles as a species come into play.

During the past century, and over thousands of years of human history, one drug or another has been banned or approved by popular legislative enactments or imperial edicts not on the basis of science, but due to the fears, prejudices, religious doctrines, and political factors unique to a given culture and a particular historical era. Social or legal approval or disapproval usually is unrelated to the actual organic harm caused by each group of drugs. The latest available U.S. government reports indicate that during 1988 at least 434,175 people in the United States died from diseases directly related to tobacco, and 40,064 from diseases directly related to alcohol (not including drunk driving) (Centers for Disease Control 1991, 53; Stinson and DeBakey 1992, 777–83).[9] Thus, the combined death toll from these two popular legal drugs in 1988 was at least 474,239. Another government report indicates that 6,756 people died from overdoses of all illegal drugs alone or in combination, often with alcohol, during the same year (National Institute on Drug Abuse 1989, 54).

Some would argue that this disparity proves the value of prohibition, that deaths from such drugs as heroin, cocaine, and marijuana are comparatively low precisely because they are illegal. Because complex causal connections of this massive nature are difficult to fathom, this

9. During the course of this and previous research, I have encountered significant variations in the number of deaths attributed to legal drugs—specifically alcohol and tobacco—as well as to illegal drugs, by different government agencies and experts. Some government estimates of deaths from tobacco and alcohol are significantly higher than those given here. However, all estimates indicate that deaths from legal drugs are vastly greater than those from illegal drugs.

is possible, but there is little evidence to support the claim. The manner in which millions of people relate to alcohol and tobacco, and especially the massive amount of organic damage these drugs cause, make it highly likely that they would continue to create the greatest harm when other drugs are legalized. My interpretation of the record of centuries of drug use in many countries is that there is no certain connection between the widespread legal availability of currently illegal drugs and a large number of deaths. Surely, that must be said of the record in the United States, as I explain in section 3.

Prohibition, Murders, and the American Gulag

Crime and violence are inextricably intertwined with drug prohibition. During periods when alcohol or drug prohibition laws are vigorously enforced, the number of homicides and prisoners rises dramatically. This has been the case in many countries. Nobel laureate Milton Friedman recently documented this trend during this century in the United States (Friedman 1991, 103–104).

Friedman estimated that each year during the 1980s there were a minimum of 5,000 extra homicides and 45,000 extra prisoners due mainly to the Reagan-Bush administrations' drug wars. While one may not be convinced of the precise accuracy of these numbers, certainly there is no doubt that when the United States made the possession and sale of certain drugs major crimes, there were vastly more major crimes, including murders.

The rise in prison populations since 1980 has been the greatest in U.S. history. Much of this rise is due to drug enforcement or to problems generated by drug laws, although it is impossible to tell precisely how many people are in prison as a result of drug enforcement because of the manner in which records are kept. For example, the arrest records of many drug offenders list the crime as burglary, robbery, or murder rather than as a drug offense. Yet there is no denying that the number of prisoners has risen dramatically during periods of strong drug enforcement.

According to official records, at the end of 1980, just a few days before Mr. Reagan took the oath of office and then soon declared our greatest drug war, the number of people in federal and state prisons (serving a sentence of one year or more) was 315,974. As of year-end 1991, that number was 823,414, a rise of 160 percent in 11 years (Bureau of Justice Statistics 1992a, 4; Bureau of Justice Statistics

1992b, 636). If the number of inmates in jails (which house prisoners awaiting trial or serving less than a year) and in juvenile facilities and boot camps are added, then the number of people behind bars in the United States exceeds 1.2 million for the first time in our history (Bureau of Justice Statistics 1992, 3–4).

Several years ago, I visited the Soviet Union, where leading officials told me proudly of how they were dismantling their gulag. However, the erection of the American gulag continues unabated. The newest 1992–93 Bush administration drug plan envisions the day, only a few years away, when fully two out of three federal prisoners in this country will be drug offenders.

The Drug Exception to the Constitution

The essential nature of U.S. drug enforcement has an alien tinge to it, more suited to an intrusive totalitarian society than to the democratic, capitalist culture that evolved uniquely here in the United States. That is because drug taking is for the most part a private, consensual matter. Like sexual activity, it normally takes place in the privacy of the home and involves consenting adults, although youths are sometimes involved. It follows that drug enforcement must break into this veil of privacy and intrude in the most intimate aspects of the lives of citizens, using the same tactics as communist officials once brought to bear against dissenters.

Without fully realizing the extent to which we have surrendered our rights, I suspect, we Americans have come to accept deeply intrusive practices as the norm because our leaders tell us that we all must give up some freedoms to save our people, especially our children, from the menace of drugs. Americans by the millions are now being told to urinate in front of strangers upon pain of not being hired or of losing their only means of livelihood. In addition to this increased power given to employers, with or without formal legal endorsement, the powers of police officials have been formally increased by judicial opinions, wherein the judges seem to have been deeply affected by drug war myths and rhetoric.

A sample of only a few of the recent drug war decisions—reliant on a principle that Justice Thurgood Marshall once disparagingly labeled the "drug exception to the Constitution"[10]—shows how the liberties of

10. The full sentence by Justice Marshall, in dissent, read: "There is no drug exception to the Constitution, any more than there is a communism exception or an exception for

all Americans have been greatly diminished by the courts in order to
support enforcement of prohibition. For example, it is now approved
constitutional doctrine for U.S. Customs officials to detain without
probable cause or indeed any evidence of guilt a person at the border,
hold that person for at least 24 hours, and release him or her only if
that person, first, defecates into a container under the eyes of an
official; second, allows the official to examine the fecal waste; and
third, thereby demonstrates that the waste does not contain any
contraband (*United States v. Montoya de Hernandez,* 473 U.S. 531
[1985], as reported in Trebach 1987, 215–20). This Supreme Court
decision, which was handed down on 1 July 1985, in the midst of the
Reagan drug war, upheld the conviction of an alimentary-canal smug-
gler caught at the Los Angeles International Airport. Justices William
Brennan and Thurgood Marshall dissented, and in an opinion written
by Brennan they declared that masses of innocent travelers would now
be subjected to many more indignities, most of which would not come
to public attention:

> The available evidence suggests that the number of highly intrusive border
> searches of suspicious-looking but ultimately innocent travelers may be
> very high. One physician who at the request of Customs officials con-
> ducted many "internal searches"—rectal and vaginal examinations and
> stomach-pumping—estimated that he had found contraband in only 15 to
> 20 percent of the persons he had examined. It has similarly been estimated
> that only 16 percent of women subjected to body cavity searches at the
> border were in fact found to be carrying contraband (Trebach 1987, 220).

An earlier case involved a quasi-military detention of all 2,780 junior
and senior high school students in Highland, Indiana, on the morning
of 23 March 1979. Teams of armed police and sixteen police dogs and
their civilian handlers were mobilized for the action. One team went
into every classroom, where the students had all been told without
warning to remain seated at their desks. "Every single student was
sniffed, inspected, and examined at least once," wrote a federal court
of appeals judge (Trebach 1987, 222).[11] He continued: "Four junior
high school students—all girls—were removed from their classes,

---

other real or imagined sources of domestic unrest." *Skinner v. Railway Labor Executives' Association* (489 U.S. 602, 641 [1989]).

11. The quotation about every single student being sniffed by the dogs comes from
the dissenting opinion of U.S. Circuit Judge Swygert in *Doe v. Renfrow* (631 F.2d. 91, 93
[1980]); the quote about the nude strip search appears on page 94.

stripped nude, and interrogated. Not one of them was found to possess any illicit material."

The parents of one of these innocent students, Diane "Doe," sued. Lower federal courts determined that the dragnet searches were constitutionally permissible even though there had been no probable cause, but that the nude searches had been unconstitutional. Diane Doe eventually collected damages for the nude search, but her parents persisted in the suit so as to obtain a court ruling that the entire procedure was repugnant to American constitutional traditions. When the case of *Doe v. Renfrow* reached the Supreme Court, the justices refused to hear it (Trebach 1987, 223; see also *Doe v. Renfrow*, 451 U.S. 1022 [1981]). In strict legal terms, no conclusions may be drawn from that refusal, but it is disturbing in itself that the highest court in the land refused the opportunity to declare that it was unconstitutional for officials to conduct dragnet searches of American schoolchildren when there was no evidence that any of them had committed a crime.

One final example of drug war judicial doctrine may be found in a Supreme Court decision that for the first time in history gave the faceless informer major constitutional approval in the United States. The police in Bloomingdale, Illinois, received an anonymous letter stating that a local couple were engaged in drug dealing and providing details of how they would soon travel by car and plane to Florida in order to obtain drugs. On the basis of this anonymous tip, along with police observance of travel by the couple, but with no evidence of actual crime, the police obtained a search warrant for the home and automobile of the couple.

The Supreme Court of Illinois threw out the conviction because it applied prior U.S. Supreme Court rulings that required the police to demonstrate, among other things, the "veracity" or "reliability" of a confidential informant before the police could obtain a search warrant. In other words, previous High Court rulings had allowed the use of confidential informants if the informants were known to the police and if the police swore that they had previously supplied reliable information. Now the police were asking for even more power than this significant grant. The Illinois court said no to faceless informers unknown even to the police. In another of the drug war's harmful court decisions, the Supreme Court overruled the Illinois court and its own previous doctrine, and on 8 June 1983, approved once again a seemingly small extension of police power to meet the needs of drug prohibition (*Illinois v. Gates,* 46 U.S. 213 [1983]). The faceless informer of totalitarian societies now has the explicit protection of the

American constitution, for which we can all thank the supporters of drug prohibition.

Mandatory Minimum Sentences and the Tears of Judges

Another practice that has received the initial constitutional blessings of the current Supreme Court has been harsh mandatory minimum sentencing. In recent years, the United States Congress and many state legislatures have passed laws meant to toughen the enforcement of prohibition by taking away the discretion that centuries of Anglo-American tradition have given to trial judges. Rigid rules and formulae now apply which, in the words of U.S. District Judge William W. Schwarzer, make "judges clerks, or not even that, computers automatically imposing sentences without regard to what is just and right" (Zeese 1991, 7).

Judge Schwarzer, a Republican appointee with a reputation for handing down tough sentences, made those remarks in the course of imposing a mandatory minimum sentence. The judge, who later became director of the Federal Judicial Center in Washington, D.C., actually cried on the bench as he imposed the required ten-year sentence without parole on Richard Anderson, a first-time offender. The Oakland longshoreman had taken $5 to drive an acquaintance to a Burger King restaurant but, he testified, he did not know he was participating in an undercover drug deal involving 100 grams (not quite a quarter of a pound) of crack. Judge Schwarzer called the sentence "a grave miscarriage of justice," and lamented, "In this case, the law does anything but serve justice. It may profit us very little to win the war on drugs if in the process we lose our soul" (Zeese 1991, 7).

Many judges are in individual and organized revolt over the injustices of the drug war, especially those imposed by mandatory minimum sentences. Some, like U.S. District Judge Robert Sweet and U.S. Magistrate Ronald W. Rose, have come out for legalization in despair over the injustices bred by vigorous, vindictive enforcement of drug prohibition.[12]

One of the worst excesses of such mandatory sentences was recently upheld by the Supreme Court (*Harmelin v. Michigan,* 111 S.Ct. 2680 [1991]). A 1978 Michigan law—reportedly the harshest in the country—

12. Judge Sweet's historic speech took place at the Cosmopolitan Club in New York City on 12 December 1989; most of it is reprinted in Trebach and Zeese (1990a, 205).

imposed a mandatory sentence of life imprisonment without the possibility of parole for those convicted of carrying large amounts of drugs.
The base amount for cocaine was 650 grams. In the case before the
high court, Ronald Harmelin had been found with 672 grams, one-and-
a-half pounds, of the drug. Even though he had never been convicted
of a crime and even though his was a totally nonviolent offense, 42-
year-old Mr. Harmelin received the mandated sentence. Since Michigan has no death penalty, Ronald Harmelin would have received no
worse a sentence had he committed a series of axe murders. The Court
refused to overturn this sentence as a violation of the Eighth Amendment's cruel and unusual punishment clause. This was the first time
that such a seemingly uncivilized drug sentencing law had been fully
reviewed by the Supreme Court.

On a positive note, the Michigan Supreme Court saw the error of
the law's ways, and struck it down in June 1992. After more than 150
people had been put away for life under the law, the court ruled that
the sentence was "unduly disproportionate," and ordered that all
those convicted be considered for parole beginning after 10 years of
prison (*People v. Bullock and Hanson,* Michigan Supreme Court,
Docket Nos. 89661 and 89662 [16 June 1992]). Michigan residents are
now protected from this incredibly harsh sentence thanks to a one-
word difference between the state constitution and the federal document. While the U.S. Constitution bans "cruel *and* unusual punishment," Michigan bans "cruel *or* unusual punishment."

For-Profit Justice: Asset Forfeiture

Slightly over five years ago, then Assistant Attorney General Stephen
S. Trott promised that the Justice Department would unleash "a
scorched-earth policy" against drug dealers. The government would
begin to seize "everything they own, their land, their cars, their boats,
everything" (Trebach 1987, 184). I wrote at the time:

> It has long been accepted in the law that a convicted criminal should be
> prevented from enjoying the fruits of his misdeeds and also that the
> instrumentalities or implements of a crime could properly be seized by
> the government. Thus, no significant issues of constitutional liberties
> were raised by seizures of rum runners' cash and boats during our earlier
> era of Prohibition nor are any raised now regarding such personal prop-
> erty of drug runners (Trebach 1987, 186–87).

However, since 1984, when amendments to the civil and criminal codes of the United States were added that dramatically changed the seizure equation, that "scorched-earth policy" has been targeted against thousands of small-time dealers, mere drug users, and the families, landlords, and lienholders of these people. Indeed, the use of asset forfeiture has produced such a windfall for law enforcers that it has spread from the drug realm and become a tool of law enforcement agencies prosecuting a whole range of criminal activities.

The first area in which drug war forfeiture laws broke with the tradition of seizing the assets of criminals was that they did not require a criminal conviction for the forfeiture proceedings to begin and succeed. This shift has turned justice on its head. Whereas the American system is the envy of the world for its commitment to equal justice before the law and the principle that a citizen is innocent until proved guilty, these cherished concepts are tossed out the window for drug-related forfeiture cases. The seizure action is technically taken against the person's property and not the suspect (in essence, the property is accused of involvement in a criminal activity), so that the individual must sue the government to regain his or her property, even if no prosecution goes forward or if a finding of innocence is returned by a jury. In short, the suspect must prove innocence in order to avoid the punishment of losing his or her property.

The second break with tradition was the system for distributing the value of the assets seized under the new laws. Federal officials decided to give local law enforcement agencies a stake in forfeitures, offering them a sizable cut of the money left when the assets were liquidated. This gives them extra incentive to pursue both drug busts of all types and the accompanying seizure actions, and it also increases the federal role in local drug cases. As it operates today, this system resembles a for-profit system of justice, in which police have a financial motivation to go after drug dealers and users more aggressively than other criminals.

Before doubting this, consider the following case, summarized in the week-long daily newspaper series on asset forfeiture, "Presumed Guilty," run in the *Pittsburgh Press* (Schneider and Flaherty 1991). A family living in Hawaii, Joseph and Frances Lopes and their son Thomas, had their home seized after a Maui detective poring over records of old drug cases found the record of their son's marijuana arrest. Thomas, 28 at the time and with a history of psychological problems, was growing marijuana for his own use in the family's backyard until the plants were spotted by helicopters in 1987. His parents had asked him several times to stop, but he threatened to hurt himself if they forced him to remove the plants, and Joseph and Frances Lopes took the threat seriously.

Because the parents, owners of the house, knew about the marijuana, their home could be taken in the same way the owner of a house where methamphetamine was being manufactured could be forced to surrender his or her property. Never mind the circumstances of the Lopeses' case. They were thrown out of their home due to zealotry, bad laws, and overeager enforcement officials seeking to fatten their agencies' budgets.

This case and countless others—*Pittsburgh Press* reporters Andrew Schneider and Mary Pat Flaherty found hundreds like it—show that a new weapon has been added to the law enforcement arsenal and is being seriously abused. The attitude of the government seems to be that it is hard to find any injustice in punishments of people in any way involved with drugs.

Confronted by a *USA Today* reporter with the fact that some surveys have shown that more than half of the people whose property is forfeited are never charged with a crime, Justice Department forfeiture chief Cary Copeland said, "What the public wants to know is: In how many cases do we take assets wrongly? The answer is virtually zero." He referred to the forfeiture weapons in terms similar to Trott's "scorched-earth" analogy, saying "it is to the drug war what smart bombs and air power are to modern warfare" (Cauchon 1992, 1A). Copeland may be more correct than he thought at the time. With both weapons, thousands of innocent people are made tragic victims.

Pleased with the success of forfeiture in the drug war, police agencies have begun using this weapon for other, non-drug-related crimes. New Jersey has written its forfeiture laws in such a way as to allow seizures to take place in reaction to all sorts of crimes. One of the more absurd examples shows what kind of future we are preparing ourselves for, with the critical ground broken in the name of fighting drugs. Former gynecologist Owen A. Chang of Burlington County, New Jersey, had his medical license stripped from him in December 1991, because he allegedly performed at least two "wrongful examinations" of patients—examinations with no nurse present. Since such an activity is illegal and because it allegedly took place in the doctor's office building, the county prosecutor is moving to take forfeiture action against the property (Forfeiture Endangers American Rights 1992, 1). Because of the way New Jersey law treats forfeiture, the prosecutor may well succeed, creating the basis for a massive and chaotic wave of forfeitures based on every conceivable crime.

These cases provide yet another example of how the precedents set in the name of the drug war can ultimately come around to affect any American who comes to the attention of our increasingly powerful law enforcement agencies.

Huge Costs, Little Return

Drug war spending is hardly an investment in the future. As of this writing, the federal government is planning to spend approximately $12.7 billion in fiscal 1993 on the drug war, much of which will simply be consumed on enforcement attempts and prison construction. If, as expected, Congress approves this request, President George Bush will have spent $45.2 billion during his term in office, making him the biggest drug-war spender in history. Indeed, Mr. Bush will have spent more on the drug war than all presidents during the past two decades. Approximately $30 billion was spent since President Richard Nixon declared the first modern war on drugs in 1971. During eight years of intense drug war activity, Ronald Reagan spent "only" $22.3 billion (Drug Policy Foundation 1992a, 126).

State and local governments can fairly be said to spend about the same amount on the drug war as the federal government from year to year, especially as the war has moved up on the national agenda. That gives a total of $20 to $26 billion a year in spending of taxpayers' dollars that virtually no one questions, much as practically no one in the recent past could find a voice to criticize the fattened defense budgets of the Cold War.

In the 1992–93 edition of *National Drug Control Strategy,* drug czar Bob Martinez issued a harshly toned demand that the states start anteing up far more for prison construction, one of the cornerstones of the drug war that makes increasing prison populations possible. Noting that the states have spent at least $7 billion on new prison construction in just the previous two years, Martinez said, "While laudable, this commitment by state governments is not enough" (White House Office of National Drug Control Policy 1992, 126).

The Drug War Diverts Attention from Real Social Problems

The greatest current dangers to our society are not drugs, no matter what form they are in, but rather racial hatred, criminal violence, and

AIDS. The war on drugs adds to every one of these major dangers and builds them up to the level of a searing catastrophe. Let us look briefly at each of these related major problems.

We Americans have almost always lived under the threat that racial hatred would tear us asunder. Today that threat seems worse than ever. For a whole variety of reasons—including especially poverty, discrimination, the collapse of too many black families, the workings of an economy that excludes too many blacks, and the perverse effects of drug enforcement on minority communities—blacks are involved in crime all out of proportion to their representation in the population. To even make such a statement often results in a charge, from both blacks and whites, of racism. Yet unless the problem is acknowledged, it can never be solved. The continued existence of horrendous levels of black crime perpetuates both the high toll of black victims and the fears of too many whites of even being in proximity to blacks whether on the job, in social situations, or in housing.

The complexity and harshness of this situation are illustrated by looking at the data on murders. In 1990, a typical year for this problem, 9,744 blacks and 9,724 whites were murdered in the United States (Federal Bureau of Investigation 1991, 11–14). In 1990 blacks constituted 12.1 percent of the population and whites 80.3 percent. (According to the 1990 U.S. Census there were 199,686,070 whites and 29,986,060 blacks in a total U.S. population of 248,709,873.) The overall black death rate by homicide was 32.49 per 100,000 and the white rate was 4.87 per 100,000 for 1990, making the black rate 6.7 times that for whites. According to the FBI, 93 percent of black murder victims in 1990 were killed by blacks, while 86 percent of the white murder victims were killed by whites. Blacks comprised 55 percent of those arrested for murder in 1990.

Between 1985 and 1989, the homicide rate for black males aged 15 to 24 years increased by 74 percent to a rate of 114.8 deaths per 100,000. According to the Public Health Service, this was the highest rate ever recorded for this group (National Center for Health Statistics 1992, 2). It is unlikely, I might add, if any group in the history of the country ever had such a rate. This was almost nine times the rate for white males in the same age group. Virtually every one of the young black male victims was killed by another young black man, in many cases during illegal drug-trade turf battles.

Blacks constitute a majority of those arrested for the fear-producing crime of robbery—61 percent of arrestees in 1990 were black (Federal Bureau of Investigation 1991, 21)—and blacks are among the most visible small-time dealers of illegal drugs. Thus, blacks are often the major targets of police action in drug enforcement. While 12 percent of the population nationwide is black, 46 percent of the prison population is black. Some studies indicate that throughout the country at least one in four young urban black men is already in prison, on parole, or otherwise under the supervision of the criminal justice system (Mauer 1991).

Whites see blacks as a major threat. Many blacks are now responding to what they perceive as racism in the justice system and in the society at large with violent racism on their part. More drug enforcement, without confronting some of the fundamental dynamics of black crime and related social issues, will increase racial hatred on all sides. This is not an argument for doing away with enforcement altogether; rather, it is a plea that we face up to the fact that the problem of black crime is incredibly complex and sensitive. Even discussing it honestly insults everyone within earshot. It cannot be solved by a simplistic domestic war that declares "get rid of the drugs and we have dealt with most of the problem." We cannot begin to deal with the complexities of black crime while we devote so much energy and attention to drugs.

Indeed, as was recently related to me by the director of an AIDS counseling center for addicts in the South Bronx, it is almost impossible to overstate the destructive effect of the drug war, meaning harsh police enforcement, upon minority communities. This is especially true, he claimed, within the context of a national economy that seems to write off significant numbers of minority youth. The tougher the enforcement, the greater the risks and the higher the prices. People with something to lose leave the scene, with the result that the most desperate criminals soon dominate the drug world. Because the prices are so high and the criminals so desperate, black (and often Hispanic) crime becomes ever more widespread and vicious. Greater drug enforcement, again, will make the situation worse, not better, this streetwise expert declared.

Similar thoughts apply to AIDS, which is another major complex problem that demands high-priority attention. AIDS affects blacks at a much higher rate than it does whites, but all races and classes have been seared by this epidemic. There is no known cure for AIDS, which, according to U.S. government data, caused 152,153 deaths between 1 June 1981 and 3 June 1992 (Centers for Disease Control 1992, 2). Intravenous drug use is now a leading cause of transmission of the virus, being involved in 32 percent of cases (National Commis-

sion on AIDS 1991, 4). So long as the war on drugs treats all users as
the enemy, it will be almost impossible to treat them as patients worthy
of being helped. Ultimately, that help must include legal medicinal
drugs and clean needles. And there is a whole host of other complex
issues regarding this public health calamity that cannot be dealt with
in the context of a war.

Drug use, considered alone and not in the context of prohibition,
could be a problem of only middling significance. However, the war on
drugs produces the same effect on drug use as it does on other social
problems: Drugs plus criminal law prohibition plus the looming threat
of AIDS transmission by drug injectors plus an army of illegal traffickers at war with an army of police and jailers, all combined, amount to
a social catastrophe. Yet this catastrophe is typically attributed to
drugs alone. The result is a periodic ratcheting up of the prohibition
enforcement machinery and a corresponding increase in the social
harm for many millions of people, most not involved in the drug scene
at all.

This section is being written as Los Angeles still smolders from the
worst race riots in American history. The flashpoint was the refusal of
a jury to convict four white police officers who had been accused of
beating Rodney King, a black man, a beating that had been recorded
by an amateur using a videocamera. Blame was also placed upon
decades of bad race relations and the neglect of America's urban
problems. The centerpiece of the response of President Bush was a
program called "Weed and Seed." This entailed the use of police
power to "weed" urban communities of drug dealers and drugs, and
then to "seed" those areas with social improvement programs. In
other words, the weed and seed program assumes that drugs are the
most prominent root cause of urban decay, crime, and even race riots.

In fact, this venerable assumption about the destructive power of
drugs on society has been the most prominent root cause of prohibition
and the war on drugs. As we have seen, like virtually every major
theory motivating current drug laws and policies, this assumption is a
myth and a very harmful one. Edward M. Brecher observed in 1972,

> Almost all of the deleterious effects ordinarily attributed to the opiates,
> indeed, appear to be the effects of the narcotics laws instead. By far the
> most serious deleterious effects of being a narcotics addict in the United
> States today are the risks of arrest and imprisonment, infectious disease,
> and impoverishment—all traceable to the narcotics laws, to vigorous
> enforcement of those laws, and to the resulting excessive black-market
> prices for narcotics (Brecher et al. 1972, 22).

In an important recent book, *Peaceful Measures: Canada's Way Out of the War on Drugs,* published in 1990 by the University of Toronto Press, British Columbia scholar Bruce K. Alexander reached similar conclusions based upon an extensive review of old and new research, including that of James Inciardi:

> The belief that drugs cause virtually all major social ills continues to serve the major justification for the War on Drugs. . . . However, this belief is unwarranted. There is no good evidence that drugs cause any substantial part of the social pathology that is attributed to them. On the contrary, there is good evidence that social pathology causes destructive forms of drug use (Alexander 1990, 17).

The Seductive Powers of Drugs Are Overrated

Bruce Alexander also made a significant related point: that those on both sides of the legalization debate make too much of the attractive and seductive properties of drugs, which he believes are overrated. In taking this position he cast great doubt on yet another myth which props up the prohibitionist structure.

The conventional view about the universal and irresistible appeal of these feared drugs is often supported by reference to experiments with laboratory animals. These experiments allegedly have shown that some animals cannot control themselves when they are provided drugs and that some seem to prefer opiates or cocaine to food.

Bruce Alexander countered this line of thinking by reference to his own experience with animal research in his so-called Rat Park, which involved a series of studies he conducted with his colleagues at the animal laboratories of Simon Fraser University. Many healthy people and properly maintained experimental animals, he declared, do not go into a feeding frenzy simply because the drugs are available to them in some form, whether injectable heroin, smokable crack and marijuana, or sniffable powdered cocaine. In the course of that research he obtained many insights, one of which he explained to a class of mine at The American University when he was giving a guest lecture several years ago.

Morphine, he said, really can be quite distasteful and unpleasant to some people and probably to some animals. While preparing opiate mixtures, including morphine—a close relative of heroin—for the rats, he found it necessary on occasion to taste the substance for consistency. On every occasion he found it unpleasant and was never tempted to try more of it, even though it was right there, sitting in his laboratory under his control. Other scientists have reported similar revulsion to opiates, including heroin (see Alexander 1990, 144).

The experiments themselves also provided insights into the conditions contributing to dysfunctional drug use. The rats in Rat Park were provided with ample accommodations, quite different from the usual solitary metal cages then in use for animal experiments. There were wood chips for digging, tin cans for general recreation, and "other rats of both sexes for social and cultural activities" (Alexander 1990, 160). Both groups of rats, those in Rat Park and those in isolated cages, were given free access to water and to a morphine hydrochloride solution. "In a series of experiments," Alexander reported, "isolated rats consumed up to sixteen times more morphine than did the animals in Rat Park." The only time the Rat Park animals drank any significant amounts of opiates was when "the solution was laced with sugar to the point of being sickeningly sweet, a taste experience that rats seemed to find irresistible" (Alexander 1990, 160). (The team resisted the temptation to draw conclusions about the comparative addicting powers of sugar and opiates.)

While the reasons for the low morphine consumption of the Rat Park residents were not entirely clear, Alexander guessed that boredom and stress motivated the isolated animals to use morphine and that the animals in a socially competitive situation felt the need to stay alert. Whatever the precise reasons, these experiments effectively exploded the irresistible-appeal theories so often promulgated by prohibitionist officials and scholars.

Bruce Alexander also discredited the standard disease-crime model of addiction that underlies the war on drugs. Alexander theorized that addiction may involve a "devotion to" or "dependence on" a wide variety of activates and substances, ranging from exercise to love to drugs. In some cases that devotion or dependence may be positive and in some cases negative in terms of the lifestyle of the addicted person. He observed that the most powerful justification for the war on drugs is the widely shared view that drugs always cause negative addiction in horrendous proportions:

> Conventional wisdom and drug-war doctrine identify certain "addictive drugs" that, once taken, induce eternal addiction and associated criminality in vulnerable people. It follows logically that traffickers in addictive drugs must be eliminated mercilessly, just as malarial mosquitoes must

be destroyed to protect a defenseless public. It also follows that Draconian legal controls can be exercised over drug users and addicts, since
their deviant behavior is a manifestation of disease . . . (Alexander 1990,
255).

Alexander could find no evidence to support this view and offered
in its place the theory that for many people negative addiction to drugs

> is a way people adapt to serious problems if they can find no better
> solution. According to this "adaptive model," the immediate cause of
> negative addiction is not a drug but a situation so dire that addiction is
> the most adaptive response a person can muster. From this viewpoint, no
> disease or criminality is necessarily involved. The adaptive model lends
> little support for the War on Drugs (Alexander 1990, 255).

Yet, the war on drugs continues to be seen as the most prominent
method of dealing with urban decay, crime, and violence. It seems
that we risk the danger that our leaders, supported by many scholars,
will forever be blind to the reality that we can never deal with any of
our worst social problems so long as drug prohibition and the war on
drugs perversely are seen as major cures, rather than major aggravating
causes, of those same problems. The Los Angeles riots and President
Bush's "Weed and Seed" program in reaction should be the last straws
for any thinking person.

I have just reviewed my major reasons, based primarily on an
assessment of the current situation, for recommending the immediate
repeal of drug prohibition. However, I have recently discovered strong
evidence to support my position in a fresh reading of the historical
record of the events leading up to the enactment of drug prohibition in
America, which I outline in the next section.

3. There Was No Reason for the Original Prohibition Laws

Many students of the drug scene, including me, have long assumed that while certain drug laws seemed unwise, at least some form of tough national criminal law control was necessary early in this century. A recent rereading of the last century of drug history leads me now to believe that the basic idea of a national law attempting to directly control the chemical appetites of the American people was extreme, unnecessary, and destructive. I was wrong in my initial assumption, and I apologize.

None of the old laws that originally criminalized drugs around the turn of the century had a rational basis, on at least two counts. First, the presence of noncriminalized drugs in great quantity was not a problem of such magnitude as to require criminalization laws and the creation of a vast enforcement machinery with the mission of controlling chemical deviance by prying into the intimate behavior of a free citizenry. As a criminologist and a lawyer, I believe in the value of criminal law. However, I also believe that acts should be made criminal only when (1) they violate widely shared values of a society which lie at the core of the democratic tradition; (2) they create the high probability of harm or actual harm to innocent third parties; and (3) the invocation of the criminal sanction will not create more harm than the act itself. Second, the original prohibition laws never would have passed the Rangel-Bennett-Inciardi test, which requires that proponents of changes in drug-control laws precisely ascertain in advance the likely effect of those laws. The framers of the early prohibition—mainly well-motivated reformers and needlessly alarmed officials—operated on the naive hope that if certain chemicals and activities were made criminal, that would handle the matter nicely, thank you. No scientific studies were made to determine precisely what the future would hold, as now is being demanded of legalizers (more properly, of course, they should be called relegalizers). The framers saw a problem—drug use—and saw the remedy—making it a crime to give powerful drugs to anyone except in the course of medical practice. There was no inquiry into what is now known as the limits of the criminal sanction, into the perverse effects of prohibition, or into the foreseeable rise of major criminal activity. It might have become apparent that such a catastrophic rise in crime could well have offset any gains for the society in terms of possible reduced drug abuse, but no such studies were made.

We need to look long and hard at an issue before creating laws as a form of social control because of the inevitable impact of these laws. Many people seem not to appreciate that by making an act a crime, we empower the criminal justice authorities to detain an otherwise free citizen, by force of arms if necessary, and then to imprison that citizen behind bars under conditions of extreme privation. For numerous types of drug-related crimes, including but not limited to simple possession of a banned substance, the resort to this sanction is out of all proportion to the offense.

My view now is that legislators earlier this century did not sufficiently consider the potential impact of their new across-the-board prohibition laws, and thus acted rashly and against the long-term interests of the country in their move to prohibit certain drugs. Accordingly, it follows that our future lies in our past, that the situation before drug prohibition was quite tolerable, and that we should rebuild the legalization system of the last century as best we can, with some modern tinkering.

While the analogy is not a perfect one, the passage of the criminal drug laws around the turn of the century is comparable to our terrible error in detaining 110,000 Japanese-Americans in concentration camps during World War II. The rationale at the time was that they represented a threat to the security of the nation, that you could not tell a loyal Japanese-American from a spy, and that the nation was demanding action against them. Yet, there was virtually no concrete evidence of disloyalty at the time. There were only fear and hysteria.

Similarly, while drugs did represent a threat to some individual citizens and families earlier in this century, there never was any evidence that drugs represented a threat to the survival of the nation. There were, however, hysterical claims to this effect that were shouted from the rooftops for decades. Eventually hysteria won regarding drugs as it did with the Japanese-Americans. Fortunately, we have recovered our good sense regarding the Japanese internment, but we continue to live in the cave we dug so many years ago regarding drugs.

Drug prohibition's framers can be forgiven their mistake to some degree. After all, they lacked the experience of national alcohol prohibition and all its disastrous effects. Like the backers of Prohibition and the modern drug warriors, they carried a faith in the power of the law's sanctions that ignored the impact of mass disobedience and that woefully underestimated the chemical desires of the American people. It was simply harder at the time to object rationally to the proposed new drug laws than it was to endorse them zealously.

Today, we have the requisite experience and analytical capability to second-guess the legislators who ushered in the era of drug prohibition. Given that legislators believed they faced a drug problem of great magnitude, they were at a proverbial fork in the road. They chose the path of prohibition, but they could just as likely have chosen a path of regulation, if their primary concern at the time had been to minimize the harm in society arising from drugs. Our job, after more than 75 years of the prohibition remedy, is to determine whether we would all be better off if we could return to that fork in the road and try the other path.

The Onset of Prohibition

The cornerstone of drug prohibition in America was the Harrison Narcotic Act of 1914, passed on 17 December 1914 and put into effect on 1 March 1915. The Harrison Act restricted the use of opiates, such as morphine and heroin, and also cocaine (which was mislabeled as a narcotic), to medical purposes. While many good scholars have argued that the law was meant only to tax drugs and not really to control them, as I have explained in detail elsewhere (Trebach 1982, 118–24), there is strong evidence that the framers of the law wanted to prevent casual or nonmedical users, frequently called "dope fiends" by congressmen during the debates on the law, from obtaining the drugs outside of medical practice.

By 1 March 1915, drug prohibition reigned wherever the United States flag waved. There was some ambiguity as to whether or not it was legal for a doctor to prescribe drugs to an addict for the purpose of long-term maintenance of a habit, which I have also discussed elsewhere (Trebach 1982, chapter 6). The answer turned out to be no, for the most part, but that issue is not in the center of this discussion. The questions here are whether there was an urgent need for criminal prohibition laws at that time, and whether there is a need for their continuation today. On that first crucial question, for years my answer had been yes. The reason for my position was the evidence before the Congress at the time of debate over the Harrison Act.

In June 1913, Congressman Francis Burton Harrison of Pennsylvania, the main sponsor of the comprehensive prohibition statute, submitted a report to the House of Representatives in support of the pending bill that spoke dramatically of the "real and, one might say, even desperate need of Federal legislation to control our foreign and interstate traffic in habit-forming drugs, and to aid both directly and indirectly the States more effectually to enforce their police laws designed to restrict narcotics to legitimate medical channels" (Trebach 1982, 121). While most states had pharmacy laws controlling the sale of addicting drugs, there was no national pattern of legal control. Harrison's report went on:

> There has been in this country an almost shameless traffic in these drugs. Criminal classes have been created, and the use of the drugs with much accompanying moral and economic degradation is widespread among the upper classes of society. We are an opium consuming nation today (Trebach 1982, 121).

Responding to this evidence, a decade ago I wrote that despite those liberal revisionists who consider the period before the Harrison Act as "the good old days," Harrison's report did point a finger at the unrestricted importation, manufacture, and sale of the opiates and cocaine "in such forms as to be available to anyone who desires them or who desires to trade on the addiction of his fellow creatures to them" (Trebach 1982, 121). This led me to conclude "that the legislators were responding to a dire situation that, in their opinion, needed controlling and not simply taxing" (Trebach 1982, 122).

Upon a fresh review of the record, however, I find myself more in agreement with the liberal writers I chided some time ago. Now I cannot find evidence of a dire situation that by any stretch of the imagination could justify the creation of the current American drug-control empire.

A review of some of the most respected authorities in the field shows that none of them can demonstrate the existence of a dire situation or a public policy disaster before 1914 that provided a rational basis for the criminalization of the activities of millions of American citizens. Yet, in effect the recognized experts often claim or imply that the evidence is there. Take, for example, the work of David Musto, M.D., professor at Yale Medical School and author of the acclaimed book, *The American Disease: Origins of Narcotic Control* ([1973] 1987). Although the book contains much historical detail, many of its conclusions flow not from historical fact but from the predilections of its author. Yet *The American Disease* is frequently cited by modern drug warriors as the definitive, objective historical text showing the rationality of the current system of prohibition.

In the preface to the expanded edition, Musto takes pains to criticize the legalization movement, which had shown new signs of vigor since his book was first released. Referring to the last century and the period before the Harrison Act, Musto observes,

> Anyone advocating that drugs should be legalized can look at a century during which our nation was one of the few in the Western world to allow unregulated drug use. The viewer will not see, however, a happy equilibrium resulting from that open drug economy in the nineteenth century, but rather an eventual demand by the public that action be taken to curb availability (Musto [1973] 1987, x).

Note for the moment that Musto does not claim that the situation was objectively dire, but simply that the public demanded action.

Musto then attempts to counter the modern critical argument that the Harrison Act "simply turned respectable drug users into criminals. If there had been no Harrison Act, this argument runs, addicts would have been free to obtain their drugs and pursue normal or relatively normal lives" (Musto [1973] 1987, 11). Musto states that even without the Harrison Act and subsequent restrictive Supreme Court rulings preventing the medical dispensation of drugs to addicts, the typical addict in 1940, and assumably thereafter, would have become more criminal anyway. Yet he presents virtually no evidence in his entire book that supports these conclusions.

Musto had to work from the same scant observations, records, and statistics available to any historian of drugs in America, and like any or all of us, his general assumptions seem to have colored his interpretations of what he found. To his credit, Musto frequently writes critically of the reasons legislators adopted prohibitionist solutions— focusing rightly on the roles played by racism and nativism in the attacks on each of the major illegal drugs. But in the end, Musto believes he had turned up evidence of such drastic and increasing social pathology related to drug use that the prohibition laws that came in reaction were ultimately justified.

With apologies to Musto, I simply restate his criticism of legalizers in order to make my essential point on the history of legal sanctions on drug use in this country. I believe that anyone advocating the continuation of prohibition must look at the last eight decades of unregulated drug use and trafficking in the black market—including the popularization of cocaine, crack, and heroin—to see that we are far from any kind of equilibrium and that in fact more innocent people in our society are now negatively affected by drugs in our society than needs to be the case. Legalization advocates do not promise a "happy equilibrium" resulting from a more open drug economy, as Musto misleadingly suggests, but rather a "better equilibrium" than we have now. Legalization—or relegalization—of drugs does not promise heaven on earth, but it does promise an opportunity to reduce to a minimum the hellish parts of our brief mortal life on this small planet.

I would gladly trade the disaster we have created with criminal prohibition for the relatively innocuous disorder of the last century. That is why I have taken the position that the future of drug control lies in the past, with some modern tinkering at the edges of the new-old system. Much of the support for this radical reform—"back to the future"—can be found in such authoritative books as *The American Disease* (Musto [1973] 1987). While Musto does not support his contention that history proves legalization a bad bet, he does provide, unwittingly perhaps, ample ammunition to prove that criminalization was utterly irrational and was a classic case of old-fashioned American overkill.

While the public eventually did demand control at the national level, time and time again Musto explains how social and governmental leaders distorted the nature and dimensions of the drug threat so as to provoke extreme public emotions. In a nutshell, Musto's story is that American drug-control policy evolved out of a mixture of many factors: very real fears about the impact of the uncontrolled sale of addicting drugs on the general population, the mercenary desires of the drug industry, imperialism, our perceived and well-intentioned duty to uplift inferior foreign peoples burdened by the opium habit, prejudice against Negroes and Mexican and Chinese immigrants, moral crusading by religious and lay leaders that painted drug users as devils, and distortions of the known scientific facts about drugs.

American leaders thus created a distorted social response to the many emerging American problems early in the century: they created a demand for drug control based upon hysteria, misinformation, and hatred of racial minorities and foreigners, who allegedly shared the blame for these problems.

Many other prohibitionist scholars, particularly James A. Inciardi, have committed Musto's error of meticulously documenting the creation and fanning of public hysteria, and then pointing to the resultant public demand for harsh laws as proof of a rational need for rigid control. This contradictory stance was particularly apparent in the first chapter of both *The War on Drugs* (Inciardi 1986) and *The War on Drugs II* (Inciardi 1992), although criticism of the hysteria of the drug warriors also appeared in other parts of these books. For example, Inciardi told of how fears of foreigners and of blacks were manipulated to support repressive controls on the drugs associated with those groups.

Inciardi documents how these distortions continued well into this century. Even the *New York Times,* he observes, weighed in with hysterical stories on the evils of marijuana. One such story, headlined "Mexican Family Go Insane" and datelined Mexico City, 6 July 1927, began, "A widow and her four children have been driven insane by eating the Marihuana plant, according to doctors, who say that there is no hope of saving the childrens' lives and that the mother will be insane the rest of her life" (Inciardi 1992, 21–22). Inciardi also accused Harry Anslinger, the commissioner of the Treasury Department's Bureau of Narcotics and the leading American force for prohibition in this century, of consistently perverting the facts about most drugs, but especially about marijuana. "Using the mass media as his forum, Anslinger described marijuana as a Frankenstein drug that was stalking American youth," Inciardi wrote. "Then there was Anslinger's 'gore file,' a collection of the most heinous cases, most with only the flimsiest of documentation, that graphically depicted the insane violence that marijuana use engendered" (Inciardi 1992, 23).[13]

Rhetoric aside, what is now clear is that at no time did political leaders sit down and mull over the best way to approach the drug problem. While it would be unfair to characterize drug prohibition as a

---

13. It is ironic that Inciardi refers to Anslinger's "gore file" when he himself is guilty of some of the same types of offenses, such as using bloody examples and making dozens of unnecessary references to obscene street talk. One is forced to wonder if both the past commissioner and the present professor were seeking to curb rational debate through these tactics.

historical accident, we can at least say unequivocally that it was not a rationally chosen option. Indeed, it should stand as one of America's most successful campaigns of distortion and demagoguery.

A Second Look at Pre-Prohibition Addiction Numbers

Since we have seen that prohibition was not a rationally chosen drug-control approach, it is worth examining whether its results have been better than the results that might have been produced by other policy options. James Inciardi seems to believe that the American drug-control system has ultimately justified itself by its results. One way to examine this question is to look at addiction rate statistics used by two leading historians to show the value of prohibition.

David F. Musto estimates that there were 250,000 addicts in the United States in 1900, a number he describes as "comparatively large," apparently in reference to the smaller estimates of opiate addicts in other Western countries (Musto [1973] 1987, 5). In a separate piece of analysis, Musto described this level of addiction as "a rate so far never equalled or exceeded" (Musto [1973] 1987, 42). In a footnote at this point, however, he mentioned a slightly higher estimate for the mid–1890s which was made by David T. Courtwright (1982): "After carefully considering contemporary surveys, importation statistics, and other estimates, Professor Courtwright concluded that the highest rate of addiction in the United States occurred in the 1890s at the maximum rate of 4.59 per 1,000" (Musto 1987, 42).

Musto then made this significant comparison: "Today that rate would result in 1.1 million addicts, about twice the current official estimate" (Musto [1973] 1987, 42). As we shall soon see this is a highly questionable statement on several grounds.

In the study cited by Musto, David Courtwright performs a massive and admirable review of almost every scrap of evidence on opium addiction available at the time, and on the basis of modern methods of mathematical interpretation, he concludes that "in round figures, there were never more than 313,000 opiate addicts in America prior to 1914" (Courtwright 1982, 9). Thus, the Musto-Courtwright thesis suggests that in the mid–1890s American opiate addiction peaked at 313,000 and then began a decline down to 250,000 in 1900. While these estimates were lower than many made by officials at the time, they were nonetheless reflective of addiction rates higher than those in other countries and higher than current U.S. rates. In effect, the thesis would conclude that before the advent of criminal laws creating prohibition, the situation was out of control and intolerable.

The official count of U.S. population in 1900 was 76,212,168. Using the Musto-Courtwright figures, the number of American opiate addicts amounted to approximately 0.41 percent of the population in the mid–1890s, and dropped to 0.33 percent by 1900.

Both Musto and Courtwright seem to support the Harrison Act and the continued use of criminal law to control most drug use, although both plead for compassion in dealing with users. Their scholarship has often been offered as scientific proof that repeal of the drug laws is an immensely complicated and very risky undertaking because addiction was rampant before the criminal law controls were enacted. Yet, no one seems to have noticed that these leading scholars have documented that before national drug prohibition, when narcotics were freely available to any citizen (over the counter in many American communities or by mail order in all areas), over 99.6 percent of the American population was not addicted to these substances.

It would seem that on the basis of these figures alone a good case has been made for the efficacy of the policy that helped create that seemingly low level of addiction with little or no attendant crime or violence related to drug trafficking. Those figures also lend support to the idea, which I and other reformers have long advocated, that there is a natural limit to the number of people who will engage in any activity or who will ingest any substance whether or not it is legal. Personal, ethical, and cultural forces control rises and falls in mass addiction trends, not the law. Even when a drug is not controlled by law and is freely available, most people do not even think about imbibing.

But what about Musto's seemingly precise calculation that the earlier rates had never been equalled or exceeded and that the rate of 4.59 opiate addicts per 1,000 population would result in 1.1 million addicts today (twice the current rate)? (Assumably, he was referring to the oft-quoted recent government estimate of 500,000 *heroin* addicts.) Certainly, this would seem to indicate that whatever the defects of prohibition and the war on drugs, scientific calculations demonstrate that the situation is much better now than in the 1890s.

This line of reasoning is one of the principal scholarly bulwarks for the war on drugs, but it has many defects—not least that there seems to have been precious little science involved in the calculations. Years ago, in preparing to write *The Heroin Solution* (1982), I went through many of the same reports as did Musto and Courtwright and concluded that the estimates of addiction rates then and now varied so widely that no responsible scholar could rely upon them, except in very general terms. The unreliability of much of the data for purposes of historical comparisons is best understood by looking at some of the extant estimates then and now.

Many of the old estimates are to be found in the classic work by Charles E. Terry and Mildred Pellens ([1928] 1970), which reports on many surveys and studies then available of the use of drugs, particularly opium. Terry and Pellens extrapolate from Orville Marshall's survey of the so-called opium habit in Michigan, which concluded that there were 7,763 "opium eaters" in the state, to estimate that there were 251,936 in the entire country for the year 1874 ([1928] 1970, 15). Such extrapolations, based upon doubtful assumptions, were often made at that time and later by researchers.

Marshall's was the earliest such survey of which Terry and Pellens had knowledge, and they reported many of its findings. However, the survey was based upon professional guesses and interpretations, many of which were in conflict. In one instance a physician reported that there was one addict in the small town of Monroe, while a druggist claimed to know of 60 in the same town. This suggests how impressionistic much of the allegedly objective data was and also suggests that many occasional users might have been reported as addicts. The drugs explicitly included in the survey were opium and morphine, but others might also have been reported. Marshall based some of his estimates of the number of addicts on reports of the amount of drugs imported into the state, a research technique that drew criticism from Terry and Pellens. On the whole Terry and Pellens thought Marshall's estimates were quite unreliable.

Another study they discuss shows the importance of extrapolation and illustrates the role of guesses in so much of our early drug sociology. Justin M. Hull's survey of a sample of Iowa druggists for 1884 found "234 users of opium in some form. Of these 86 were men and 129 women. The form of drug used was morphin [sic], 129; gum opium, 73; laudanum, 12; paregoric, 6; Dover's Powder, 3; McMunn's Elixir, 4." Hull extrapolated on the basis of his data that there were at least 5,732 chronic users of these drugs in the state of Iowa; Terry and Pellens estimate, on this basis, that there were 182,215 chronic users in the entire country during 1884 (Terry and Pellens [1928] 1970, 17–18).

Another study they cite demonstrates that even careful reporting could be useless if the drugs recorded were mixed. A. P. Grinnell studied "the enormous consumption of narcotics or stimulating drugs" in the state of Vermont for the year 1990. He reported large amounts of the drug sold but came to no conclusions as to the precise numbers of chronic users. He did, however, shed some more light on the broad definition sometimes given to "narcotics or stimulating drugs" in the old surveys (Terry and Pellens [1928] 1970, 22). His questionnaire to druggists included the following detailed description of the drugs included in his survey:

Opium (gum or powder)
Morphine sulp. (powder or pills)
Dover powder
Paregoric (tinct. opii. camph.)
Laudanum (tinct. opii.)
Cocaine
Chloral
Indian Hemp (Cannabis Indica)
Quinine (powder or pills)

It is unknown how often such a wide array of drugs—many non-narcotic and non-opiate—were included in estimates of "opiate" use or addiction. The confusion is not completely surprising, however, since top government officials still incorrectly refer to cocaine as a narcotic and even classify marijuana enforcement programs under "narcotics enforcement."

Terry and Pellens ([1928] 1970) also report a number of other, wildly different estimates of addiction for the period around 1900, when Musto estimates there were 250,000 addicts. The American Pharmaceutical Association made surveys in 1902 and 1903 of opium, cocaine, and other habit-forming drugs and issued a statement in 1902 that there were at least 200,000 users in the country. In 1903, however, the association stated that there were "over a million opium smokers" in the country, and did not try to reconcile the apparent conflict (Terry and Pellens [1928] 1970, 23–24).

When he was the medical officer for the city of Jacksonville, Florida, Charles Terry himself estimated that in 1913 0.93 percent of that city's population was addicted to opiates. When he applied the figure to the entire country, he came up with a figure of at least 782,118 addicts (Terry and Pellens [1928] 1970, 25). Lucius P. Brown, the state food and drugs commissioner of Tennessee, reported that on 1 January 1915, a few months before the Harrison Act took effect, there were 2,370 registered opiate addicts in the state, of which 784 were men and 1,586 were women (Terry and Pellens [1928] 1970, 27–28). (Tennessee and other states provided a process of registration which often allowed better care and easier access to drugs for some addicts.) Using these figures, Brown estimated that there were a minimum of 215,000 and as many as 269,000 opiate addicts in the United States in 1915 (Terry and Pellens [1928] 1970, 28). A Special Committee of Investigation appointed by the secretary of the treasury reported in 1919, several years after the Harrison Act had been in effect, that there were a million heroin and cocaine addicts in the country (Terry and Pellens [1928] 1970, 32). Each such national projection by various writers and groups was based upon widely varying methods and produced questionable results.

I encountered similar confusing and conflicting reports in the 1970s when I was seeking to nail down the best estimates of the number of heroin addicts in the country. As I reported (Trebach 1982, 298), the Federal Bureau of Narcotics (FBN) and the National Institute of Mental Health placed the number of "opiate addicts" in 1971 at between 215,000 and 315,000. The successor agency to the FBN, the Bureau of Narcotics and Dangerous Drugs (BNDD), reported only two years later, in January 1973, there were 626,000 "heroin addicts" in the country; the successor to BNDD, the Drug Enforcement Administration, told me that there were an estimated 725,000 "narcotics addicts and abusers" in the country in 1975. In 1977, the House of Representatives Select Committee on Narcotics Abuse and Control reported that "we have more than 800,000 heroin addicts" (Trebach 1982, 298). I have no idea whether any of these estimates were correct or even in the ballpark.

One of the most reflective reports I saw at the time was from the Carter White House Office of Drug Abuse Policy, which stated in 1978 that on any given day there were 500,000 daily heroin users or addicts and 1.5 million less-than-daily heroin users—and that as many as 4 million people had used heroin at least once in the preceding year (Trebach 1982, 245). This estimate dealt only with heroin and not with other opiates or cocaine. In 1992 a congressional committee placed the number of heroin addicts at 750,000 (U.S. Congress 1992).

If modern estimates on addiction to other opiates such as dilaudid, methadone, morphine, and codeine are added to this figure of 750,000, then the number of opiate addicts in modern America could well exceed 1.5 million, yielding an addiction rate of 6.03 per 1,000 (using the 1990 U.S. Census Bureau population figure of 248,709,873). Such a figure—based on estimates and information similar to that used by modern scholars looking at the drug situation before prohibition—

would appear to contradict any confident claim that opiate addiction was demonstrably worse before prohibition was enacted than it is now.

If, as was often done in the early studies, we added in estimates of the number of those addicted to many other drugs today, especially the roughly 2 million cocaine addicts, the current total for the country would be at least 4 million, with a comparatively huge addiction rate of 16.08 per 1,000. Conceivably, the figure for all drug addicts, excluding alcohol and tobacco, could be much higher than 4 million. In launching the Center on Addiction and Substance Abuse at Columbia University in the summer of 1992, Joseph A. Califano, Jr., estimated that, in addition to the high numbers of addictions to other drugs, 10 million Americans abuse barbiturates or other sedative-hypnotic drugs. This figure, if believable, would yield an abuse rate of 40.2 per 1,000 (Califano 1992, 2). Such drugs are often prescribed by doctors for middle- and upper-class patients, but they have many of the same beneficial and addictive attributes as the opiates.

Thus, the charge that prohibition enforced through the criminal law has succeeded in reducing the total number of addicts or the rate of opiate addiction in the United States cannot be supported by the evidence at hand, despite the claims of leading experts to the contrary. Conclusions based upon seemingly precise mathematical comparisons between the rate of addiction at the turn of the century and today are, to put a fine point on the matter, irresponsible.[14] The prohibitionist scholars should admit they are only guessing and apologize for their misleading conclusions, which provide seemingly learned support for destructive policies—even though, as in the cases of Musto and Courtwright, they may oppose the excesses of many current drug enforcement methods.

Setting aside the question of cause and effect from the drug-control

14. James Inciardi claims the current system is working today to reduce heroin addiction, using methods similar to those used in historical claims debunked throughout this chapter. He writes, "In the United States, where the number of heroin addicts has remained relatively stable at 500,000, the addiction rate actually declined over this same period [1985 to 1990], from 209.3 per 100,000 population in 1985 to 198.8 in 1990" (Inciardi 1992, 266–67). What Inciardi offers here, while sounding typically precise, is in fact a guess. He takes an old rough estimate of the heroin addict population from 1978—500,000, a figure which may well be in the ballpark of accuracy—and compares it with two precise figures for the U.S. population, which expanded slightly between 1985 and 1990. This calculation gives scientific-looking numbers that show a decline in addiction. Perhaps addiction rates did decline during this period, but Inciardi fails to show it, and he reveals a willingness to rely on doubtful figures without qualifications in order to make the point that prohibition works.

system, it is worth noting that the major explosions in drug use over the last three decades—including the massive outbreak of marijuana and psychedelics use in the 1960s and 1970s, the peak of upper-class use of cocaine in the 1970s and 1980s, and the so-called epidemic of crack use nationwide in the 1980s and 1990s—all took place under conditions of strict prohibition. This is not surprising, in that there have always been doubts about the ability of criminal law to police the private behavior of the people. It is especially noteworthy, however, that scholars seeking to demonstrate the value of prohibition in keeping drug use and addiction at allegedly lower-than-natural rates avoid discussing these explosions in drug use, preferring to focus primarily on limited statistics that show only the cyclical declines in drug use.

If by this point some readers' eyes are glazing over because they have been wading through these contradictory and mushy statistics, allow me to summarize the major points of this section:

■ The statistical information on the size of the addict population historically has been and is now indeed mushy and confusing; there are no reliable comparable data about the size of the addict population before and after prohibition.

■ Certainly there is no evidence that there was a huge population of addicts before prohibition when drugs were freely available.

■ Accordingly, there is no support in the available addiction data for a policy as harmful as prohibition.

The Early Addicts Were Not a Social Threat

However many addicts there were at the turn of the century, it appears clear that these "opium eaters," as they were often called, did not create major social problems. They were feared and hated by many, as were the witches of Salem, but like those unfortunate victims of an earlier American hysteria, the factual record gives no civilized support for the criminal punishments inflicted upon them. Their major "crimes" were that they used chemicals not approved by people in power, that they often seemed to enjoy themselves too much, that many of them were Chinese or Mexican or Negro, that these alien types sometimes attracted white folks to their ways of pleasure, that they seemed too devoted to their chemical pleasures and not enough to material and social advancement, and that they represented a vague but wide array of threats to the established order of things as they should have been in decent American society.

There were also contradictory charges that, on the one hand, opium eaters were especially to be found among the ranks of fallen women and seamy male gamblers, and, on the other, that the vice was so insidious that society matrons and business tycoons could be compulsive opium eaters for years without anyone knowing of their disgrace. Yet none of the respected scholarly authorities provides any evidence that narcotic addicts as a group at the turn of the century committed more predatory crimes because of taking drugs, that there was a major criminal underworld of anything approaching the proportions of the current drug trade, or that industries could not function or ships could not sail because the workers or crews were intoxicated on freely available opium, heroin, and morphine, not to mention cocaine and other drugs. While all of these drugs were freely available in abundant quantities, the vast majority of the American people made free choices not to use them. Americans did not make up a nation of drugged, criminal zombies.

Before prohibition in 1914, we enjoyed more freedom to choose and we chose not to use drugs, and if we used them, we chose not to abuse them. Those who did become addicts constituted a minor nuisance to society. They were not the menace that many, then and now, have seen them to be. The pre-prohibition addicts as a group did not amount to the social threat that our martial drug repression policies have created out of addicts today. When I review realistic stories and analyses of addicts' lifestyles at the turn of the century, I am reminded of nothing so much as the addicts of the United Kingdom whom I have met or read about during the last twenty years. The British addicts are at worst a nuisance, but they are not a threat to the social order.

Perhaps the majority of American addicts at the turn of the century, as far as can be guessed from the objective facts available, were white women. Many of those female addicts were from the middle and upper classes who used opiates regularly in large doses and yet were able to hide their addiction from almost everyone, including sometimes from their closest relatives. The majority might well have been housewives who probably became addicted in the course of medical treatment by a physician or other medical practitioner and who probably used opiates in the form of pills or liquid nostrums in the same way that tranquilizers and stress-relievers are used today. These female opiate addicts often appear in American literature, such as Mrs. Henriette Lafayette Dubose, a sympathetic character in Harper Lee's *To Kill a Mockingbird,* who was a rich widow living in a small Alabama town who became addicted in the course of medical treatment for a painful condition.

After reviewing a great mass of data found in the early surveys about addicts, David Courtwright observes,

> Although fictitious, Mrs. Dubose personifies the American addict of the late nineteenth and early twentieth centuries. If all of the foregoing statistics were condensed into a single, modal type, it would closely resemble Mrs. Dubose: a native Southerner, possessed of servant and property, once married, now widowed and homebound, evidently addicted since late middle age. In all respects—her sex, age of addiction, race, nationality, region, class, and occupation—she is typical. Typical, too, is the origin of her condition: she was addicted by her physician (Courtwright 1982, 42).

In other parts of his work, Courtwright builds on this last point about physicians. He seems to argue that the venality or ignorance of the medical and pharmaceutical professions and trades regarding the dispensation of narcotics provided major justification for the rigorous drug-control laws that were enacted around the turn of the century.

Yet this depiction of the typical early addict could argue for precisely the opposite conclusion. Older, housebound women of the middle and upper classes were not a criminal threat to anyone, no matter what peculiar habits they might have had. It made no sense at the time to pass laws that made instant criminals of both these decent female citizens and the people who provided them with their drugs of choice. Concerns about opiate intake could have been dealt with far differently, with more compassion and effectiveness.

At the other end of the social spectrum, however, there is seemingly reliable evidence that many criminals at this time were opiate addicts. Experts then believed that whole classes of criminals were created by the ingestion of narcotics. Many believe that now. For example, James A. Inciardi argues that drugs drive crime, that the taking of drugs makes addicts commit crimes. Yet, there is scant evidence to support this cause-and-effect relationship in regard to large groups of addicts, especially those who take narcotics.

The weight of evidence suggests that for those who are social deviants, the same unorthodox drives that move them toward crime move them toward narcotics, and also that the illegality of drugs is a major force moving poor addicts toward more crime, in order to obtain funds to buy drugs. (The drugs-crime connection is dealt with more extensively in section 4.)

Before prohibition, such sensible arguments about the true relationships between drugs and crime were rarely heard, although many doctors argued that their "drug fiend" patients were really quite decent people who were no more criminal or deviant, except for their drug habits, than anyone else. It was only after the foundation for the vast prohibition machinery had been set in place that more influential voices were consistently heard voicing this more tolerant message.

Starting in the 1920s, Lawrence Kolb, M.D., assistant surgeon general of the United States, provided overwhelming evidence that the assumptions that had forced national drug prohibition upon an unknowing nation were false. "No opiate ever directly influenced addicts to commit violent crime," he concluded in 1925 after an intensive psychiatric and personality study of 225 addicted prisoners. Kolb explained further:

> No addict who receives an adequate supply of opium and has money enough to live is converted into a liar or thief by the direct result of the drug itself. The direct effect is to remove the irritability and unrest so characteristic of psychopathic individuals. The soothing effect of opiates in such cases is so striking and universally characteristic that one is led to believe that violent crime would be much less prevalent if all habitual criminals were addicts who could obtain sufficient morphine or heroin to keep themselves fully charged with one of these drugs at all times (Terry and Pellens [1928] 1970, 505).

Kolb illustrated "the effect of morphine and heroin in reducing courage and aggressiveness" among addicts by stories such as "the experience of the wife who said she could turn her husband around her finger when he was under the influence of heroin, but that other times he was irritable and disagreeable." Quotations directly from addicts further illustrated the calming nature of heroin for many users:

> If there is any yellow in you, heroin will bring it out. A man could slap you in the face and you would not resent it. You have no guts when you take this drug (Terry and Pellens [1928] 1970, 507).

Kolb did see many problems for heroin users, especially in a society where the drugs were illegal. He observed, "Although the immediate effect of all opiates is to curb criminal tendencies, the continued effect of the drug is to create petty thieves because the lethargy, loss of ambition, idleness, and physical depletion produced by the drugs, together with the social and legal difficulties of an addict's career,

result in moral deterioration and financial embarrassment'' (Terry and
Pellens [1928] 1970, 507). He added the thought that the greatest
difficulties were suffered by people who originally were neurotic or
mildly psychotic and that

> only a few who had in the beginning potentialities for growth into first
> class citizens became thieves in order to satisfy their addiction. The more
> normal addicts continued to work and support themselves honestly. When
> this became impossible, they as a rule sought cure in order to relieve the
> financial burden (Terry and Pellens [1928], 1970, 508).

The writings of Kolb about narcotic addicts remind me of the gentle
approach taken by many British, Dutch, and, more recently, Austra-
lian drug experts. There is the assumption that drugs, even heroin, do
not deprive a human being of basic dignity or rationality. Had such
different assumptions been operative in America, the history of narcotic drug control in the United States would have been a more positive
one.

Opium Smoking: The Original Sin

More evidence of the comparatively gentle nature of the drug problem
at the turn of the century is found in the largely forgotten custom of
opium smoking in the United States. Indeed, the modern era in drug
control may well have started with the fear that white people, especially the young, as well as defenseless females of all ages, were
succumbing in epidemic numbers to the lure of opium smoking.

This peculiar practice originally had been thought to have been
restricted to Chinese immigrants brought here in the mid-nineteenth
century as coolie laborers to help develop a wild continent. By the
1870s it had become apparent that a significant number of white people
of all classes, ages, and genders were to be found in opium dens
sharing the pipe with Chinese smokers. This was particularly true in
the West and not only in an urban cosmopolis like San Francisco, but
also in many small towns scattered throughout the prairies. It is likely
that many cowboys came off the dusty trail into a frontier town looking
for the opium pipe either in place of or in addition to the other more
well-publicized diversions then available.

The thought that this foreign habit was reaching and ruining the
decent white population galvanized the growing anti-opium movement

into action. Thus, it might be said that opium smoking was the original sin which launched criminal prohibition and ultimately the modern war on drugs. Many of the original war zealots openly used the language of bigotry to justify their actions. Their call to prohibitionist arms sounded much like the intolerance of those who led campaigns of persecution of Jews on the basis of religion and blacks on the basis of skin color. Contemporaneous accounts by writers documenting what they felt was the need for repressive laws and for imprisonment of opium smokers instead reveal just how irrational and biased those laws were.

A review of this record reveals that virtually every problem that the anti-opium crusaders placed at the door of opium smoking—including addiction, broken families, and crime—is worse now in the United States and the other countries.

Those opposed to opium smoking believed that they could rid the country of this practice by declaring it illegal and by directing the police to relentlessly pursue opium smokers. The anti-opium warriors never examined whether the new local prohibition laws and ordinances would create more problems than the original vice, thus flunking the Rangel-Bennett-Inciardi test, which requires predictions of the precise impact of drug-reform laws prior to their passage.

Initially there were scattered local ordinances, the first in the 1870s in the West, that prohibited opium smoking and the keeping of opium dens and often carried only a fine.

When the police and other informed observers reported that the laws could not really control opium smoking and that arrests simply seemed to motivate smokers into more ingenious ways of hiding their smoking, the reaction of officials was to demand harsher, more comprehensive, and more intrusive criminal laws. There followed prohibition statutes that penalized opium smoking by imprisonment in the state penitentiary. The Nevada prohibition law, a taste of future statutes, made it a crime for a person to be found in possession of opium, unless it had been prescribed by a physician (Kane 1882, 3).

American crusaders soon were involved as leaders in a major national and international campaign against all forms of opiates, but especially opium smoking. A treaty of 1880 with China prohibited the importation of opium by Chinese subjects in the United States (Terry and Pellens [1928] 1970, 745). The Internal Revenue Act of 1890 provided for a high tax on all opium manufactured in the United States and restricted the manufacture of smoking opium to citizens of the United States. The first national criminal drug-control law came on

9 February 1909, when Congress passed a law entitled "An act to prohibit the importation and use of opium for other than medicinal purposes" (Terry and Pellens [1928] 1970, 745). It became obvious within a few years that criminal prohibition of opium smoking was not working and that other, even more destructive, forms of disapproved drug use were spreading. After much national and international agitation at the highest levels of power, as we have seen, the Harrison Act, a comprehensive national prohibition law, was passed in 1914 and went into effect on 1 March 1915. The intent of the Harrison Act was to make criminal the use of all narcotics as well as cocaine, not merely opium smoking, unless they were prescribed by a physician. It is of interest in this context that the foundation for national drug prohibition was enacted originally as an amendment to the 1909 national law seeking to curb opium smoking.

Looking the New Evil in the Face

Typical of contemporaneous accounts of the evils of opium smoking of the time is that found in a small tome by Harry Hubbell Kane, M.D., apparently the owner and director of the DeQuincy Home, Fort Washington, New York City (Kane 1882). Published in 1882, the book was entitled *Opium-Smoking in America and China*. Kane treated drug addicts at his sanitarium and also did research on the subject of addiction. He explains that until a few years before he wrote this book, he believed that opium smoking was a vice confined entirely to Orientals. Now, he said, there was cause for great alarm since "the practice, comparatively unknown amongst us six years ago, is now indulged by some six thousand of our countrymen, male and female . . ." (Kane 1882, iii). As has become typical in the drug field, no solid basis was provided for that national estimate of the extent of the use of this new drug. Kane placed a good deal of the blame for the problem in the world on the selfish actions of the British in compelling the Chinese by force of arms to accept the opium trade, but he focused most of his attention on the growing use of opium smoking in the United States. A typical, shocking story was how the habit reached Virginia City, Nevada:

> Opium smoking had been entirely confined to the Chinese up to and before the autumn of 1876, when the practice was introduced by a sporting character who had lived in China, where he had contracted the

habit. He spread the habit among his class, and his mistress, "a woman of the town," introduced it among her demi-monde acquaintances, and it was not long before it had widely spread amongst the people mentioned, and then amongst the younger class of boys and girls, many of the latter of the more respected class of families. The habit grew very rapidly, until it reached young women of more mature age, when the necessity for stringent measures became apparent, and was met by the passing of a city ordinance (Kane 1882, 3).

While Kane relays reports that some addicted smokers were engaged in petty crimes, the overwhelming impression he creates in every eyewitness account of his own or others that he recounts is that of a largely peaceful opium-smoking scene. In his eyes (and those of other experts of the time), the opium smokers were obviously immoral, sinful, vicious, and a threat to the good people of society. However, the pictures he paints are of people who wanted literally to hide in dens, withdraw from the world, relax, reflect, and talk and laugh together quietly—all the while taking the real risk that they would become addicted to a very powerful drug that could in time cause immense personal distress for them and their families.

Kane's first visit to an opium den occurred one dark night about 9 P.M. "in the company of an old smoker." Kane found that Mott Street in New York City "was alive with swarthy-faced Celestials," and he and his companion made their way through several rooms, in one of which they saw "a pleasant-faced Chinese who, with scales in hand, was weighing out some opium." Eventually they found themselves in "the smoking room" which he describes in these terms:

> In the back part of the room there were two tiers of bunks. Close to the ceiling was a narrow grated window, the only means of ventilation. Upon these bunks were stretched transversely, in parties of two or three, some twelve men and women—Americans—engaged in cooking and smoking opium. The whole place was rank with the odor of the drug.
> The recumbent forms, the quiet faces half lit by the little opium lamps, the subdued conversation, the sizzling and bubbling of the pipes, served to impress us with astonishment, and suggested something uncanny (Kane 1882, 7–8).

It is unclear why Kane and his companion were astonished or found what they saw somehow uncanny. However, it is clear that these smokers, while deviant in American terms, were peaceful and did not represent a threat to society. Yet Kane and the leaders of the nation advocated sending the police after these generally unthreatening people, time and time again. Kane wrote approvingly of a raid that had been reported in a Stockton, California, newspaper on 2 August 1881, when four officers "raided an opium den located in a wooden building back of a house of ill-fame . . . and captured four smokers—a white man, a Chinaman, and two white women—all stretched out on bunks and enjoying a quiet smoke" (Kane 1882, 9). The newspaper reported another raid in the same edition under the lead, "One Man Arrests Twenty." The story related that

> Officer Chris. B. Ryer of Oakdale, Monday night, raided an opium den kept by a Chinaman named Tuck Tye, who is a merchant in that thriving village. The officer, single-handed and alone, arrested two white men and eighteen Chinamen, and locked the whole party in a room over which he stood guard all night (Kane 1882, 10).

Kane's book is full of accounts documenting the perverse effects and futility of prohibition: "The very fact that opium-smoking was a practice forbidden by law seemed to lead many who would not otherwise have indulged to seek out the low dens and patronize them, while the regular smokers found additional pleasure in continuing that about which there was a spice of danger. It seemed to add zest to their enjoyment" (Kane 1882, 2). The *San Francisco Chronicle* ran a story on 25 July 1881, retold by Kane, that foretold the future of prohibition, although it was not seen as such at the time:

> "We didn't pretend to have broken up the habit of opium smoking," said the Police-Officer James Mahoney, who has figured extensively in the raids on Chinese opium and gambling dens. "That can't be done by any number of ordinances, no matter how rigidly enforced. We have, however, closed up the opium dens. I mean by that, the places formerly kept by Chinese in Chinatown, where anyone could go and smoke opium by paying for the privilege. These places were supported principally by the patronage of white men and women. The likely chance of having to pay $20 in the Police Court for the privilege has made the white smokers find other means of hitting the pipe."
>
> "What means have they found?"
>
> "All of them who can afford it now have their own lay-outs for smoking and sleeping-rooms. Those who are too poor for that beg the privilege from more lucky friends. We can keep pretty good track of the number of these lay-outs around town by the number of whites who come into Chinatown for opium."

"How many rooms where opium is smoked do you suppose there are outside of Chinatown?"

"The number probably would not fall under 200. You see we can do nothing to prevent it" (Kane 1882, 10–11).

When asked if the habit would gradually die out now that the white smokers have been driven out of Chinatown, Officer Mahoney replied, "It will rapidly increase."

What about the effect of opium smoking on the health and behavior of the user? While Kane clearly believed that the general effect was negative, he sought to be balanced in his assessment:

Between opium-smoking and chronic alcoholism there can be no comparison. The latter is by far the greater evil, both as regards to its effects on the individual and on the community. The opium smoker does not break furniture, beat his wife, kill his fellow-men, reel through the streets disgracing himself or friends, or wind up a long debauch comatose in the gutter. He is not unfitted for work to the same extent that an inebriate is. True organic lesions rarely follow.

Many Chinamen smoke, and we should expect to find them incapacitated for work by it. But it is not so. From the overwhelming testimony given before . . . [a] Congressional Committee to the effect that Chinamen, placed side by side with American, Irish, and British miners, do more than they in a given time on the hardest kind of work, we are fain to believe that the extreme physical deterioration claimed to result from opium-smoking must need some modification before being admitted to full belief (Kane 1882, 74–75).

Here and in other parts of his work, Kane seems to have stumbled upon the truth, documented by modern science, that all of the opiates are generally benign in terms of causing organic harm, unlike alcohol. While many users of opiates suffer ill health, their poor condition may result from poor living and eating conditions—which of course may be propelled by a state of addiction—but not directly from the impact of opiates upon organs and tissues.

What about overdoses and deaths? If there exists a single documented case of an overdose death from opium smoking in the entire record of centuries, I have not yet uncovered it, even though such deaths may have occurred. Certainly, there were none reported in the works of the modern prohibitionist scholars. Kane hints at reports of such deaths in his book, but he doubted their veracity, as he suggests in the above quotation.

What about the related issue of longevity? Did opium smoking shorten life, particularly from long-term deterioration as distinguished from overdoses? Here there are a good many reports that opium smokers live much shorter lives than non-smokers, partly because many addicted smokers ignore their health. Yet the objective medical evidence, if assessed fairly, is mixed on this issue also. And that is precisely what Kane reports. He explains how many medical experts were absolutely convinced that opium users invariably shortened their life spans, but he also quotes authorities such as Dr. O'Shaughnessy of Calcutta, who declared flatly, "The longevity of the opium eater is proverbial." After reviewing all of the conflicting reports, Kane judiciously concludes, "We can only say from *a priori* reasoning that it is *probable* that the natural term of life is abridged somewhat, if the drug is used to decided excess. To ascribe the early death of every opium smoker to opium, as has been done, is, however, unjustifiable and nonsensical" (Kane 1882, 142–43).

The First Prohibitionist War: Was It Worthwhile?

While many opium smokers were, as we have seen, deviants and criminals, there is no evidence that the opium trade or the ingestion of the drug was related to any significant amount of crime of any kind. There was a considerable amount of smuggling to avoid customs duties and other legal regulations, such as those meant to keep opium away from Chinese immigrants, at the end of the last century and at the beginning of this one. However, it appears that this illegal activity was largely peaceful and nonviolent. Indeed, I have encountered no reports in the last century or this of a homicide in the American opium trade, although some might well have happened.

David Courtwright (1982) provides an extensive review of the literature, revealing many important insights into how opium smoking spread rapidly across the country a century ago, but he suggests there is little indication of crime resulting from these activities or in connection with them. Quite the contrary. One New York addict, according to Courtwright, said that fights were practically unknown in the dens. "Instead, the smokers passed the time between pipes by chatting, smoking tobacco, telling stories, cracking jokes, or even singing in low voices," Courtwright said, adding:

> Within the den a rigid code of honor prevailed: smokers would not take
> advantage of other smokers, or tolerate those who did. "I have seen men

and women come in the joints while under the influence of liquor,'' continued the New York addict, ''lie down and go to sleep with jewelry exposed and money in their pockets, but no one would ever think of disturbing them'' (Courtwright 1982, 73).

The reflections of one white girl of good family who began smoking at age 16 in San Francisco are instructive. She started smoking in 1880, became addicted, and then entered into a life of prostitution. While she showed some regret about the path of her life, she observed in testimony to a Canadian Royal Commission in 1884 while in a Vancouver opium den:

> There is too much nonsense talked about opium smoking. Life without it would be unendurable [but] I am in excellent health. . . . [I]f opium houses were licensed as drinking saloons are, one need not to come into holes such as this to smoke. There would be nice rooms with nice couches, and the degradation would be mitigated. At all events I think the government that will not license an opium saloon should shut up public houses and hotels where they sell vitriol for whiskey and brandy, and where men kill themselves with a certainty and a rapidity beyond the power of opium (Brecher 1972, 43).

What then did the nation accomplish when it launched its first prohibitionist war, that against opium smoking? It destroyed a sometimes personally unhealthful but almost always peaceful practice by a nonthreatening and nonviolent group of people. It invaded their privacy and dignity and that of many others. It set in motion a series of campaigns in this never-ending drug war that has required the creation of an intrusive drug-control army of police and prison keepers unmatched in the history of democratic societies. That drug-control army also targeted as enemies the peaceful female opiate addicts, perhaps the largest group of dependent persons at the time, and their doctors. This extensive martial power has been one of the main reasons why we have witnessed the replacement of those peaceful opium smokers, those quiet woman addicts, and their peaceful suppliers with larger groups of addicts and suppliers, many of whom are much more violent and many of whom now have the funds and the disposition to match the state virtually weapon for weapon and bullet for bullet in terms of force.

After 110 years of police drug raids, we have created a situation where, in some raids at least, the police-arrestee ratio would have to be almost completely the reverse of the 1-to-20 ratio of the 1881

California arrest mentioned above, in order to assure the safety of the officers. Borrowing a phrase from Harry Hubbell Kane, the suppression of opium smoking, an action he urged, was in retrospect unjustifiable and nonsensical. The suppression, not the vice, is indeed the original sin for which all of us now pay penance every day.

But What about Soldier's Disease?

For many thoughtful scholars, the principal counter to my line of reasoning—that drugs in the last century did not constitute a major social problem—would be the oft-cited cautionary tale about Soldier's Disease. The liberal dispensation of morphine by doctors to wounded and sick Civil War soldiers, the story goes, created a massive amount of addiction. There were so many dependent veterans of the Civil War that morphine addiction earned the sobriquet "the Soldier's Disease." All of this allegedly proved the generally accepted idea that the widespread use of drugs, even in medical settings, almost always results in a large number of abusers and consequent major disruptions of the entire society.

In a seminal paper, however, addiction expert Jerry Mandel makes an impressive case for a different interpretation (Mandel 1989). Mandel reviews the records of the time and comes to the conclusion that while there was evidence of a good deal of drug use, there was none indicating a major social problem stemming from drugs. He observes, "Even the moralistic anti-opium writers of about a century ago, with rare and often unbelievable exceptions, did not point to a publicly noticed problem" (Mandel 1989, 110).

Mandel goes on to confront the reality and the implications of Soldier's Disease. The crux of his argument is:

> The paradigm justifying U.S. opiate policy—availability leads to use; use leads to addiction; addiction is long-term; and addiction becomes a publicly manifest problem—conveys the idea that unavoidable social consequences of free access to opiates justify the enormous costs of contemporary U.S. policy. Of all the stories about the "bad old days" when opiates were legal, only Soldier's Disease provides convincing "evidence" that opiate availability led to a publicly manifest problem . . . (Mandel 1989, 110).

Mandel also relates how the story of Soldier's Disease grew over the years until, like so much else in the addiction field, it was uncritically accepted by leading authorities. Since 1964, he claims, it was mentioned, usually in uncritical terms, in over 100 works, including books by leading critics of American drug policy (such as me). Mandel's research confirms only one part of the story. He found it was true that opium and morphine were handed out liberally, sometimes—in the case of morphine—on the point of a helpful doctor's knife, who thus passed it on to wounded or sick soldiers. Often it was dusted or rubbed directly into wounds. Just after the Civil War, the secretary of war reported that the Union Army alone had issued 10 million opium pills, over 2.84 million ounces of other opiate preparations, and almost 30,000 ounces of morphine. There was nothing new in those numbers. Mandel found no truth, however, in the claim that large numbers of soldier addicts were created. "Yet for all the quantities dispensed," he wrote, "there was not one report from 1861–65 of an addicted soldier" (Mandel 1989, 113).

Such findings *were* new, at least in my eyes. Moreover, Mandel found that "As with morphine, there is not a single report during the Civil War of a soldier using opium for pleasure, and the single claim of opiates used to stave off withdrawal pains (published 16 years after the war) was the 'confession' of an officer charged with 'deserting in the face of the enemy and sentenced to be shot' " (Mandel 1989, 114). There were many reports by journalists and army physicians on the conditions of wounded and sick soldiers (sickness was the major cause of death for soldiers on both sides), yet neither the physicians nor the journalists saw any reason to mention opiate addiction or withdrawal. "In Walt Whitman's description of the 80,000 to 100,000 sick and wounded he saw in 600 hospital visits during three years of the Civil War, he notes that many patients craved tobacco, sweets, or alcohol, yet he never once mentions opium," Mandel observes (1989, 115).

Mandel's search also convinced him that there was no solid support for the claim of widespread addiction by veterans immediately after the war. In taking this position, he directly contradicts the position taken by David Courtwright (1982), who put forth the theory that while Soldier's Disease did not amount to an epidemic, addicted veterans had a major impact on postwar society. Because 63,000 veterans continued to suffer from chronic diarrhea and at least 20,000 were survivors of amputations, it might have been expected that they would have continued to use the most helpful medicines of the time for such conditions. They probably did use opiates, which restrict the motility of the lower bowel and control pain, but Mandel at least found almost no evidence of widespread addiction at the time.

His arguments are convincing. When veterans filled such prisons as Auburn and Sing Sing in New York State, prison keepers told of all types of contraband smuggled into those tough institutions: whiskey, tobacco, sugar, tea, coffee, pies, cakes—"yet opiates were not mentioned" (Mandel 1989, 115). The Mississippi State Hospital reported its first narcotism admission in 1884. The major cause of the wide acceptance of Soldier's Disease may well have been its naive endorsement by Terry and Pellens ([1928] 1970), but, as Mandel reminds us, there was virtually no mention of the problem in all of the extensive surveys performed in the latter part of the nineteenth century—surveys that Terry and Pellens reported in their seminal volume in 1928 and some of which I have discussed earlier. Mandel states that

> Not one case of addiction [by soldiers] was reported in medical records or the literature of the time; under ten references were made in the Nineteenth century to addiction the cause of which was the Civil War; and no pejorative nick-name for addicted veterans, like Soldier's Disease, appeared in the literature until 1915, and it did not become part of the Conventional Wisdom of drug experts until almost a century after Appomattox (Mandel 1989, 110).

Mandel's conclusions do much violence to the entire basis for prohibition in modern American society:

- "Soldier's disease . . . is a myth" (Mandel 1989, 110).
- "[T]here is no other pre–Harrison Act example of a currently believable social problem" (Mandel 1989, 119).
- "It is in the illegal context that the modern 'opiate problem' arises, rather than in a legal context such as the Civil War. The chemistry lesson of the Civil War is that opiates per se do not cause the problem, the context does" (Mandel 1989, 119).

And the chemistry lesson of the last century, one might add, is that none of the drugs caused the American people as much difficulty as the public policies meant to save us from them.

Legal Drugs Did Not Produce Significant Crime

National drug prohibition has been in effect in the United States for over 75 years. In this section I have argued that there was no rational basis to impose prohibition on the country, that we are much worse off because of it, and that there is no good evidence that prohibition has met its primary goal of curbing the addiction rate. However, there is still more evidence of how mild drug-related problems were before prohibition.

The writings of many conventional scholars and the stories of journalists in the popular press would lead one to believe that social chaos inevitably results when masses of people have easy access to powerful drugs. We have already seen that there is no evidence of any major type of social disruption in the known record from the turn of the century. In the following review of new data, which I and my research assistants gathered in 1992, it becomes clear that crime rates before prohibition were a small fraction of what they are today. A comparison of statistics from a century ago and today shows that crime, the most troubling side effect of drugs in our society, was not at such outrageous levels before drug prohibition as to necessitate tight controls on drugs. Free availability of narcotics, cocaine, and other substances to adults did not lead to substantial crime.

The data that follow are meant only to make that negative point: massive crime was not caused by wide drug availability. It is quite possible that prohibition was the leading cause of the huge increases in crime evident in the last 100 years. However, I do not attempt to make that argument here because so many other social and environmental factors—urbanization, economic dislocations, class conflicts, the breakdown of old family values and controls, to name only a few— have emerged over the last several decades that help explain crime. Moreover, the greater size and skill of local police forces may have contributed to the discovery of more crime in modern times. Nonetheless, I believe the data here seriously undercut the modern argument that legalizing drugs would certainly lead legions of citizens into lives of crime.

Crime data sufficiently similar to be comparable across a century of American history were difficult to find. Today, the FBI issues the Uniform Crime Reports, which use reports from almost all local police departments in the nation to measure "offenses known to the police," which in turn are used to calculate the widely used "crime index." A century ago, there were no equivalent national crime reports. I sought an alternative method of comparison, settling on arrest reports, which have advantages and disadvantages. An arrest report indicates that some definitive official action was taken and a suspect apprehended, thus providing solidity to a crime report. An arrest implies that there was enough evidence to meet the legal standard of probable cause. On the other hand, the number of arrests is always significantly lower than the number of offenses reported to the police. Nevertheless a comparison based on arrest data, even a hundred years apart, should still provide insights that have some degree of consistency.

For convenience, I sought data wherever possible on two years precisely a century apart, one well before and one long after drug prohibition went into effect. It turned out that the best years I could find were 1889 and 1989. In order to calculate crime rates per 100,000 population, I was forced to use the census data from 1890 and 1990, which should in no significant way distort the findings.[15]

Dozens of cities were contacted, most of which did not have data on arrests for 1889. Eventually ten cities were found that had arrest data for both 1889 and 1989 (see table 1).

Homicide is a good indicator of crime trends, in part because record-keeping is generally good and also because the definition does not usually change over time as it does for some other crimes. Generally, homicide is defined as the intentional, unlawful killing of another human being. With one exception, the homicide rates for each city under study went up dramatically from 1889 to 1989. For example, there were 26 arrests for homicide in Chicago during 1889, and 865 in 1989. The homicide arrest rate per 100,000 population in 1889 was 2.4 compared with 31.1 in 1989, an increase of 1,214 percent. On a per capita basis, murders went up over 12 times in Chicago during the 100 years in question.

Similar trends are visible in the murder arrest rates for Boston, Manhattan, and Washington, D.C. Drug-trade murders now are perhaps the single largest cause of homicides in the nation's capital. Washington's 1989 arrest rate for homicide was 47.9 per 100,000. Yet, in 1889, before national drug prohibition, there were only 13 homicide arrests in Washington, for a rate of only 5.6. There seems little doubt that the District of Columbia was a far safer place then.

15. The material for these crime comparisons was gathered primarily by direct contacts with the police departments and the public libraries in the cities involved. The U.S. Census Bureau was consulted for population data. The published material consulted was: Baltimore Police Department (1890, 45–46; 1990); Boston Police Department (1890, 1990); Chicago Police Department (1890); City of Minneapolis (1890, 346); Cleveland Police Department (1890, 1990); D.C. Commissioners (1890, 88); Detroit Police Department (1890, 59; 1990); Macguire and Flanagan (1991, 415); Minneapolis Police Department (1990, 26); New York City Police Department (1890, 28–29); Office of Management Analysis and Planning (1990, 40); Philadelphia Police Department (1890, 22–23; 1990, 23); San Francisco Police Department (1890, 1990); State of Illinois (1991, 118).

Both Detroit and Minneapolis had extremely low levels of arrests in 1889, leading one to wonder whether this was due to poor enforcement or good social conditions or both. Detroit had an arrest rate of 2.4 in 1889, compared with 178.1 in 1989—72 times as high as a century earlier. This was the largest rise in the homicide category. Detroit also had the highest 1989 homicide rate of any city in the sample. Minneapolis went from 1 homicide arrest in 1889 to 32 in 1989, creating a huge rise in percentage terms over the century but still leaving that city with a comparatively low homicide rate.

Of all the comparative numbers generated by this analysis, only those for homicides in San Francisco went heavily against the general trend. In 1889 there were 37 homicide arrests, for a rate of 12.4, while in 1989 there were 63 arrests, for a rate of 8.7. While the drop in the rate was only 30 percent, it was the only significant drop encountered. It was not the purpose of this limited research to speculate on the reasons for this drop, though perhaps others may find it worth exploring in the future.

Robbery is one of the most fear-producing of the crimes since it involves the use of force or a threat of force to take property from a victim. (Fear, of course, is in the eye of the beholder; for many women, fear of rape far outweighs any apprehension about robbery.) In 1889, Manhattan must have been a relatively safe island, since there were only 257 robbery arrests in a population of 1,515,301, resulting in a rate of 17. By 1989, the population had actually dropped slightly but the number of robbery arrests skyrocketed to 9,051, resulting in a rate of 608.5—a 3,488 percent rise over 100 years. It is possible therefore that before prohibition the rate of robberies in Manhattan was roughly 1/35 of what it is today.

With the reservations expressed above about the possible lack of records, it must be observed that the highest rate of increase for any offense was for robbery in Detroit: 18,236 percent or a 182-fold rise. Thirteen robbery arrests were reported in that city during 1889, compared with 11,902 in 1989.

Burglary does not involve personal violence but it is another crime that creates fear, outrage, and a sense of defilement. It involves breaking and entering a structure, often a home, for the purpose of committing a crime. For many victims the impact of a burglary in the home is a sense that their privacy and sense of security will never be the same.

Addicts today are more often involved in burglary than in violent crimes such as homicide and robbery, although many addicts are

Table 1. Arrest Rates in 10 American Cities Before and After Drug Prohibition: 1889 and 1989

	1889			1989			Change in Arrest Rates (%)
	Population*	Arrests	Arrest Rate†	Population‡	Arrests	Arrest Rate†	
Baltimore	434,439			736,014			
Homicide		38	8.7		245	33.3	+281
Robbery		46	10.6		1,801	224.7	+2,211
Burglary		190	43.7		4,252	577.7	+1,221
Boston	448,447			580,095			
Homicide		20	4.5		50	8.6	+93
Robbery		109	24.3		1,471	253.6	+943
Burglary		554	123.5		1,219	210.1	+70
Chicago	1,099,850			2,783,726			
Homicide		26	2.4		865	31.1	+1,214
Robbery		350	31.8		5,027	180.6	+467
Burglary		895	81.4		8,262	296.8	+265
Cleveland	261,353			505,616			
Homicide		4	1.53		168	33.2	+2,071
Robbery		24	9.2		733	145	+1,479
Burglary		17	6.5		1,076	212.8	+3,172
Detroit	205,876			1,027,974			
Homicide		5	2.4		1,831	178.1	+7,234
Robbery		13	6.3		11,902	1,157.8	+18,236
Burglary		22	10.7		3,914	380.7	+3,463
Manhattan	1,515,301			1,487,536			
Homicide		119	7.9		338	22.7	+189
Robbery		257	17		9,051	608.5	+3,488
Burglary		659	43.5		3,383	227.4	+423
Minneapolis	164,738			368,383			
Homicide		1	0.6		32	8.7	+1,331
Robbery		2	1.2		447	121.3	+9,895
Burglary		40	21.3		687	186.5	+668
Philadelphia	1,046,964			1,585,577			
Homicide		24	2.3		477	30.1	+1,212
Robbery		109	10.4		4,774	301.1	+2,792
Burglary		93	8.9		4,603	290.3	+3,168
San Francisco	298,977			723,959			
Homicide		37	12.4		63	8.7	-30
Robbery		360	120.4		866	119.6	-0.7
Burglary		118	39.5		1,661	229.4	+481
Washington, D.C.	230,392			606,900			
Homicide		13	5.6		291	47.9	+750
Robbery		N.A.	N.A.		1,239	204.2	N.A.
Burglary		106	46		1,089	179.4	+290

NOTES TO TABLE 1: Arrest Rates in 10 American Cities Before and After Drug Prohibition
*Population figures in this column are from the 1890 census.
†Arrest rates are per 100,000 population. **Note:** The numbers in these columns are rounded and may not result in the precise calculation shown in the last column.
‡Population figures in this column are from the 1990 census.
N.A.: not available.

Sources Baltimore Police Department, *Report of the Board of Police Commissioners for the City of Baltimore to the General Assembly of Maryland for 1889 and 1890* (Baltimore: Baltimore Police Department, 1890), 45–46; Baltimore Police Department, *Summary of Index Crimes* (Baltimore: Planning and Research Division, 1990); Boston Police Department, *Boston Board of Police Annual Report, December 1889* (Boston: Boston Police Department, 1890); Boston Police Department, *Annual Report of the Boston Police Board 1989* (Boston: Boston Police Department, 1990); Chicago Police Department, *Report of the General Superintendent of Police for the City of Chicago* (Chicago: Chicago Police Department, 1890); City of Minneapolis, *Annual Reports of the Various City Officers of the City of Minneapolis for the Year 1889* (Minneapolis: Harrison and Smith, 1890), 346; Cleveland Police Department, *Annual Report of Police Commissioners: I. L. Morris, James Macneil, Frank D. Bosworth, E. B. Cornell, Commissioners, Year Ending 1889* (Cleveland: Cleveland Police Department, 1890); Cleveland Police Department, *Annual Report of the Police Department, Cleveland, Ohio, 1989* (Cleveland: Cleveland Police Department, 1990), 768–69; D.C. Commissioners, "The Report of the Police Commissioner," in *Report of D.C. Commissioners 1890* (Washington: District of Columbia Government Printing Office, 1890), 88; Detroit Police Department, *Twenty-fifth Annual Report of the Board of Commissioners of the Metropolitan Police to the Common Council of the City of Detroit* (Detroit: Raynor and Taylor, 15 February 1890), 59; Detroit Police Department, "Arrest and Disposition, 1989" in *1989 Annual Report* (Detroit: Detroit Police Department, 1990); Kathleen Macguire and Timothy J. Flanagan, eds., *Sourcebook of Criminal Justice Statistics 1990* (Washington: U.S. Department of Justice, 1991), 415; Minneapolis Police Department, *1989 Annual Report* (Minneapolis: Minneapolis Police Department, 1990), 26; New York City Police Department, *Report of the Police Department of the City of New York for the Year Ending December 31, 1889* (New York: Martin B. Brown, 1890), 28–29; Office of Management Analysis and Planning, *Complaints and Arrests: Police Department of the City of New York, 1989* (New York: Office of Management Analysis and Planning, 1990), 40; Philadelphia Police Department, "Third Annual Message of Edwin H. Fiddler, Mayor of Philadelphia," in *Public Safety 1889*, vol. 2 (Philadelphia: Philadelphia Police Department, 1890), 22–23; Philadelphia Police Department, *Meeting Tomorrow's Challenge: Annual Report* (Philadelphia: Philadelphia Police Department, 1990), 23; San Francisco Police Department, *Annual Commissioner's Report—City of San Francisco, 1889* (San Francisco: San Francisco Police Department, 1890); San Francisco Police Department, *Arrest Report*, cable (San Francisco: San Francisco Police Department, 1990); State of Illinois, *Crime in Illinois, 1990* (Springfield: Authority of the State of Illinois, 1991), 118.

involved in the latter as well. All of the cities surveyed suffered a significantly lower rate of burglaries during the period before national prohibition. This included San Francisco, where the rate of burglary arrests in 1889 was only 39.5 per 100,000 of population, and rose to 229.4 in 1989, a comparatively high gain of 481 percent. This suggests that many of the same dynamics found in either cities regarding most crime data were operating in San Francisco as well.

The highest rate of increase in burglary arrests was in Detroit, where the rate in 1889 was 10.7 per 100,000 and 380.7 in 1989, a rise of 3,463 percent.

Virtually all of the data support my central thesis: the absence of national prohibition and the generally easy availability of drugs cannot be shown to have pushed significant numbers of people into crime. Under prohibition, on the other hand, crime rates have risen dramatically.

Drug abuse will always constitute a threat. However, as I hope I proved in the previous pages, a calm assessment of history demonstrates that we can live better with the threat posed by the availability of legalized drugs than with many of the other threats to health and the social order that we currently face. During the only time that we had widespread experience with virtually complete legalization, before 1 March 1915, the great majority of people withstood the allure of easily available drugs quite nicely.

In light of the information laid out in this section about the situation before drugs were prohibited, it seems appropriate to turn our attention to just how we should go about relegalizing drugs.

4. The Repeal of Drug Prohibition

The repeal of drug prohibition is, in my opinion, clearly more important than the creation of a finely tuned plan of legalization. Many drug policy experts, both prohibitionists and legalizers, see the priorities exactly reversed: plan first, then repeal. While I am certainly willing to lay out a series of plans in connection with the repeal proposal, the most important priority is repeal, no matter what the initial plan of legalization. My contrarian recommendation for immediate action flows from my current assessment of the unacceptable damage being caused by the war on drugs to American society, on the one hand, and the quite tolerable threat that would be posed by legalized drugs, on the other.

Basic Principles of Repeal and Legalization

It follows that any sensible plan for legalization will work so long as it adheres to certain basic principles of realism about the manner in which people actually relate to drugs. Legalization is as much an approach to drug policy as it is a specific plan, as this section will make clear. In that spirit, I offer the following summary list of drug realisms, of new ways of thinking about drugs, that any legalization plan must take into account.

■ We must stop thinking about drugs and drug users in terms of war and hate. As an antidote to such destructive conceptualization, in 1987 I coined a new word that should dominate our initial thinking about this field: drugpeace. My explanation was:

The two words "drug" and "war" are now so joined in the minds of our leaders that they tend to think of them as one, drugwar, something like damnyankee in certain regions of the country. A new word might be coined; perhaps "drugpeace" will do. That word and the ideas associated with it could form the foundation for the profound ideological change that must take place if we are to move down the road away from war and toward a vast range of peaceful options (Trebach 1987, 353).

In the wake of the riots of 1992 and revolutionary discontent of the American public over the inability of the government to cope with harshly divisive social problems, the need for drugpeace is more vital than ever. We cannot have peace in our cities in the midst of the constant attacks and counterattacks of a drug war.

■ Multitudes of people, most of them perfectly decent and respectable human beings, like drugs. Any program that demands, upon threat of criminal punishment, that these people always repress those desires so as to create a drug-free society is unrealistic and harmful. It is the equivalent of attempting to repress the natural and diverse sexual appetites of our people. As the recent revelations about pedophile Catholic priests have demonstrated, the rule of sexual abstinence, even when backed by the threat of burning in hell, cannot create a sex-free clergy. Moreover, in too many cases it has perverted normal sex drives into destructive paths of sexual expression. In the same vein, our war on opium smoking and opium dens set in motion conditions that helped replace them with crack smoking and crack houses. Some way must be found to allow those so inclined to obtain drugs within a set of reasonable rules. Repression of natural drives inevitably creates worse forms of the so-called vice.

■ The criminal law must not be allowed to occupy the center of the new drug-control system. Police and prison keepers should not be the primary agents for controlling the admittedly bad effects of many drugs. We should attempt to put parents, educators, clergy, and cultural leaders in their place. The criminal law should operate only at the edges of the system—when there is the imminent possibility of harm to an innocent third party arising from drug use. It should not be a crime to use heroin at home in your bedroom, for example, while it should remain a crime to be under the influence of any mind-altering drug, say prescribed Valium, while driving.

■ "Harm reduction" should be the overarching theme of all new drug laws and drug-control policies. This enlightened operational concept had its start during recent years in Liverpool, England, and

Amsterdam, Holland (Trebach and Zeese 1990, 45–60, 141–49). It is now widely endorsed by drug-control experts in Australia and in Europe. Harm reduction accepts the reality of both the desire for drugs by millions of people and the related fact that millions of people may be harmed by drugs every year. Accordingly, the philosophy suggests, we must bend our energy and ingenuity to convincing people that they must make careful choices and that in a free society they may choose no drugs at all (as most will), comparatively harmless ways of using drugs, or very destructive methods. Whatever their choices, they must be assured that they will not be treated as enemies of the state and that help will be available if they encounter trouble.

■ Every civilized (meaning, in this context, nonforceful) attempt should be made to counteract any move toward more potent forms of drugs such as has taken place recently in the illicit drug market. Conversely, the effort should be made to replicate the current movement in the licit market toward more temperance, meaning moderation as well as abstinence, in regard to legal drugs. For example, there has been a move toward milder forms of alcohol, to light wines and beers, and away from more potent distilled spirits. It is to be expected that sellers of the newly legal drugs will want to offer a wide variety of less concentrated and more natural products. They should be encouraged to do so.

The more natural the drug, the less harmful it is to people who use it. The more natural the drug, the less potent it is, dose for dose. Primarily through the use of public education and persuasion people should be encouraged to use drugs in the most natural way, namely, by oral ingestion and not by sniffing, smoking, or, worst of all, injecting. Cocaine hydrochloride, for example, is a highly potent stimulant in the form of a white powder that is sniffed and often creates problems for users. Coca leaves, from which the cocaine is taken, cause very little difficulty for millions of people in the Third World, where they have been chewed for centuries. For those who like the stimulation of coca products, chewed coca leaves or even coca leaf tea may well satisfy their desires without causing them any observable harm.

■ The pursuit of highs and altered states of consciousness, far from being destructive as is widely assumed, is natural and good for individuals and society. The best highs are very probably those brought about without the help of chemicals—through, for example, religion, meditation, cheering on a favorite sports team, exercise, and making love. This is because natural highs avoid the risks of drugs and demonstrate to people the powerful truth that each individual has the inherent ability to achieve internal happiness. Yet, the great majority of people who use drugs, legal or illegal, to achieve highs do so without causing observable harm to themselves or others. Only a small minority of opium, heroin, cocaine, crack, and marijuana users get into trouble with the drugs (and with other elements of their lives) and come to public attention. Sadly, the universe of drug users is defined in the public mind by that tiny percentage who draw so much attention to themselves and their troubles.

■ Education and public relations campaigns should stress these principles of drug realism and harm reduction. While the Partnership for a Drug-Free America may well continue its distorted television commercials meant to scare people away from drugs (it's a free country, after all), major efforts should be made also to have on the air spot commercials and informative programs that express the different values espoused herein. The same should be true of public education. Instead of the current biased, one-sided drug-war curriculum now offered in most schools, American students should be presented with the rich array of conflicting ideas about drugs that is now available in any decent library or video center.

■ As we design new drug-control systems, we should remember our revolutionary democratic roots. For centuries, the great mass of people were considered inferior clods, certainly incapable of choosing rulers, who were instead anointed by God and the accident of royal blood. In a shocking reversal of these established, hallowed truths, the Declaration of Independence declared that the people had a natural right—based upon natural law which was superior to written law—both to throw out their divinely appointed rulers by force of arms if necessary and also to choose all future rulers. If we can put faith in the people to make the awesome choice of who will rule their nation, it seems an easy step now to ask those rulers to relinquish control once again over what substances people may choose to put in their own bodies. In the end, that is all that is involved here: returning the power of individual choice to the citizens of a supposedly free country over a very intimate matter.

My Preferred Plan of Legalization: The Real Trebach Model

A treasure trove of ideas on the specifics of drug-law reform has developed during the past two decades. These ideas are contained in dozens of bills now pending before state legislatures and in the literature of the reform movement. While traditionalists deny the existence of this rich array of specific proposals, they are easily found—especially in the publications of the Drug Policy Foundation, many of which are comprised of papers presented at its annual meetings, the International Conferences on Drug Policy Reform (see, for example, Trebach and Zeese 1989, 1990b, 1991, 1992).

There is a great deal of disagreement among the reformers about the specifics of reform; indeed, they raise many of the same questions that prohibitionists do. However, the reformers' rhetoric is serious rather than satirical or derisive. Moreover, the reformers start with the assumption that eventually the nation will have to bite the bullet and select one model of legalization or make a choice from among elements of several models for implementation. Thus they see the questions raised as hurdles to be intelligently surmounted rather than as insurmountable barriers to change.

Richard M. Evans, a Massachusetts attorney and experienced reform activist, provides an excellent summary of the range of worthwhile proposals, which he places in three broad categories: decriminalization, limitation, and regulation and taxation (Evans 1990). Under decriminalization, drugs would remain illegal but the offense of possession would be treated like a traffic violation, with relatively little loss of liberty for the transgressor. Limitation models would make drugs legally available but with clearly defined limits as to which institutions and professions could distribute the drugs. Included here, for example, would be the distribution of drugs to addicts through doctors, an approach I labeled "medicalization" many years ago. Regulation and taxation models would involve a wide array of looser controls, similar to those currently applied to alcohol.

Choosing a path for future policy from among these proposals is complex. There are many conflicting choices, for example, within the regulation and taxation models, as is reflected in the great variety of alcohol-control systems throughout the United States and the world. Different aspects of various models might very likely be applied to different drugs. For purposes of brevity, I will not review all of the reasons why I have selected the one model outlined here, which is actually constructed out of pieces of several. It will suffice to say that I was seeking a model that would create radical reform as quickly as possible.

My preferred plan of legalization seeks essentially to turn the clock back to the last century, before we made the terrible mistake of starting the war on opium smoking. With some modern adaptations—such as sensible rules regarding purity, labeling, places and hours of sale, and age limits for purchasers—we should return to the people the freedom of choice regarding drugs which was unwisely taken from them at the turn of the century. This plan springs from a judgment that we should trust our adult citizens more than government officials to make choices as to what goes in their bodies.

In concrete terms, then, my major proposal is what we deal with virtually all illegal drugs as we now deal with alcohol. This idea, which has been suggested by many commentators, including me, during recent years, has often been derided by prohibitionists as being naive on the grounds that alcohol is allegedly less harmful and easier to control than the currently illegal drugs. There is simply no proof of this assumption; in fact, dose for dose, alcohol is one of the most toxic and violence-producing drugs human beings regularly consume.[16] For those very good reasons, the nation prohibited alcohol from 1920 to 1933. However, we soon came to see that as bad as alcohol was, Prohibition was worse for the country and its people. National alcohol prohibition was therefore repealed.

That is where the process of reform should start now: repeal national drug prohibition. Just do it—in the same way Prohibition was repealed in 1933, in the same way its people dismantled the former Soviet Union—with speed, courage, and the confidence that the future cannot be worse than the present. Because national alcohol prohibition had been created by a constitutional amendment, the Eighteenth, another constitutional amendment was necessary to repeal it. Accordingly, section 1 of the Twenty-first Amendment reads: ''The eighteenth article of amendment to the Constitution of the United States is hereby repealed.'' Section 2 reads: ''The transportation or importation into any State, Territory, or possession of the United States for delivery or use therein of intoxicating liquors in violation of the laws thereof, is hereby prohibited.''

In the context of this discussion, it is significant that this economically worded amendment did not make alcohol legal in the states. Rather, it removed the blanket federal prohibition and allowed each state to choose how it wanted to control alcohol. At the same time, it committed the federal government to support state prohibition.

Such an approach could well be taken regarding drugs, but a consti-

16. Andrew Weil, M.D., has made such statements on numerous occasions. For example, he writes ''No illegal drug is nearly so addictive as tobacco in the form of cigarettes. No illegal drug approaches alcohol in medical harmfulness'' (1986, 41).

tutional amendment would not be necessary. Since national drug prohibition was created by statutes passed by Congress, Congress has the power to repeal them by a simple majority vote of both houses, assuming that the repeal law is also signed by the President.

The Question of Political Reality

At this point, it might be wise to pause for a moment and reflect on the political reality of repealing drug prohibition. The very idea of Congress passing a law today to do so would seem impossible, a laughing matter, to most people. I share that reaction—but only in regard to the present. We live in cataclysmic, revolutionary times where the unthinkable today may well become the norm the day after tomorrow. Traditional ways of thinking and sacred icons are regularly and rapidly smashed. The repeal of alcohol prohibition happens to be one splendid example of this phenomenon.

Even though it was widely disliked and disregarded, there was a general belief that Prohibition was here to stay. An Associated Press story of 24 September 1930 quoted the main author of the Eighteenth Amendment, Senator Morris Sheppard of Texas, as gloating, "There is as much chance of repealing the Eighteenth Amendment as there is for a hummingbird to fly to the planet Mars with the Washington Monument tied to its tail" (as quoted in Kyvig 1985, 14). A few years later, in 1933, the Twenty-first Amendment was proposed and, quite remarkably, actually ratified the same year. It was the only amendment to have been ratified by the difficult route of state conventions rather than by state legislatures. And the Eighteenth Amendment stands as the only one ever repealed.

In a similar vein, it was utterly unthinkable and laughable to contemplate the dismantling of the Union of Soviet Socialist Republics and the rejection of communism by its leaders. Certainly, it would have seemed absurd to imagine that it could have been accomplished comparatively peacefully and without the use of armed force by the West. To my knowledge, not a single intelligence officer among the thousands on either side of the old Iron Curtain ever made such a prediction.

It would be a rational assessment to conclude that if one were calculating probabilities a few years before each event, the mathematical odds against either (1) the repeal of Prohibition or (2) the peaceful dismantling of the Soviet Union should have been calculated as much higher than (3) the possibility that Congress would pass a national drug–prohibition repeal law by the year 2000. Of course, such cosmic calculations are extremely difficult, but I would like to place one large thumb on the scale.

As an activist professor at The American University and as the founder and president of the independent Drug Policy Foundation, I have been more or less in the front lines of reform for two decades. I have received my fair share of both brickbats and bouquets for my heretical positions. Now the latter almost exclusively predominate. The drug-law reform movement has more and more supporters throughout the United States and the world. The movement is getting positively respectable (although not so much so as to be boring). I have never seen such high-level support for change. The Drug Policy Foundation now regularly receives letters and calls from federal and state judges and other officials prodding it to greater action and asking that it more aggressively mobilize its resources and fight more openly to repeal prohibition once and for all. At times I feel I must run to keep up with the seemingly conservative judges and others of that respectable ilk who want complete legalization now, today.

However, my major task at this point is not to calculate the political possibilities for repeal but to lay out the best approaches to thinking about change and to organizing the new system in legal and practical terms. If the experience with repeal of alcohol prohibition is repeated, we would create a committee of lawyers and legal draftsmen who would provide the most experienced and expert advice in crafting the new statutes. Fortunately, as we have seen, such experts have already started to express their ideas in detail—despite protestations to the contrary by such critics as William Bennett, Congressman Charles Rangel, and James A. Inciardi—and this section is meant to explain some of these basic ideas. In the future more details will certainly be added.

Repeal Goals and Options

The major goals of the new drug laws at the national level would be, first, to eliminate the key federal laws imposing criminal penalties on the manufacture, sale, and possession of drugs; second, to dismantle the Drug Enforcement Administration and assign some of its staff and functions to the Federal Bureau of Investigation or other federal agencies; and third, to carve out a new supportive role for the federal government that recognizes the primacy of the states in drug control.

Thus the federal government would not be totally eliminated from the drug field, but rather there would be an attempt to recognize the unique contributions that national agencies could perform under the new system. The federal government should continue to play a major role in the drug field, particularly in the areas of drug education, treatment, and research—ongoing needs regardless of the legal status of drugs. Thus, we will be invoking a venerable conservative concept, states' rights, as the cornerstone idea for reform (yet another idea from the past that will help design our future).

As it did with repeal of alcohol prohibition, the federal government would return to the states the primary power to determine which drugs could be legally sold and under what conditions, a power the federal government took away early in this century. The major federal statute affecting currently illegal drugs is the Comprehensive Drug Abuse Prevention and Control Act of 1970, which has been amended numerous times in the past two decades. This prohibition statute (although not named that, of course) is listed in the United States Code starting in section 801 of volume 21. The first task is to excise that law.

Recently, Daniel K. Benjamin and Roger Leroy Miller of Clemson University faced up to that task (1991) and suggested two main legal options. Alternative 1 would change the U.S. Code to read:

THE ENHANCED STATES' CONTROL OVER DRUG ABUSE ACT
Section 1. Sections 801–904, 21 USCA are hereby repealed.
Section 2. The transportation or importation into any state, territory, or possession of the United States for delivery or use therein of any controlled substance, in violation of the laws thereof, is hereby prohibited (Benjamin and Miller 1991, 267).

This proposed law uses the language of the alcohol repeal amendment and would accomplish almost complete repeal of drug prohibition at the federal level. It would virtually put the Drug Enforcement Administration (DEA) out of business because that agency has the distinction of being perhaps the only police organization in the country with the sole responsibility to enforce only one statute, the one being repealed. Of course, under section 2 of the repeal statute, the federal government would have the duty to assist the states in the enforcement of their own prohibition laws, and this could require the work of federal drug enforcement agents.

Also, the national government would retain responsibility for international law enforcement duties in the drug field, the precise shape of which are now impossible to determine. They would certainly, however, be quite limited compared with today. In my opinion, such limited duties could well be handled by the Federal Bureau of Investigation, the major national law enforcement agency in the United States. There would seem no need, except political appearances, to pay for a separate agency in the future, whatever form of legalization statute is crafted.

Benjamin and Miller suggest a less comprehensive reform law, Alternative 2, as follows:

> Amendment to 21 USCA Section 903
> THE RETURN TO THE STATES CONTROL OVER DRUG ABUSE AMENDMENT Section 903, 21 USCA, shall be revised to read as follows: No provision of this subchapter shall be construed as indicating an intent on the part of the Congress to occupy the field in which that provision operates to the exclusion of any state law on the same subject matter which would otherwise be within the authority of the state. Any conflict between that provision of this subchapter and that state law so that the two cannot stand together shall be resolved by construing the law so as to give full effect to the relevant state law (1991, 268).

This alternative new statute would leave the major federal prohibition law in place but would recognize the primacy of state law wherever there was a conflict. The authors claim it would accomplish the same result as the first alternative. I much prefer the more comprehensive approach because it would definitively remove the federal government almost totally from its dominant role in prohibition enforcement. However, Alternative 2 should also be considered as a bargaining option, as should other approaches to repeal. Over the next few years all legal innovations should be considered that might possibly contribute to achieving the main objectives: a radical, rational diminishment of the role of the federal government in drug control, and the institution of a series of rational systems of drug regulation to replace the current federal policy. This effort should concentrate on removing the great majority of armed federal drug police officers from American life, forever.

Another new law might provide for the appointment of a major national commission to study alternatives to prohibition. Such a commission has been recommended by a number of leading public figures in recent years, most prominently by Mayor Kurt Schmoke of Baltimore in a 1988 speech before the U.S. Conference of Mayors that had a profound impact on public thinking. However, many people believe that the idea of a national commission is often put forth as a substitute for action—indeed as a means of delaying seemingly unpleasant action. Study first; then act, maybe, some time in the distant future. My proposal is, of course, repeal as quickly as the language of the repeal statute can be settled, then settle the details of the new models of control, primarily at the state level. Of course, both functions can proceed on parallel tracks.

A logical sequence of events would be that Congress first passes a repeal bill, roughly along the lines of the Benjamin and Miller (1991) Alternative 1. This would mean that the criminal law jurisdiction of the federal government over domestic illicit drugs would largely cease. While the rapid removal of the federal government from most domestic drug control would cause uncertainties, it would not mean that drug control would cease. All states now have overlapping laws and agencies that perform many of the same functions as the federal government. Under the new system, the state systems would simply become dominant.

Congress would then pass a law, under this scenario, setting up the new national commission that would study all of the major issues about the future of drug control, but especially the various approaches being taken in the states to implement new systems. If the current approach to dealing with alcohol is any guide, it is to be expected that there would be wide variations from one state to another in drug control. (As in the first years after alcohol repeal, many states might exercise their legal option to retain drug prohibition within their borders.) It is likely that the national commission would continue working for some years, monitoring and reporting on the results of the different state models and about new American policies on the international scene.

There would be other important roles in the future for the federal government, some being simple extensions of current functions now being carried out by research agencies such as the National Institute on Drug Abuse, which should be retained and expanded. Current federal and state drug-control systems usually take entirely separate approaches to dealing with legal and illegal drugs. This makes no sense and ought to be remedied in the future. All of the drugs present many common problems and should be considered together. For example, there is a good deal of prescription drug abuse, especially among the elderly. Existing federal grant-in-aid programs would be extended to include grants to help states to develop good models of control for all drugs, including the currently illegal ones as well as those with a long history of legal use, especially alcohol, tobacco, caffeine, and mind-altering prescription drugs, such as tranquilizers.

Another federal function that ought to be retained is the regulation of the legal drug industry. This is carried on primarily by the Food and Drug Administration, which has the responsibility to see that drugs sold in interstate commerce are "safe and effective." Thus the FDA approves new drugs for use in the country. Because the legal drug business is national, even international, it makes sense for a national agency to continue to have some control on assuring the safety, efficacy, purity, and proper labeling of these sometimes potent substances. The FDA also participates in the scheduling process, which is primarily controlled by the DEA, through which the regulations are set for the manufacture and prescription of legal drugs. Too often the FDA's participation in this process has been characterized by the martial spirit of the drug war in general and the tough-cop mentality of the DEA in particular. During the long, continuing fight to get marijuana rescheduled so that it could be prescribed by doctors for medicinal use, for example, I saw FDA officials sometimes indicate a desire to show compassion but later suppress it out of fear of retribution by the DEA. Primarily because of DEA intransigence, marijuana remains a Schedule I substance prohibited for use in medicine. With the DEA out of the picture, it would be hoped that the FDA would be more compassionate and intelligent in approving and scheduling legal drugs. Of course, under the new legalization system, scheduling would take on an entirely different meaning and style since there would be a great deal more freedom for all adults in selling and using almost all drugs. The future in this regard is not entirely clear, though it might well include devising new sets of standards for products in the new drug marketplace. It would depend to an extent on the manner in which the states set up their new models of control.

State Models

It is possible that once federal drug prohibition is repealed, many states would continue prohibition within their boundaries. However, I make the assumption that the same political forces that would have effected reform at the federal level would be pushing for change within many states. This certainly was the case with the repeal of alcohol prohibition. My preferred model for the states, which would be largely free from federal control, would be one that provided great freedom to adult residents to obtain the drugs they desired. At the same time there would be less stringent control on the selling and marketing of drugs. The preferred new state model could involve two options: the medical option, and the nonmedical option.

The first option would be quite similar to the current prescription system. Under this medical option, a person desiring drugs would go to a doctor or—and this is an important addition—other licensed drug expert and obtain advice and, if the expert agreed, a prescription. The prescription would then be filled by a pharmacist under many of the current rules. It is to be expected that this option would be used by the great majority of people, certainly by almost all of those who see themselves as patients in a medical setting with traditional organic illnesses, such as asthma, cancer, and heart disease. They would have the comfort and protection of familiar methods of obtaining and using drugs, which they would properly think of as medicines.

The one major change I would make in the current system is to break the monopoly that medical doctors now enjoy regarding the power to write prescriptions for drugs deemed to have the greatest potential for abuse. There is no good reason, either scientific or ethical, to retain that monopoly, and this would seem a good time to break it. While many doctors have great knowledge of drugs and medicines, many others are ignorant of all but those few they use in their practices daily. States should be encouraged to experiment with new procedures that would allow drug experts without medical degrees—including pharmacologists, pharmacists, and nurses—to be tested and licensed to write prescriptions. However, it would seem wise to prevent those who wrote prescriptions from also selling the drugs to fill them. Thus, there might be, for example, consulting pharmacists and dispensing pharmacists.

Second, the nonmedical option would avoid the prescription system altogether. It would allow an adult citizen who had passed certain modest requirements or even tests, similar to those for a driver's license, to obtain the drugs he or she wished directly from a licensed seller without the need of professional advice or prescription. Thus, the state would be treating adults like adults, responsible thinking people who are given choices and are deemed capable of making them.

Those who chose to use drugs under the second option would, in effect, be the adventurers and risk-takers because of the dangers presented by drug use. The great majority of them would be marijuana smokers, at least in the first years of legalization, since marijuana is the most popular currently illicit drug. If the truth be faced, however, few marijuana smokers will be taking great risks, unless they use the drug heavily while attempting to work, drive a car, or use other machinery. Of course, all drugs, including marijuana, present dangers which the state and private sellers would have a duty to fully disclose.

Some people might prefer to operate under neither or under both of these options. Many heroin addicts I have known see themselves simply as people who love heroin and who probably would initially choose the nonmedical option to obtain drugs. I have also known many such addicts as they got older and more troubled, at which point they might turn to the medical option in a fervent effort to stop using. Under this new system, even the lowest street addicts would be treated as basically rational people who have to make choices about their options. There are great risks in this approach, but I submit there are even greater risks in continuing the current method which assumes that all addicts have lost their ability to make rational decisions.

Senator Galiber's Model

There are many detailed proposals laying out how radical legalization systems might work, as outlined, for example, by Benjamin and Miller (1991). While none shares precisely the same features, all move in the direction of full legalization of drugs. One of the most far-reaching and comprehensive has been that proposed by New York State Senator Joseph L. Galiber of the Bronx. First introduced in 1988, the bill has been reintroduced and redrafted regularly and remains an active proposal before the Senate of New York (as do similar bills before other state legislative bodies).[17]

The Galiber bill would set up a comprehensive, rational legal control system for drugs which in most vital respects would mirror New York State's system for controlling alcohol. As a State Liquor Authority

17. An earlier version of the Galiber bill appears in Trebach and Zeese (1989, 400). Also in that volume, with an introductory analysis (p. 371), is a proposed law titled, "A Bill to Reduce the Violence Associated with the Trade in Illicit Drugs," by Nancy Lord, M.D., J.D., who was the Libertarian Party candidate for Vice-President of the United States in 1992, as well as a detailed proposal (p. 429)—The Cannabis Revenue Act—that was composed originally by the National Task Force on Cannabis Regulation in 1982. Taking a lead role in that latter project is Richard Evans, Esq., of Northampton, Massachusetts. The latest version of the Galiber bill is no. 4094-A, New York State Senate, entitled in part "An Act to Establish a Controlled Substance Law," dated March 21, 1991.

now controls alcohol in New York, in the future a State Controlled Substances Authority (SCSA) would control drugs. (Of course, alcohol is a drug and a very powerful one and it is possible to argue for one state control system dealing with both alcohol and other drugs, but we should attempt one step at a time—and the new SCSA would be a giant step forward.)

The law would first repeal those sections of state law that impose criminal sanctions for the possession and sale of all illegal drugs. The SCSA would move into this gap and act to determine the manner and means of dispensing controlled substances in order to promote the welfare and safety of the public. The authority would be headed by a five-person commission appointed by the governor with the advice and consent of the senate. Members would serve five-year terms and could be reappointed by the governor. The SCSA would have a typical budget, staff, and a physical presence in Albany, New York City, and perhaps other cities of the state. All members and staff would be disqualified from holding an interest in any establishment being regulated.

The manufacture and sale of drugs would take place within regulations set up by the SCSA, which would bear many similarities to those now established for alcohol. While it is easy for an adult to purchase alcohol almost anywhere in the state, few people are aware of the extensive network of laws and regulations, most at the state and local level, that control the industry. Some of these controls are established by the legislature, with most being imposed by the executive rule-making power of the liquor authority. This would also be the case with the new drug agency. The new law would establish the minimum requirements, for example, for a person to be eligible to obtain a license to manufacture or sell drugs: over 21 years of age; U.S. citizen or lawfully resident alien; no convictions of a felony other than drug offenses before the enactment of the law; and no past revocation of a liquor or drug license for cause. In addition, the law would require that drugs be sold only within the channels of the new system, that there be no house-to-house sales or sales in public parks, that manufacturers and sellers keep complete records open for inspection by the authority, that advertising be modest and subject to review by the authority, and that individual purchasers be at least 21 years of age.

The new law would also impose specific packaging and labeling requirements. For example, controlled substances would be sold only in separate, clearly labeled packages containing "no more than ten usual doses." The authority then would be delegated the responsibility to determine in each case the definition of "a usual dose" (section 43-1). It would be unlawful for any person to sell a controlled substance that did not meet any of the new labeling and packaging requirements. Each package would contain a full disclosure of the contents and the potential dangers. Samples of warning labels that would be required by the law are as follows:

> WARNING: This drug is addictive. You may not be able to quit using it.
> WARNING: This drug may cause seizures, convulsions, and death.
> WARNING: If you are pregnant, this drug may cause serious birth defects in your child, including missing limbs and brain damage.

The law would also require that such warnings be rotated on a quarterly basis by those who package the drugs (section 43).

While the law would not require that sellers have any special professional qualifications, there is a provision for "addiction care centers" operated by licensed physicians. Under this section, physicians could operate a treatment center and obtain a license to dispense drugs for addicts in treatment within the new system. While this may sound like the current system or the medical option I recommended above (which is my own proposal and does not appear in the Galiber bill or any of the other bills in state legislatures), it is somewhat different. Under the Galiber bill, the doctor would be licensed to dispense drugs within medical treatment but no prescription would be necessary.

The SCSA would have jurisdiction over a new "controlled substances treatment fund." Monies would be placed in this fund from general tax revenues and also from taxes imposed on controlled substances, which could be quite substantial. The new authority also would be given responsibility for coordinating, directing, and funding all public treatment programs in the state. These would cover a wide range of treatments, including those that were drug free and aimed toward complete abstinence (section 52). Not later than one year after the effective date of the law, the new authority would have to report to the legislature on changes in the crime rate, changes in the number of people in prison, the quantities and types of drugs legally sold under this law, "estimates of number of people using controlled substances in each category, with a breakdown by frequency of use," and estimates of the number of "controlled substance related motor vehicle and industrial accidents, and hospital admissions" (section 50).

There are many other provisions in this proposed law which now covers 19 single-spaced, printed pages. If the law were to be passed, the SCSA would, in accordance with directions in the law, develop additional rules for the orderly marketing and control of the newly legalized drugs. The system envisioned here appears well conceived, comprehensive, and rational. It is only one of many such proposals, as I have said, now pending before legislatures across the country. Even though I find much to support in each of them, if I were consulted I would suggest amendments in each one. Indeed, when I testified in general support of the Galiber bill on 16 June 1989, I made several specific suggestions for amendments (Trebach 1989). Among them:

■ Put the law into effect and thus formally legalize all of the drugs but then allow the SCSA to set up a timetable for gradual implementation. This could mean that a mild drug like marijuana would be placed on sale first in a few selected localities around the state. Once the SCSA had worked out the practical and administrative details with that drug in those places, the authority could then move on to other drugs and other localities.

■ Experiment in the first years of legalization with a provision that drug purchasers be required to pass a test on the drugs, their dangers, and the applicable law. The test would bear some similarities to the written section of the test for a driver's license. Thus at the start of this experiment only those who had passed the test and obtained a drug user's license could purchase drugs under the new system. (I should report that Senator Galiber told me during the hearing that he thought this was a bad idea and would simply keep too many people in the black market.)

■ Institute a "harmfulness tax," an idea that has been championed in recent years by Lester Grinspoon of Harvard Medical School, among others. In this context it might mean that at first taxes would be roughly equal on all drugs. The SCSA would be given power to conduct research on the relative harm caused by each drug to the health of individuals and to the general society. On the basis of that research, the SCSA would establish tax rates, none of which would be prohibitive. It is likely that, for example, crack would be in the highest tax category and marijuana in one of the lowest. Heroin, powdered cocaine, alcohol, and tobacco might well be grouped just below crack. A vote of the SCSA governing body, hopefully based upon realistic research, would decide. The new revenue would be devoted primarily to new treatment and education resources. It is possible that billions in taxes, now lost to the underworld, would be realized, even in New

York State alone. Finally, there might be enough money for drug treatment on demand.

■ Include exemptions for personal use. Most illegal drugs are relatively easy to produce. Given the availability of the basic ingredients, it is harder to produce, say, a good Scotch than to grow marijuana or to synthesize heroin. Another reason for such a personal-use exemption is found in basic principles. A free society should recognize that individual privacy is at the core of the democratic experience. In 1975, the Alaskan Supreme Court did recognize these factors when it interpreted the right to privacy clause in the state constitution as granting adult Alaskans the right to grow and possess marijuana in the privacy of the home for personal use and not for sale. Thus, marijuana is legal, not simply decriminalized, in the privacy of Alaskan homes. (A state recriminalization law was recently passed by referendum, which had the strong backing of former drug czar William Bennett, but the constitutionality of that law has not yet been litigated.) The exact details of such a personal-use exemption would be worked out over time by the SCSA in the form of executive regulations. For example, the growth of four marijuana plants per year in the home or in a nearby garden might be exempted from regulation and taxation under this law, so long as the adult citizen were in possession of a drug user's license. Similar exemptions might be developed regarding other drugs.

In addition to the suggestions I made in my testimony, other ideas should be considered when creating new legalization systems in each state. Each state should establish ground rules for places and hours of sale. Nonmedical drug stores should be subject to the same type of local community controls as are liquor stores; they should not be located in residential areas nor near schools or religious establishments. Regulations should allow the stores to be open for as long as local liquor stores are. The exteriors of the new stores should contain no advertising and the signs on them should be for purposes of identification only. Here again the concepts of moderation and of harm reduction would apply.

A New Direction in Drug Policy

At this point I realize many readers may be offended by even the idea of thinking about the normal hours of sale of establishments offering legal marijuana, heroin, and cocaine! For many, these ideas are simply too jarring to deal with calmly. Yet that is what must be accomplished if we are to move away from the terrible costs of keeping full drug prohibition and waging an intrusive, expensive, permanent war on drugs.

The Dutch government came up with a concept that should be brought into play in this discussion: "normalization." While the Dutch have not fully legalized drugs as I am here recommending, it is the spirit of normalization that is most helpful to those thinking through reform. Normalization is a companion idea to harm reduction. In essence it means, in the words of Eddy Engelsman, the former head of Dutch drug policy, "a destigmatization of drug users" (Trebach and Zeese 1990, 53). This means treating drug users not as accomplices to murder, as Nancy Reagan once referred to them and as many Americans now think of them, but as potentially decent citizens and as members of our national family, with all the responsibilities of any other citizen. Surely then we should treat the new stores that would sell drugs legally to these users in America as normal places of business functioning according to normal rules and regulations.

All of these calm concepts—moderation, harm reduction, and normalization—should also apply in regard to the selection of the products offered for sale. Within recent years, as we have seen, there has been a tendency in the United States for the illegal drug scene to move toward more potent drugs and toward more concentrated pockets of destructive behavior. It appears that there are fewer casual users who take their drugs in moderation and more addicted users who cannot seem to leave the stuff alone. Public and private leaders in each state should design campaigns aimed at building true temperance—meaning moderation—into the entire new drug scene that will be the result of legalization. Advertisements and television programs could explain the techniques of moderation and control, rather than extolling only the virtue and necessity of total abstinence.

Moreover, the new state control authorities and market forces could well spur the development and sale of a wide range of less concentrated drugs. Customers who use the more potent drugs constantly are much more likely to get into difficulty, require the attention of the police and public hospitals, and cease being regular customers. Thus, marijuana, coca leaves, and smoking opium, among many other comparatively less-potent intoxicants, make a good deal more sense than crack, powdered cocaine, and heroin—even though all would be legal. The parallel case would hold that beer, wine, and wine coolers are generally better for alcohol drinkers than high-proof bourbon, scotch, and rye. Wholesale and retail sellers should receive guidance on how to develop new lines of such milder drugs. Public service announcements in the mass media and at the point of sale should encourage users to consider the milder forms of drugs. This is not to say that these drugs are harmless; certainly beer and wine are not. Rather, the spirit of harm reduction should move us to accept the use of these drugs but also to recognize that there is a world of possibilities in devising less harmful mind-altering substances.

While it may seem impossible to imagine, we should not discount the thought that ingenious capitalists working in a free market will soon come up with substances that have the general feel of current drugs but have only a tiny percentage of the most active ingredients. Think of the growing popularity of nonalcoholic beer and decaffeinated coffee, two substances that millions of Americans now regularly use, perhaps to their surprise, almost to the exclusion of the original versions. Also think of the current growth of what are sometimes called "water bars" where no alcohol is served and where people often seeking sexual adventures meet over a variety of exotic sodas and mineral waters.

Moreover, publicity campaigns should be mounted that, as contradictory as it may sound to some in the context of a drug legalization discussion, provide realistic information on the values of abstinence and the joys of achieving highs without drugs. Social leaders would be saying to the people of the country what I have told virtually every meeting I have addressed of the National Organization to Reform Marijuana Laws: you really do not have to use this stuff to feel good, but if you do, I do not think you should be treated as criminals. These campaigns would not be like the current distortions put forth by the government and the Partnership for a Drug-Free America. Instead, they would accept the reality that the pursuit of highs is not evil but healthy, especially if done without drugs. Concrete information should be provided about the nondrug methods now in use that could be expanded. Even an increase in one venerable method, disciplined meditation, could be beneficial to multitudes of people.

We also might bring back another old, seemingly scandalous, idea, the opium den, but we would reshape its function somewhat and give it a new name. If we think back and compare the gentle opium-smoking scenes of the past century with the rowdiness and violence of many modern alcohol bars and crack houses, the opium den would seem to be superior in the context of a harm-reduction strategy. We should also be guided by the wisdom of that opium-smoking prostitute who observed in 1884 that if opium houses were licensed like saloons, the society would benefit (Brecher 1972, 43).

Moreover, there have been some reports in this century that, while not discounting the dangers of the practice, have documented the often peaceful nature of the opium-smoking scene. Author Somerset Maugham visited an opium den in China in 1922 and had the same surprised reaction to its calmness that so affected Harry Hubbell Kane in New York in the 1880s. Maugham wrote: "It was a cheerful spot, comfortable, homelike, and cozy. It reminded me somewhat of the little intimate beer-houses of Berlin where the tired working man could go in the evening and spend a peaceful hour" (as quoted in Alexander 1990, 146).[18]

While I and other reformers have always been troubled by the idea of drug bars similar to alcohol bars, it may be time for us to overcome our reluctance to contemplate that innovation also. If we face reality, all sorts of drugs (in addition to alcohol) are now used in alcohol bars every day, except that such use is normally ingeniously hidden. Some states should encourage harm-reduction ideas in regard to bars that would license private entrepreneurs to experiment with various forms of controlled establishments that might be called "drug bars" or "smoking parlors" or some such similar name. They could combine peaceful elements of the old opium dens, venerable respectable coffee houses, and current Dutch youth clubs. In these youth clubs, even though the drugs are formally illegal, the Dutch authorities now allow "house dealers" to sell small quantities of soft drugs, mainly marijuana and hashish, to the young customers. Often there are rock musicians and revolving lights, all enjoyed by youth from many countries wearing what I would term outlandish clothes. Yet, it is a generally peaceful, nonviolent scene.

These new drug bars might initially be licensed to sell no alcohol or tobacco and only the less-potent drugs such as smoking opium, marijuana cigarettes, hashish, and coca leaves for tea and also for chewing.

18. Alexander also reports on more recent accounts by Joseph Westermeyer, an American opium expert who spent years studying the subject in Laos. In the company of eight Caucasian visitors, he visited local opium dens and all tried an occasional pipe. Westermeyer wrote in 1982: "None of them reported anything resembling pleasure or euphoria. One man having a bout of diarrhea at the time found that two pipes greatly relieved this condition (much as one would expect from a dose of the old nostrum, tincture of opium). I have followed the lives of these eight people (seven men and one woman) over a six- to ten-year period since their smoking opium in one or another Laotian den. None has become an opium addict, or, for that matter, an abuser of any other substance" (quoted in Alexander 1990, 143).

They might also find it popular to offer a wide variety of good coffees and mineral waters.

The greatest danger here, in my opinion, is intoxicated people driving home from the drug bars at night, as in the case of alcohol bars. While none of the currently illegal drugs mentioned here should produce anything like the aggressive irresponsibility of the alcohol-impaired driver, all mind-altering drugs impair driving ability. Accordingly, all patrons of these new establishments would have to be impressed with the dangers to good driving posed by their drugs, with the fact that driving while intoxicated on any substance would continue to be a crime, and that at least one person in every car should be selected as a "designated driver" at the beginning of the evening, as should be done now with alcohol drinkers in bars. That person would not consume any mind-altering substance, except for perhaps some cappucino.

I worry more about the danger of an increase in drugged-driving deaths than I do about any single potential difficulty in the future under legalization. In large part, that is because the drunken driver has for decades been a greater threat to the safety of all of us than almost any other danger. Some of the best, and some of the worst, people in our society regularly drink and drive. Despite the magnitude of the danger, automobiles and alcohol remain quite legal. The same should be true of drugs. At the same time we must recognize that while the problem of impaired driving will not go away, we do not have to throw up our hands and lament that that's the price of freedom. We must be constantly researching the matter and seeking new ways to reduce the harm from impaired driving, even though we cannot hope to stop the practice completely. For example, we should contemplate a coordinated national, state, and local campaign against impaired driving. This might involve, first, more punitive laws and regulations, particularly those that give greater power to the police to seize driving licenses of impaired drivers summarily under certain defined circumstances. Second, we should develop more effective educational and media programs to get the message across that driving while impaired by any substance constitutes the greatest threat of violent death and injury in modern society. Spot television commercials carrying such messages would be worthy substitutes for the misleading ads of the Partnership for a Drug-Free America. Thus we must constantly be striving for a rational balance in social relations. Greater freedom of choice for adults in regard to drugs should be balanced by more rational governmental intervention in related arenas—and also by greater personal attention by individual citizens to safety.

In the future, each of these reform ideas would be tested, enlarged, and adjusted on the basis of experience. Whatever one may think of the specific proposals made in this section, it is difficult to see how Congressman Charles Rangel, former drug czar William Bennett, or James Inciardi, among other prohibitionists, could refer to these legalization proposals as superficial, disingenuous, shallow, shoot-from-the-hip, or lacking in detail. However, critics and supporters of legalization have raised specific questions about the possible results of these far-reaching changes in the machinery of drug control, which will now be addressed.

5. Contemplating the Future under Legalization

In all human endeavors there is a great fear of the unknown. Certainly this is true in regard to proposals to strip away the protections seemingly provided by the criminal drug laws. What will happen to the people of the country, especially the poor and racial minorities? Will we become a society of drugged zombies? Will the country slide deeper into the historic decline that so many commentators claim we are now in?

When I contemplate the reality of legalization, I see that apparently drastic step not as offering the solution to all of our criminal and social problems, but as creating the opportunity to deal with many of our more pressing problems in a rational fashion. This country is being torn apart by hate, especially racial hate, and by violence that often but not always has a racial component to it. Because the war on drugs escalates both the racial hate and the level of violence in general, legalization offers the hope of reducing the destructive levels of hate and violence.

I readily admit the possibility that we could legalize drugs and continue to have massive drug abuse, crippling levels of crime and violence, the rapid spread of AIDS, the collapse of our cities, and vicious racial conflict. However, it is much more conceivable, and indeed more likely, that legalization will allow us to greatly curb all of those searing problems. Thus, legalization is not a solution but a door that must be opened if we hope to come to grips with the problems that are tearing us apart. It is utterly inconceivable that we can deal effectively with any of these divisive problems while at the same time continuing drug prohibition and the repressive war on drugs.

There you have it. There is no promise of a free lunch or Camelot. Both prohibition and legalization carry great risks, as do all serious social programs. Any legalizer who claims that repeal of the drug laws is a sure bet does not understand the situation. My plea for reform now is based on a balancing of probabilities and a balanced review of all of the best evidence from the historical record. On the basis of those balancing processes, I conclude that legalization, with all of its risks, must be tried and it must be tried now because the continuation of prohibition and the war on drugs is certain to cause all of us further serious harm.

A number of major criticisms and questions have been raised about the potential impact of legalization, many by prohibitionist officials like Congressman Charles Rangel and former drug czar William J. Bennett and prohibitionist scholars such as James A. Inciardi who claim that they can confidently predict that repeal of the drug laws is sure to cause disaster. Let us examine each of the major areas of concern.

Drug Maintenance and the Fate of Addicts

I advocate that drug maintenance should be one of many treatments available to addicts under either our present legal system or legalization. As part of maintenance treatment, I support the provision of injectable narcotic drugs and clean needles by doctors. At present, oral methadone is the only narcotic legally available for addict maintenance, and the federal government, especially Bush drug czar Robert Martinez, has actively opposed the few needle exchange programs in existence around the country.

In a *Parade* magazine article published just before the historic congressional hearings on drug legalization held in September 1988, Congressman Rangel raised several questions about drug maintenance: "And how much will you give an addict? A maintenance dose? They don't want to be maintained. They need to get high" (Ryan 1988, 20). This is archetypically misleading and reveals the basic misunderstandings at the highest levels of power that prevent rational consideration of new drug policies—ones that might work. Some addicts need to get high. Some do not. Some do not want drugs at all but simply need a strong, sympathetic hand and close supervision while being detoxified. Many heroin addicts, like many alcoholics, function quite well for long periods on their drug of dependence.

On the same day that the misleading *Parade* article appeared, I had the joy of attending the wedding of Warren, a recovering heroin addict. Years earlier he claimed I saved his life when he came to me in London, where he was a student in one of my American University seminars. In an embarrassed voice, he told me he was in trouble with heroin and Diconal, a synthetic opiate much in fashion among British addicts at the time. I asked him what he wanted to do. He replied that he was totally out of control and that he needed to be "locked up." I immediately made arrangements and deposited him at a good psychiatric hospital. While in the locked ward, Warren was detoxified. Over a week later, Warren returned to class, took the final examination, and despite his intensive abuse of drugs and his absence, he received a high grade. He has gone on to a good career in the field of drug treatment and to a happy marriage.

Under the legalization plan I propose here, addicts like Warren would need to make some serious choices. If they chose the nonmedical option, they would be able to purchase the heroin and needles they need at reasonable prices from a nonmedical drugstore. While James Inciardi scoffs at the idea that such an option would change the heroin addict's lifestyle (see Inciardi 1992, 247), I believe that for some addicts, at certain points in their lives, this freedom could be quite advantageous. There are many addicts in this and other countries who are mature and quite stable in many respects, especially if they have a good, affordable source of drugs, legal or illegal. This is not to say they are without problems, but like some alcoholics, they live tolerable lives for many years, committing few or no crimes, save for the crimes of selling, buying, and possessing drugs.

But legal drugs do not always equal a good life for all addicts, because the lives of addicts change over time and because one addict may be quite different from another. Many heroin addicts, like many alcoholics, eventually get into trouble in their relationship with their drugs. At that point, the new system would offer the addict another choice, to change his behavior. This would be a matter for the addict and his or her family, religious counselors, and doctors to decide; it would not be a matter for the police, which would be a major improvement.

Addicts who seek medical help should be treated with compassion and care that is inexpensive and readily available, virtually on demand. Care should be available time and time again, since relapse is part of the healing process. There should be a full range of possible treatments: locked psychiatric wards, drug-free detoxification, religious counseling, group therapy, outpatient psychiatric therapy, drug maintenance with clean needles, among others. We must include drug maintenance and clean needles because we do not now have, and never will have, a method for forcing addicts off drugs immediately, even when they desperately want to be rid of them. Drug maintenance, supervised by doctors, is not a surrender, as prohibitionists claim, but a recognition of realities. In many cases it is an essential part of harm reduction, keeping many addicts functioning, working, and paying taxes for years until that great day when they are ready to quit. When an addict is ready to come off drugs, experienced treatment doctors tell me it is fairly easy to gradually accomplish that feat.[19] But it is not easy before the patient, rather than a doctor or the police, is ready. For too many, that day never comes, but society and the patient are still better off when drug maintenance is available: a lifetime of responsible narcotic use, however contradictory that may sound, is possible for some people and quite preferable to a lifetime of hiding like a feared and fearful nocturnal animal.

It is difficult to determine the proper dosage for drug maintenance and to determine when an addict is ready to be weaned from powerful narcotic drugs. While these are not new issues, as it is difficult to determine the proper dose of narcotics for any condition (for example, cancer pain), these questions should be important elements in the treatment experiments a democratic government should launch.

British doctors have openly debated maintenance issues for decades. In 1924, the minister of health put some of the central questions to a group of leading doctors, which became known as the Rolleston Committee, "to consider and advise as to the circumstances, if any, in which the supply of morphine and heroin . . . to persons suffering from addiction to those drugs may be regarded as medically advisable" (see Trebach 1982, 90–96). The historic Rolleston Committee report, issued in 1926, described two types of patients for whom long-term maintenance on these powerful narcotics was considered proper and helpful: "those in whom a complete withdrawal of morphine or heroin produces serious symptoms which cannot be treated satisfactorily under the ordinary conditions of private practice," and "those who are capable of leading a fairly normal and useful life so long as they take a

19. See, for example, the thoughts of Dr. Dale Beckett of England, who wrote that once an addict has been helped to deal with his emotional pain, he no longer needs heroin and at that point, "a sensitively designed withdrawal from heroin is easy for the addict to handle" (quoted in Trebach 1982, 203).

certain quantity, usually small, of their drug of addiction, but not otherwise'' (Trebach 1982, 94).

In other words, the Rolleston Committee saw the prescription of powerful narcotic drugs not as a means of destroying normal lives or of killing off a worthless addict, but rather as a means to make it possible for an addict to survive and to lead a fairly normal life outside a hospital. This medical advice, both compassionate and timeless, is the original intellectual basis for modern harm reduction. Applied under a future legalization system, it would mean that if an addict chose treatment by a physician, rather than choosing to buy drugs from the nonmedical drugstore, the doctor would provide drugs, along with clean needles, at a dosage appropriate for that patient, allowing him or her to function as a good citizen, employee, and family member.

This entire line of thought runs counter to most of the dominant prohibitionist thinking about addicts, as reflected in James Inciardi's writings. His assumptions are that drugs drive addicts into crime and that addicts who take drugs regularly can rarely function in a productive fashion. As this section illustrates, such thinking ignores a major segment of experience and research.

Will Abuse Rise to Destructive Levels?

We all should be concerned about the possibility of a great rise in drug use and abuse should the criminal drug laws be repealed. If I believed that legalization would bring about a destructive explosion of use, I would rethink my position. However, my review of the evidence leads me to believe that drugs are not so seductive nor the American people so gullible as some doomsayers seem to believe. There is particular comfort in the historical record.

For me the most powerful historical argument is the low incidence of opiate abuse and related social problems during the last century when drugs were legal and available to almost anyone, as discussed in section 3. While people have certainly changed in a century, there is no indication that the basic character of American society is different. Accordingly, the experience with opium during the last century must be weighed heavily on the side of legalization now.

Similar thoughts apply to a review of the historical record from several countries on the experience with marijuana. There have been at least seven major studies of marijuana use by impartial bodies of experts over the years in various countries. One of the most notable was the first, the Indian Hemp Drugs Commission,[20] composed of British and Indian experts, who patiently and calmly secured testimony from 1,193 witnesses from throughout the Indian subcontinent where marijuana and other "hemp" products were freely and legally available. The 3,281–page, seven-volume classic report (Indian Hemp Drugs Commission [1894] 1969) contained some salient summary conclusions, including:

- It has been clearly established that the occasional use of hemp in moderate doses may be beneficial; but this use may be regarded as medicinal in character. It is rather to the popular and common uses of the drugs that the Commission will now confine their attention.
- In regard to the physical effects, the Commission have come to the conclusion that the moderate use of hemp drugs is practically attended by no evil effects at all.
- In regard to the alleged mental effects of the drugs, the Commission have come to the conclusion that the moderate use of hemp drugs produces no injurious effects on the mind.
- In regard to the moral effects of the drugs, the Commission are of [the] opinion that their moderate use produces no moral injury whatever.
- . . . [T]here is little or no connection between the use of hemp drugs and crime.
- Viewing the subject generally, it may be added that the moderate use of these drugs is the rule, and that the excessive use is comparatively exceptional (Solomon 1966, 192).

Nothing of significance in the report's conclusions has been proved wrong in the intervening century.

The congruence in basic findings of these seminal studies is truly remarkable: None found marijuana to be harmless; all found marijuana to present some dangers to some people but concluded that the actual level of harm was consistently exaggerated and that control measures were frequently too harsh. Several of the studies stated flatly that rigid criminal prohibition laws were harmful.

The two most recent reports, by the National Commission on Marihuana and Drug Abuse (1973) and the National Research Council

20. The others are: The Panama Canal Zone Military Investigations, carried out between 1916 and 1929 and reported in various publications, including Siler et al. (1933); the LaGuardia Committee Report (Mayor's Committee on Marijuana 1944); the Baroness Wooten Report (Advisory Committee on Drug Dependence 1968); the LeDain Report (Government of Canada 1970); the National Commission on Marihuana and Drug Abuse (1973); and the National Research Council (1982).

(1982), are among the most significant national drug studies performed by impartial groups of experts in American history. The report of the National Commission on Marihuana and Drug Abuse was mandated by Congress and carried out by a generally conservative commission appointed by President Nixon. After a massive series of studies of the entire illicit drug situation in the United States, the first recommendations of the commission were, to the dismay of President Nixon and many supporters of harsh drug laws, as follows:

> 1. Possession of marihuana for personal use would no longer be an offense, but marihuana possessed in public would remain contraband subject to summary seizure and forfeiture.
> 2. Casual distribution of small amounts of marihuana for no remuneration, or insignificant remuneration not involving profit, would no longer be an offense (National Commission on Marihuana and Drug Abuse 1973, 458).[21]

These proposals for moderate compromises have been treated with disdain by the United States Congress and ignored by drug-abuse experts—but not by the prestigious National Academy of Sciences, a quasi-governmental body, in the latest comprehensive American report.

The report, by the Academy's National Research Council (1982), supports the recommendations of the Nixon commission a decade earlier, but then goes dramatically further. It recommends that carefully prepared and researched experiments be considered that would involve removal of federal criminal penalties for cultivation and distribution of marijuana. Under this thoughtful plan, states would be encouraged to devise individual methods of control, an idea consistent with the basic legalization plan here recommended (National Research Council 1982, 16–30). Before making those recommendations the council carefully reviewed the available evidence on the relationship between the proposed cautious changes in the criminal law and the possibility of an increase in use and abuse. Some of the most important evidence was found in the 11 American states that had decriminalized possession during the 1970s. The Council found that these relaxed criminal laws had no significant impact on use but did help curb massive criminal justice expenditures and injustices to many people. The council projects that even more far-reaching legal distribution and

---

21. These recommendations were originally announced in the first report of the commission in 1972 and repeated in its final report.

sale would not likely produce significant changes in use—if governments, opinion leaders, and families enjoyed sensible, noncriminal
control methods.

The National Academy of Sciences report places great emphasis on
building up public education and informal social controls, which often
have a greater impact on personal behavior than the criminal law. The
report also has these comforting thoughts for those who would expect
to see disaster for our young in a change so radical as to allow regulated
marijuana sales:

> . . . there is reason to believe that widespread uncontrolled use would not
> occur under regulation. Indeed, regulation might facilitate patterns of
> controlled use by diminishing the "forbidden fruit" aspect of the drug
> and perhaps increasing the likelihood that an adolescent would be intro-
> duced to the drug through families and friends, who practice moderate
> use, rather than through their heaviest-using, most drug-involved peers
> (National Research Council 1982, 27–28).

Powerful support for fundamental revisions in our attitudes and
policies toward marijuana was also contained in a historic decision
handed down on 6 September 1988 by Francis L. Young, the chief
administrative law judge of the Drug Enforcement Administration.
Judge Young's decision, while focused on the issue of medical use,
calls into question many of the fundamental ideas underlying the drug
war. Some excerpts from his decision, *In The Matter Of Marijuana
Rescheduling Petition* (Docket No. 86-22 [6 September 1988]):

- There is no record in the extensive medical literature describing a
  proven, documented cannabis-induced fatality.
- In strict medical terms marijuana is far safer than many foods we
  commonly consume.
- Marijuana, in its natural form, is one of the safest therapeutically active
  substances known to man (as reprinted in Trebach and Zeese 1989,
  325).

The decision of Judge Young stands as a major official refutation of the
basic assumptions about the nature and uses of the most popular
currently illicit drug.

When the historical record of marijuana use is combined with that
of opiate use, there seems little solid basis for the widely held fear that
legalization will produce catastrophic levels of addiction. The major
argument against the notion that drug abuse would rise destructively

because of a change in the legal status of certain drugs is common sense—people tend to act in their own best interests. Most people will resist drugs, but even if they dabble in drugs or even suffer a period of abuse (a period that would undoubtedly be related to many more personal and social issues than the drugs being ingested), people tend to come to their senses and get out of destructive cycles and off of drugs without tremendous outside intervention. That seminal revelation colors nearly every objective major report on drug abuse done over the last century.

Of course, the worst might happen, and drug use may increase dramatically, but the odds, based upon a calm assessment of the facts, are strongly against such a dire outcome. The legalizers' seemingly naive leap of faith—that drug use will not go through the roof—is a great deal more logical than the prohibitionists' cynical lack of faith—that the repeal of drug laws will suck multitudes into lives of despair and addiction because the American people cannot be trusted to make rational choices about their own bodies and lives.

An Opinion Poll: Drug Appetites Are Small

In 1990 Richard J. Dennis, chair of the Drug Policy Foundation Advisory Board, commissioned Targeting Systems, Inc., an Arlington, Virginia, firm with extensive experience in nationwide polling, to design and execute a drug opinion poll. A scientific national probability sample of 1,401 adult Americans was questioned by telephone between 24 January and 4 February 1990. The result was the largest and most comprehensive independent national opinion poll ever conducted on the drug issue (Dennis 1990a).

The poll produced some pessimistic results, by my lights. Fifty-two percent of adult Americans, for example, believe that heroin makes people crazy, violent, and psychotic. (The prevalence of drug hysteria and misinformation was thus confirmed.) Seventy-one percent said they would grant the military police powers to patrol their neighborhoods and fight drugs more aggressively. These and other findings seem to endorse the prohibitionists and the drug war. However, there was comfort also for reformers, including the fact that 36 percent of the respondents were in favor of some form of legalization, the highest level of such support from any known scientific national survey.

The most significant findings of the poll for this discussion were those regarding the respondents' propensity to use legalized drugs in the future. The interviewees were asked how likely they were to try marijuana or cocaine if it were legalized. The answers showed that today, as in the past, the American people are not as fascinated with the idea of using these drugs as some of their leaders seem to think or fear. This was especially true among those who had not tried the drugs in the past. Of those who had never used marijuana, 1.1 percent said they would be "very likely" to try it if it were legal, and 3.1 percent said they would be "somewhat likely" to try it. Of those who had never used powdered cocaine, 0.5 percent responded that they would be "very likely" to experiment with it, and 0.4 percent answered "somewhat likely." Thus, 4.2 percent of those who had not tried marijuana might use it if it were legal, while 0.9 percent of those who had not tried cocaine might do so if legalization came to pass.

As table 2 shows, the worst-case scenario seems to be that 9.6 percent of the adult population might try marijuana and 1.7 percent might try cocaine after repeal of prohibition, based on combining the answers of those who have tried the drugs with those who have not. This would mean that 90.4 percent of American adults would not try marijuana and 98.3 percent would not try cocaine.

It is important to note that these numbers deal only with use, not addiction. While such calculations must be made with great caution, it is possible to speculate on the number of addicts or abusers that might result from this level of use. Assume for the purpose of argument that

Table 2. How Likely Americans Would Be To Try A Given Drug If It Were Legalized

Likelihood of trying if legalized:	Marijuana Have tried in the past			Cocaine (powder form) Have tried in the past		
	YES* (35% of respondents)	NO (65% of respondents)	TOTAL (100%)	YES* (11% of respondents)	NO (89% of respondents)	TOTAL (100%)
Very likely	8.5	1.1	3.7	1.5	0.5	0.6
Somewhat likely	11.0	3.1	5.9	7.5	0.4	1.1
Not very likely	13.0	5.8	8.3	12.8	3.1	4.1
Not at all likely	66.8	88.9	80.5	78.4	95.1	92.8
No opinion	0.8	1.1	1.6	0	0.9	1.4

Source Drug Policy Foundation/Targeting Systems, Inc.
Telephone survey, January–February 1990.
Reprinted by permission.
*Figures do not add up to 100% because of rounding.

one in twenty marijuana users might become dependent on the drug and one in ten cocaine users would become addicted (I recognize that these ratios could be subject to attack by scholars on both sides of the legalization issue, but all would admit, I suspect, that they are within the range of possibility). If these suppositions were borne out, then 0.46 percent of the adult public would be addicted to marijuana and 0.17 percent would be addicted to cocaine after repeal of drug prohibition. Put in other terms, after legalization, 99.54 percent of the adults in the country would not be addicted to marijuana, and 99.83 percent would not be addicted to cocaine.

It is not wise to push such projections too far to predict the number of addicts there might be under legalization (although, truth be told, these are the types of calculations the government now uses to arrive at current addiction figures). It is possible to analyze these figures to show that there would be a rise in the number of addicts after legalization but that a cost-benefit analysis, factoring in a drop in crime and other social costs, would show legalization worth the risk. Indeed, Richard J. Dennis made such an analysis in *The Atlantic* (1990b, 126).

My purpose in making these projections is simply to refute the claims of those prohibitionists who confidently predict that there will be a public policy disaster if legalization is enacted: there is an absence of evidence that huge numbers of people would become addicted to these drugs once they were made available legally.

The Alleged Health Success of Alcohol Prohibition

Many prohibitionists base their claims of future disaster in part on the alleged health success of alcohol prohibition.[22] The standard argument is that while alcohol prohibition was an overall failure in America, especially because of the crime and corruption it engendered, it was a resounding success in terms of public health. Support is found in such statistics as those on alcohol consumption: during the period 1916–1919, per capita consumption of absolute alcohol for the drinking age population in the United States was 1.96 gallons; during Prohibition, it dropped by more than half to 0.90 gallons; after repeal, during 1936–1941, it went up again to 1.54 gallons. By 1986, it had reached 2.58 gallons, alleged proof of the value of Prohibition.[23]

---

22. See, for example, the speech by William Bennett at the John F. Kennedy School of Government, Harvard University, December 1989, reproduced in Trebach and Zeese (1990a, 17).

23. Figures on alcohol consumption in this paragraph and the next are taken from

This argument ignores a number of salient facts, starting with the observation that the low figures for the 1920s are suspect because during Prohibition many people hid their alcohol use. Moreover, the highest periods of known mass alcohol consumption were during our earliest years as a nation when popular culture and private predilections made us a nation of hard drinkers. The high point was in 1830, when Americans consumed 7.10 gallons of absolute alcohol per capita! By 1871–1880, consumption had dropped to 1.72 gallons. Even in recent years there have been significant variations in use, with a clear downward trend in recent years. In 1977 consumption was approximately 2.63 gallons; it rose to 2.76 gallons in 1981 and 1982; then it dropped continually to 2.43 gallons in 1989, the latest data available. All of these changes took place within an atmosphere of legality.

Similar trends can be seen in the use of the other major legal drug, tobacco. Tobacco use has dropped dramatically: the percentage of cigarette smokers 18 years of age and older dropped from 42.3 percent in 1965 to 32.2 percent in 1983, and to 25.4 percent in 1990 (National Center for Health Statistics 1992). And all the time, tobacco was fully legal.

What about Crack?

Yes, I would even legalize crack. It is a very dangerous drug, but the dangers of prohibition are on balance a greater threat to us all. I know that for many people the very thought of making crack legal destroys any inclination they might have had for even thinking about drug-law reform. For others, the arrival of crack in the 1980s created the most profoundly felt barricade in their defense of the current system. The latter seems to be the case with conservative scholar James Q. Wilson of the University of California at Los Angeles. In an important and influential article (1990), Wilson laid out some of the best arguments "Against the Legalization of Drugs." As it happens I disagree with the factual basis for most of his arguments, but I disagree in particular with his position on crack.

Wilson seems to say that there is something new and peculiarly destructive about cocaine and especially crack that simply changes everything in the drug arena. Cocaine and/or crack, he wrote: "de-

Lender and Martin (1982, 196–97), Secretary of Health and Human Services (1990, 13–14), and National Institute on Alcohol Abuse and Alcoholism (1991, 17).

stroy[s] the user's essential humanity''; "alters one's soul''; and "corrodes those natural sentiments of sympathy and duty that constitute our human nature and make possible our social life" (Wilson 1990, 26). Moreover, he writes, "crack is worse than heroin by almost any measure" (Wilson 1990, 23). He goes on to explain that heroin produces a pleasant drowsiness and few other major side effects, while bingers on crack "become uninhibited, impulsive, hypersexual, compulsive, irritable, and hyperactive. Their moods vacillate dramatically, leading at times to violence and homicide" (Wilson 1990, 23).

Even if all of Wilson's (and Inciardi's, since they are similar to Wilson's) dire claims about crack's chemical destructiveness were true, I would still work to legalize it. My support of legalization is not a vote of confidence in any drug; in fact, I think it is a very bad idea for anyone to use most of the drugs, legal and illegal, now available. I support legalization because I believe that the facts show convincingly that the criminal law is too crude and too harsh an instrument to be unlimbered and launched at the personal habits of our citizenry. If an adult wants to purchase crack, I would prefer he or she have the option of walking into a nonmedical drugstore, asking the clerk politely for the desired drugs, paying the modest price that they are actually worth, and walking calmly out the door. The thought of this occurring does not make me happy, any more than the thought of someone buying very high proof alcohol does. It is a matter of social trade-offs. I place a higher priority on destroying the illegal crack trade than I do on preventing the use of crack. Crack is bad for people. Bullets are worse. In supporting legalization, then, I am not voting for crack but against bullets.

It is also important to recognize that almost all of the facts cited by Wilson in his article (like those mentioned by Inciardi in his writings) are either not true or are severely distorted, as I shall hopefully demonstrate. For example, despite Wilson's objective-sounding warnings, all of the reliable evidence suggests that people very rarely die of crack and that they often die of bullets in the crack trade. More important at this point is to recognize that claims such as that crack destroys a user's essential humanity and that (Wilson really says this) women seem more susceptible to crack than heroin (Wilson 1990, 23), would have fit right into the hysterical campaign against opium smoking over a century ago. Wilson has ignored our history. If he read it, he would also see that such demonic attributes have been laid at the door of almost every new drug on the scene during the past century—and of all the old drugs, such as alcohol.

Certainly that's how heroin—which ironically Wilson now chooses
to declare almost housebroken—was described in the 1920s. Harken
the testimony of Sidney W. Brewster, a deputy prison warden in New
York City, at the 1924 congressional hearings on heroin: "The man
who uses heroin is a potential murderer, the same as the cocaine user;
he loses all consciousness of moral responsibility, also fear of consequences" (quoted in Trebach 1982, 50–51). When asked at that hearing
if heroin produced insanity, one of the country's leading medical
experts, Surgeon General Rupert Blue, immediately replied, "Oh,
yes" (quoted in Trebach 1982, 50). This is what Wilson seems to be
saying about crack. Of course, the objective facts support neither the
surgeon general in the 1920s nor the professor in the 1990s.

The Crack Scare of the 1980s   The modern story of crack started in
1986.[24] Before that year, relatively few people had heard either of crack
or of college basketball star Len Bias. Soon, both had become tragic
household words.

Dr. Arnold Washton, a nationally renowned expert in cocaine treatment, by 1986 had been quoted frequently about the dangers of crack,
declaring at times that "crack is the most addictive drug known to man
right now" and that it caused "almost instantaneous addiction." In
May 1986 he expressed a typical view when on national television he
countered my plea for calm measures by declaring, twice, that we
should get hysterical about crack.

Virtually all major print and electronic media joined in the emotional
stampede. Reports were frequently made and repeated that females,
including young girls, would go into houses where crack was sold, find
that they were unable to stop taking the stuff, and would sell their
bodies to man after man in order to buy more and more crack. The
stories were never balanced with an inquiry into the extent to which
drugs, mainly alcohol, and sex were intertwined in legal establishments
known as bars. Nor did anyone know that such stories had been heard
a century before about another feared drug that was smoked in so-
called dens.

Newsweek seemed particularly hooked on the compulsion to run
story after story on the drug, emphasizing the most sensational aspects
of its impact on society and individuals. Its 16 June 1986 issue stands
as one of the most hysterical issues of a major American publication in

24. Some of this material on the story of crack originally appeared in Trebach (1987,
5–16).

recent history, and rivaled the sensationalism of the movie "Reefer Madness" about marijuana in the 1930s. Editor-in-chief Richard Smith unbosomed himself of a lead editorial entitled, "The Plague Among Us," in which he compared the drug problem to medieval plagues and to the Japanese attack on Pearl Harbor. Smith saw all drugs but especially crack—"the . . . most addictive commodity now on the market"—as creating a crisis that threatened the survival of the nation. The drugs themselves, mind you, not the governmental and social reaction to them.

A few days later, in one of those sad and unpredictable events that change the course of history, Len Bias, a star basketball player at the University of Maryland, died suddenly in his room at the university. Bias was a black 22-year-old who was liked and admired by his friends and fans, a nice American kid, a model of clean living. The Boston Celtics had drafted him to play in the National Basketball Association, and he had just signed a rich contract. The youngster even had a jersey number. Total strangers with no interest in basketball were elated for him. Then, headlines screamed the awful news that crack might have killed Len Bias.

Within a short time, another young black sports star, professional football player Don Rogers, died of a cocaine overdose—which many people heard as "crack" overdose. Coming after all the previous hysteria, the tragic deaths of these two young Americans pushed the governmental and social leadership of the most powerful nation on earth into frenzied action in all directions.

Bills were tossed into legislative hoppers all over the country, as if they were sandbags heaved onto dikes being hastily erected to control a rampaging flood. Measures were proposed on both ends of Pennsylvania Avenue in Washington, D.C., to demand mass random urine tests of government officials, to deploy the military to control drug trafficking, to impose the death penalty for certain homicides connected with drug sales, to water down the exclusionary rule so that evidence seized without a warrant and in violation of the Fourth Amendment could be introduced in drug prosecutions so long as the officer had acted in "good faith," and dozens of other more repressive recommendations.

The Evolution of Crack   What do we know about the drug that has caused all this furor? There seems nothing terribly new about the chemical process that produces crack. Entrepreneurs have for ages sought to produce more potent forms of mind-altering drugs that could be transported more cheaply, be sold at a higher cost per unit, appeal to different tastes, and produce more immediate effects. Fermenting grapes and grains to make wine and beer is fine for many millions of people, but distilling them produces spirits, sometimes called brandy-wine, that are more potent. Wine and beer create trouble for many people, but the greatest difficulty seems to come from the more concentrated distilled spirits of alcohol. The less natural the drug, as has been said, the more trouble for humans.

The same for opium. Smoking the dried powder that comes from the opium poppy sap is both calming and potentially addicting. Not nearly so alluring or dangerous, however, as using morphine, the main active ingredient in opium. Neither is as thrilling or as dangerous as diacetyl-morphine, which, for convenience, could be called the essence of morphine plus a bit of vinegar-like acid; this concentrated and refined drug is also known as heroin.

Chewing the leaves of the South American coca plant produces, along with numbness of the mouth and tongue, a mild sensation of stimulation and good feeling. When chemists managed to isolate what might be called the essence of coca, the most powerful ingredient in the leaf, they produced a very potent white powder: cocaine hydro-chloride. Largely ignored for years, cocaine, as it is usually called, suddenly became very popular to millions of Americans who now like to snort it through their noses. For many thrill-seekers (and that is what is truly involved here) both the stimulation and the risks of the cocaine powder were enough. Then some bored soul decided to refine the powder further for smoking, which is the most rapid way (even quicker than injection) to get drugs to the brain. Thus, freebasing was born.

Traditional freebasing involves heating the powder with volatile chemicals, such as ether, which sometimes results in explosions and fires. (This, apparently, is what injured comedian Richard Pryor in June 1980.) The preparation of crack is easier and safer. Cocaine powder is mixed with water and baking soda or ammonia. The result is a highly concentrated chemical that looks like bits of coagulated soap powder, often slightly off-white, about the size of large green peas. It is frequently smoked in a pipe and makes a crackling sound when lit. In some cities, it is known as rock or cooked cocaine.

A gram of cocaine, less than a teaspoonful, costs at least $100 in many communities. Crack pellets are sometimes sold for as little as $10 each in the same areas. Of course, this drug is more addicting than powdered cocaine. That should be no surprise. Any drug that is more refined and then smoked will be more potent than its less-concentrated relatives. However, there is no reliable evidence that crack is the most addictive drug now known. While I believe that anybody who tries this relatively unknown compound is taking a great risk, my guess is that it is no more addicting than smoked tobacco or smoked heroin, which by my lights is quite bad enough. I also believe that anyone who uses either of those latter substances in any form is taking a major risk. As with those dangerous drugs, however, many risk-takers use crack and do not get hooked.

On an anecdotal level, I have spoken to perhaps several dozen crack users. Several had become addicted and felt they had to stop before they got into serious trouble. However, each of them did so, suggesting again that the drug operates like many others and can be conquered. Most of the smokers I spoke to said that it simply was not that significant an event in their lives.

This was the experience of journalist Jefferson Morley, who smoked crack and told about it in a series of articles and media appearances starting in 1989. Because his stance was not pure anti-crack ideology, many assumed Morley was endorsing the drug. Yet, he wrote that in his very limited experience "crack's pleasure quickly gave way to its side effects, combining the worst of marijuana and cocaine and inducing both stupefaction and paranoia" (quoted in Trebach and Zeese 1990a, 79). He also observes that "if all you have in life is bad choices, crack may not be the most unpleasant of them," and "crack can make sick sense to demoralized people." Morley's balanced approach also makes clear that while he saw dangers in the drug, his occasional use did not cause him to become addicted.

The Ignored Official Data We do not know how many addicted crack customers there are out there. When I heard and read the major news stories during July 1986 on the crack epidemic and related deaths, I was confused because they were inconsistent with my reading of the available federal data. My calls to officials in the National Institute on Drug Abuse (NIDA) and the Drug Enforcement Administration brought honest humility and admissions that the officials didn't know very much about crack and often relied on reports in the newspapers. There is not even a separate listing for crack, in NIDA's authoritative Drug Abuse Warning Network (DAWN), which collects data on drug-abuse deaths and injuries. Crack injuries and deaths are listed under cocaine, because, according to NIDA officials, it is usually not possible for a coroner to tell crack from powdered cocaine in the body of a deceased person.

Totally ignored in the cries to save our children from crack were the NIDA data which showed that the total number of children who died from cocaine in 1984 was eight—yes, eight, from all forms of cocaine, including crack. In the great majority of all of the cocaine mentions, death apparently was caused by use with other drugs. The most common fatal chemical companion to cocaine was alcohol, which was cited in 224 episodes during 1985. This is how the death of Len Bias should have been reported by DAWN when the 1986 reports were issued—because it turns out that the poor young fellow may not have died from crack at all, but perhaps from a combination of massive amounts of powdered cocaine and alcohol during an all-night celebration with his friends. Alcohol will probably forever remain, long after legalization of crack and other feared drugs, the single greatest "drug" threat to our youth.[25]

How many overdose deaths can be definitively attributed to crack as the major cause? I have searched. My assistants have searched. We have gone through many government reports. We have quizzed government statistical experts. During the summer of 1986, we did not discover one overdose death in which the presence of crack was confirmed as the major factor. Some six years later, during the summer of 1992, we searched again for confirmed crack deaths. Again, we could not find one in the DAWN reports. Calls to NIDA met with the same response.

We also checked again on the number of American children who might have died of crack. Again, such deaths were usually impossible to distinguish from those caused by powdered cocaine, but the total of all cocaine deaths for children up through the age of 17 during 1990, the latest year available, was 14 (National Institute on Drug Abuse 1990, 20). (The total number of overdose deaths from all illegal drugs for children through the age of 17 was 57 in 1990.) The presence of crack is demonstrably one of the least significant threats known to American children, perhaps because they have sense enough not to use or abuse it very frequently.

Yet the hysteria about crack has continued. Alleged crack deaths are regularly reported by major media, including the *New York Times*.

25. For some interesting recent editorial commentary on the enduring threat of alcohol, see Peter Passell, "Less Marijuana, More Alcohol?" *New York Times* (17 June 1992): D2.

The claim also has been made in that prestigious paper and in others that legions of babies are now being born addicted to crack; the number most often quoted has been 375,000 crack babies. As best as rational inquiry can determine, such claims have no basis whatsoever in fact. While too many babies are, sadly, damaged by drugs, including crack, there is no indication that anyone knows the exact number and the best guess is that the most threatening drug remains legal alcohol. An objective review of the known facts suggests that it is likely that all babies damaged by cocaine (including crack) might be about equal to those damaged by alcohol. In a recent article, Dale Gieringer estimated the numbers at perhaps 4,000 to 12,000 per year for each (1990, 71). Every one of these damaged infants is a tragedy, but that is a lot fewer than the number of 375,000 so often mentioned by experts. Even those numbers were an educated guess on the high side. Moreover, the great majority of those infants recover with good medical care and go on to lead normal lives. The greatest danger to infants does not lie in drugs, by the way, but in parental violence and neglect. I have yet to discover a single case, although I do not doubt that one might have occurred, where it has been definitively established by a pathologist that the consumption of crack by a pregnant woman was the major cause of death of the fetus. This is no recommendation for the use of crack by pregnant woman—a thought that repels me—but a simple objective reporting of the known facts.

There has been a recent move to combat the stories about crack babies by leading medical experts. Dr. Ira Chasnoff, frequently cited as the source of the scare stories, observed in 1992 after a major new study:

> They are no different from other children growing up. They are not the retarded imbeciles people talk about. . . . As I study the problem more and more, I think the placenta does a better job of protecting the child than we do as a society (quoted in Sullum 1992, 14).[26]

An article in the *Journal of the American Medical Association* by leading medical researchers about the impact of prenatal cocaine exposure concluded in a similar vein that "premature conclusions about the severity and universality of cocaine effects are themselves potentially harmful to children" (Mayes et al. 1992, 406). There are even reports from doctors that some women, upon learning that they

26. For a series of brief critiques of current conventional wisdom about crack, see Trebach and Zeese (1990a, chap. 4).

are pregnant, demand abortions because they once used cocaine and
believe the popular propaganda about the terribly deformed children
they almost certainly will produce (Koren et al. 1989, 1440).[27] It would
seem that abortion is much more harmful to a fetus than crack or
powdered cocaine ingestion by the mother.

Prohibition: More Toxic than Crack   In a seminal study on a related
aspect of the crack issue, researchers Paul J. Goldstein, Henry H.
Brownstein, and their colleagues (1990) showed how prohibition may
well be more toxic than crack. With the assistance of the New York
City police department, the team studied a sample of 414 homicides
that occurred during 1988. A total of 218, or 52.7 percent, of them
were classified as being drug-related. These were broken down into
three categories: psychopharmacological, those where the presence of
the drug in the body seems to have caused the violent action; systemic,
those where the violence was based upon participation in the black-
market drug trade; and economic compulsive, where the violence
occurred because the assailant wished to obtain money to buy drugs.

According to current mythology in the popular media, echoed by
scholars such as James Q. Wilson and James A. Inciardi, the major
problem with crack is in the psychopharmacological arena: the drug
drives people to violence. Objective research often refutes this mythology, as it does so much in the drug arena. Such were the results of this
study. There were in fact only five psychopharmacological cases out
of the 414 studied that involved crack. Only three involved crack alone,
and two of those cases were victim-precipitated. This leaves only one
case that fit the public mythology: a 22-year-old man who beat his
infant daughter to death while high on crack. The great majority, 74
percent, of the drug-related homicides studied were systemic. They
arose in violent disputes between participants in the black market
created by drug prohibition in the same way that bootlegger murders

27. The authors, located at the Division of Clinical Pharmacology, Hospital for Sick
Children, Toronto, found that the hysteria about cocaine (and assumably crack) has
affected supposedly objective scientific judgments. In a study of scientific articles
submitted to leading medical journals, they found that articles that found adverse effects
of cocaine on the fetus were much more likely to be published than those that found
none. They concluded: "This bias against the null hypothesis may lead to a distorted
estimation of teratogenic risk of cocaine and thus cause women to terminate their
pregnancy unjustifiably" (p. 1440). The authors also reported they encountered requests
for abortions among their Toronto patients in part because of sensational newspaper
stories to the effect that "even one dose of cocaine in pregnancy can harm the baby"
(p. 1441).

cast a pall over many cities during alcohol prohibition. The largest single category of homicides, a total of 106 out of 414, were those involved in the crack trade. An additional 45 involved those in the cocaine trade. Only 11 of the systemic cases involved drugs other than crack.

It is not possible to tell why the crack-cocaine trade is more violent than the trade in other illegal drugs. However, this rigorous study adds considerably to the mountain of existing evidence to the effect that prohibition and the drug laws are major contributing factors to the huge amount of homicides and other violent acts making sections of some American cities virtually uninhabitable.

These are only some of the facts that lead me to believe that we could live with legalized crack but that our society cannot survive in recognizable form much longer while it remains illegal.

Crime and Violence

There are many benefits that will be brought to our society with the legalization of drugs. For example, the suffering of millions of sick people will be eased because their doctors should face less control on the use of pain-killing drugs. Also, such banned drugs as heroin and marijuana will be easily available to those who need them in medical settings. The number of criminal cases could drop considerably, I would guess from 25 percent to 60 percent, depending on conditions in each community. The prison population might be cut at least in half over a period of a few years, with the help of an amnesty program that would release drug offenders incarcerated for nonviolent offenses. There would be less need for vast urine-testing programs and for widespread police invasions of privacy and constitutional rights. There would be other benefits as well, some of which I have not dealt with extensively here.

However, the biggest benefit will be great reductions in crime and violence. Murders and maimings, often of innocent bystanders, in the drug trade are what motivates most thinking people to be willing to take the risk of legalization. Many people are also motivated by having been the victims of drug addicts who commit crimes in order to obtain money to buy drugs. A crippling amount of crime and disruption for innocent third parties arises from the fact that many popular drugs are banned by the criminal law. The monetary toll of prohibition runs into billions of dollars every year in the United States. Elsewhere I have reviewed the extensive amount of research documenting the connection between the illegal drug scene and crime (see Trebach 1982, 212–18, 242–53).

Legal drugs should cost a small fraction of their artificially inflated illegal prices. I estimate that a gram of cocaine, which now costs $100, might cost $7–$15 in the future. Ten marijuana cigarettes, which now cost $100, might cost $5–$10. And so on for heroin, opium, and other drugs. Most of these drugs come from plants that are easy to grow in many parts of the world. They do not have a high intrinsic value in a free market, as do gold and silver.

It appears likely that these economic realities will force almost everyone in the illicit drug trade to seek other lines of work—as repeal of alcohol prohibition made multitudes of those in the illegal alcohol business consider their employment options. Violent, illegal drug markets should disappear from the streets of our cities, replaced largely by peaceful, legal nonmedical drugstores, selling their wares at prices most people could afford from legal employment. For poor street addicts, it is to be assumed that they would be able to obtain free maintenance drugs through the doctors under the medical option of the new legalization system.

It would seem to follow logically, moreover, that the disappearance of the drug trade would mean the virtual disappearance of systemic crime—which Goldstein, Brownstein, et al. (1990) define as homicides in drug-trade turf battles—and economic compulsive crime—attempts by addicts to obtain money for drug purchases. It would seem that other crimes, especially burglaries and thefts, impelled by these motivations would also decline.

This would leave one type of crime that would still be relevant under legalization: psychopharmacological, those caused primarily by the impact of the drug upon the body and emotions of the users. It is conceivable that this kind of crime could increase somewhat under legalization. However, even a significant increase in such crimes would be quite tolerable as compared with today because, according to Goldstein, Brownstein, et al. (1990), the base amount is so low. For example, only one out of the 414 homicides they studied (0.24 percent) involved an assailant high on crack. A total of 7.5 percent of the homicides involving any of the drugs was classified as psychopharmacological. The most common element in those was alcohol. Thus, the presence of crack or heroin in the legal market should not have, if one reads the research objectively, a significant effect on the number of crimes committed in the society.

Yet, this is not how many leading prohibitionists, including Inciardi and Wilson, interpret the evidence.

Referring to the Goldstein, Brownstein, et al. typology, for example, Inciardi acknowledges that the extensive systemic violence associated with the drug trade had spurred calls for legalization recently and that "if heroin, cocaine, and marijuana were legal substances, systemic violence would indeed decline significantly" (Inciardi 1992, 249). In my eyes, with that admission he has conceded the entire debate. Reducing systemic drug-trade violence is so important to our survival as a decent society that almost any downside impact of legalization is worth this gain.

However, Professor Inciardi goes on to observe that "to achieve the desired declines in systemic violence, it would be required that crack be legalized as well." Next, he says that there was a great deal of psychopharmacological violence associated with both heroin and cocaine, assumably including crack. He then reaches this conclusion: "Given the fact that drug use would certainly increase with legalization, in all likelihood any declines in systemic violence would be accompanied by corresponding increases in psychopharmacological violence" (249). Thus, even though Inciardi admits that the major goal of legalizers would be achieved, he then retreats to the standard distortions that prohibitionists have used for over a century to justify their destructive system: Drugs would drive multitudes of our people crazy and into major amounts of crime.

Of course, there is no proof of any of Inciardi's major arguments. During the past century, as we have seen, there has been no proof that any drugs, alone and not in the context of the drug laws, have caused major criminal problems. Not opium. Not heroin. Not marijuana. Not cocaine. Not even crack, the latest devil drug which appears so seductive that most people, including some scholars, appear revulsed by the very thought that it would be sold legally.

To reach the standard dire conclusions about crack, one must ignore history and turn much objective research, including that of Goldstein, Brownstein, et al. on its head; this is what Professor Inciardi does. Their research on crack shows that there was only one homicide out of 414 in the sample in which the major cause seems to have been the intoxication of the assailant on crack—as compared to 106 due to the illegal crack trade. There is no indication in that research or in any other objective study that demonstrates the probability that there would be over a hundredfold increase in psychopharmacological crimes under legalization. That level of increase would be necessary to achieve the "corresponding increase" that Inciardi predicts.

It is admittedly possible, but by no means certain, that there would be some increase in psychopharmacological crime after legalization. However, past experience, research findings, and logic suggest that this rise would not be crippling. There is every indication that the peoples of many countries have shown a good deal of sense and moderation in dealing with most drugs under conditions of wide availability. Even if there were a temporary breakdown at first and, say, psychopharmacological crack homicides increased to the seemingly unlikely level of five times the current tally, this would be unfortunate but not intolerable. Among the New York sample, this would have meant an increase of from one to five homicides. That increase would most likely be offset by a decrease in the total of systemic murders. Thus, we would be trading off an increase of four murders with a decrease of as many as 106. While one must be cautious in making projections from limited data, nevertheless these ratios suggest that while legalization would not eliminate all drug-related homicides (and other crimes), on balance it could well be a very good bargain for society.

Prohibitionists also make much of another important argument about crime: the presence of legal drugs will make very little difference in the criminal lifestyles of drug addicts (see, for example, Inciardi 1992, 247). Many authorities support this argument against legalization, but that support fails in the end to counteract the evidence about the benefits of legalization as compared with the costs of prohibition. This argument is often referred to as the theory of pre-addiction criminality and declares that most addicts were criminals before they became addicts, that the same deviant tendencies led them to both drugs and crime, and that providing them with a regular source of drugs will have no effect on their criminal behavior. There is some truth to these arguments about some addicts at some points in their lives, but none whatsoever in regard to other addicts at different times in their lives. Drug addicts are not robots nor, as I have explained, are they all alike.

Many addicts I have known simply love the deviance and defiance of it all. They use whatever drug is available to them, whether alcohol or heroin or crack. They never even think about the legal status, only the price and the source. They are urban adventurers and risk-takers and criminals. I believe that this set of thrill-seeking attitudes toward life is much more important to their behavior than their dependence on drugs, although that is a powerful influence also. This is especially true of some, but not all, young urban male addicts in their teens and twenties.

Changes occur in addicts' attitudes, sometimes in their early twenties, more often in their late twenties or, if they survive the streets that long, in their early thirties. A vast body of criminological research demonstrates that young people are much more deviant than their elders in all sorts of activities, including crime and drug-taking, and that the simple process of maturing creates much more conventional behavior. Indeed, in the drug field it is recognized that the dynamics of "maturing out" of drug use are a most positive force.[28] People mature in their attitudes at different rates and often because of different life experiences. I have known addicts who were walking crime waves at 21, and bragged about it, but who turned into reflective, decent citizens by the time they were 30. In addition to age and growing maturity, the single most prominent factor told to me by the addicts I have known was, although it sounds too simple, meeting the right woman at the right time in their lives. (Almost all the street addicts I have known were male.) A typical story I have heard from addicts: I was getting a little bored with my so-called exciting life on the streets; I met this girl; and she eventually said to me, it's me or the streets— and the girl won over the streets, over crime, and over drugs.

At this point, despite the notion that heroin or crack, for example, is all-powerful, many addicts give it up without any professional help because they are ready to do so. Indeed, so-called spontaneous cures of this nature occur without professional intervention in perhaps half of all cases of those who come off drugs, including alcohol. The difficulty is that many of this group relapse and there is the other group that needs help of various kinds. Here is where the availability of drugs under legalization, whether from doctors or from the nonmedical option, becomes vital. An addict reaching out for some semblance of normality or legality should find that his or her drugs of addiction are obtainable without resorting to crime, a thought which of course goes

28. Edward Brecher was particularly insightful in writing of the venerable process of youthful deviance and maturing out in connection with the drug problem. In one section of his masterwork (Brecher et al. 1972), he goes to great lengths to praise the understanding of Canadian officials at the time of the release of the LeDain Report (Government of Canada 1970). He cited with approval this statement by Canadian Minister of Health John Munroe in 1970: "After all, it is our children we are talking about. Will they come to power with a fierce dedication to destroy everything we now represent—the good along with the bad—because of the way we now treat the drug problem?" (Brecher et al. 1972, 506).

against the grain of current prohibitionist thinking but which is quite consistent with modern notions of harm reduction.

For many addicts the availability of legal drugs would be important also during their early criminal careers. Because the drugs would be much cheaper than during prohibition, many if not most addicts would find they could buy their drugs from legal income and that there was no need to rob and steal to get the money. Those who continued their crimes would find that they had to commit fewer crimes—perhaps only 10 to 20 percent of the prelegalization rate—in order to get enough money to buy the cheap legal drugs they needed. We legalizers never claimed that drug-law reform would magically make all addict crime disappear, as Inciardi declares we have, but huge percentages of such crime clearly would cease.

One of the most revealing studies of the impact of legal drugs on the criminality of addicts was reported in 1974 by Dr. Paul Cushman, then director of the Methadone Maintenance Clinic at St. Luke's Hospital in New York (reported in Trebach 1982, 261). Cushman reviewed the frequency of arrest of 269 narcotic addicts over a period of time. Before they became addicted, many of the addicts were involved in crime, which confirms part of the pre-addiction criminality thesis. During this pre-addiction stage of their lives the rate of arrest was 3.1 per 100-person years, a rate calculated to reflect the total criminal activity of each group during a given time period. However, after they became addicted, which for many meant using drugs daily, and before they went on methadone, the rate of arrest went up over ten times, to 35.1 arrests per 100-person years. After they started getting maintained on methadone—which for them was in a sense a legal drug—the rate went down almost to the previous level, to 5.9 arrests per 100 person-years.

The patterns in this one piece of research are, I suspect, characteristic of a broader reality. They answer effectively the argument that legal drugs will not make criminals into innocent choirboys and so legalization will be a failure. If the access of addicts to legal drugs, whether from a nonmedical drugstore or from a doctor, cuts the rate of crime approximately 83 percent (the difference in the Cushman study) among a group of urban street addicts, it is difficult to imagine a better bargain for society. This would be true even if the reductions were only half that amount. The fact that these addicts were criminals before they became addicted and that many of them continue to commit crimes after legal drugs were available only tells us that no drug control solution will create a perfect world. Prohibition certainly has not done so.

In sum, the evidence strongly suggests that the future under legalization could well be vastly improved for casual users, for addicts, and for their drug-free neighbors. The numbers of casual users and addicts should remain within tolerable bounds, even though millions of Americans will be in trouble with drugs. Those with drug problems will be treated more humanely and effectively. There will be a dramatic drop in the level of serious crime that has created a scared society. When this probable future under legalization is contemplated, it appears that drug prohibition endures primarily because it is a familiar but bad habit.

6. Epilogue: The Satirical Questions

There remains the matter of the long lists of often derisive questions asked of legalizers by prohibitionists. These questions were not raised about the current system a century ago when it was being proposed, but appear to prohibitionists to be essential to showing whether legalization of drugs could be workable. Many seem to emanate from that same intolerant spot in the human psyche that reacts to any proposed major innovation with fear, ridicule, and insults.

Such a list appears in James A. Inciardi's book, *The War on Drugs II,* in a section, "Shooting from the Hip" (1992, 241–43). Some of the questions raise serious issues. Too many are simply satirical or derisive and serve to prevent any serious discussion of the real issues. To save space here, I have edited out some of the questions' offending language. In any event, I have already answered many of them in the previous pages. What follows is a summary of my previous answers plus some additional information on a few questions that might not have been answered adequately.

1. "[W]hich drugs should be legalized, according to what criteria, and who should determine the criteria?" In time, very probably all of them. However, it would make sense to start with the milder drugs, such as marijuana and coca leaves. Cocaine, crack, and heroin might follow in short order. The criteria would be determined under my preferred plan, the Galiber model now pending before the New York senate, by a State Controlled Substances Authority, similar to the State Liquor Authority. The authority might base its own criteria on whether or not a significant number of adult citizens wanted to obtain the drug through either the medical or nonmedical options. This is a

democratic test and thereby stands in direct contrast to the totalitarian test of the prohibitionists, that is, that the government knows what drugs are best for the people. Of course, each state could determine which drugs to legalize and which to keep illegal.

2. "[W]hat potency levels should be permitted?" Every effort should be made to discourage the trend toward the use of purified and high-potency drugs, which is of course the trend in modern medicine and in the illicit market under prohibition. Government warnings and free-enterprise pressures should move users toward a whole new array of low-potency, natural drugs. It will be good for public health and for business if users choose coca leaves over crack or marijuana over 151-proof rum. Yet, if there is a demand for high-potency drugs, it is best that they be made available legally—along with warnings on their dangers and advice on how to use them so as to minimize harm.

3. "[S]hould there be age limits?" Yes. They may well vary from state to state, and if a state so decides, even from drug to drug. As with alcohol, many underage youth will delight in defying the age limits and deceiving the legal sellers about their age. There is no ultimate remedy for youthful defiance. However, it should be easier for states to enforce age limits on all drugs and alcohol because in the future only a tiny fraction of drug sales will be illegal, those made to youth.

4. "Should certain drugs be limited to those already dependent on them? . . . And if this approach is deemed viable, what do we say to the heroin addicts who want to buy cocaine? In other words, do we legalize heroin and cocaine sales but forbid speedballing? And then, what about drug experimenters? . . . [I]n what amounts can users . . . purchase heroin, cocaine, marijuana, Quaaludes, and other chemical substances?" Like many of the other questions, this one assumes that it is absurd on its face to allow such feared drugs into the legal market under any guise. However, such drugs are widely available to anyone with the price under the current prohibitionist system. Under the system I prefer, no drugs would be limited to addicts. Under some state systems, there could be sensible limits, to be determined by the state authority, on the amount anyone, whether an addict or a recreational user, could purchase at one time or on the same day in a retail establishment. There should be widespread observance of those limits, since a purchaser might well be able to come back day after day in many states.

That of course is the great danger: that lower price and greater availability will result in too many people coming back day after day, with disastrous social consequences. As I have said repeatedly, I worry about such a worst-case scenario but do not believe it will come about, based upon a study of current and past history. On balance, I have more faith in the good sense of the masses of the people than in the rule of government autocrats on such personal matters.

5. "Where should the drugs be sold? Over the counter in drug and grocery stores as is the case with many pharmaceuticals? Through mail order houses? In special vending machines strategically located in public restrooms, hotel lobbies, and train and bus stations? In tax-supported 'drug shacks' as Rep. Charles Rangel (D-NY) satirically asked?" While much of this multi-faceted question is crafted in satirical terms, all of these outlets are possible at some point in the future. Under the system I prefer, at the outset of legalization, the State Controlled Substances Authority would very probably restrict the sale to a limited number of outlets with strict licensing requirements. There will be no vending machines in the first years, one may safely assume, nor will such a system be forced on a state that objects to it.

6. "Where should the raw material for the drugs originate? . . . Should legalization policies permit the introduction of currently little-known drugs of abuse into the U.S. from foreign ports such as *qat* from Yemen or *bekaro* from Pakistan?" I am recommending a new drug-control system based on capitalism and free enterprise. It is not that I have blind faith in free-market economics. Rather, after 20 years of direct involvement in the field, I have reached that point where I now have no faith whatsoever in the benefits of the current state-controlled system, which is close to old-fashioned communism. Accordingly, the new system would allow for the greatest possible economic freedom in production and marketing. Yes, of course allow new drugs from Yemen and Pakistan or anywhere else—if there is a demand for them and if they are packaged and sold according to the regulations established in each state, including health warnings.

7. "If drugs are to be legalized, should the drug market be a totally free one, with private industry establishing the prices as well as levels of purity and potency? . . . Should Timothy Leary and Manuel Noriega be permitted to endorse certain drugs or brands of drugs as part of advertising programs?" There is no totally free market in any commodity in the United States. We have a system that combines elements of capitalism and socialism. I would like to see the former emphasized at the expense of the latter under drug legalization. However, as we have seen, under the Galiber model the state authority would have some controls on the type of advertising that would be permitted. In the first years of the new system, I would prefer very modest amounts of

advertising, like a simple listing of products and prices in a newspaper. The reference to Messrs. Leary and Noriega does not deserve a response.

8. "If drugs are to be legalized, what types of restrictions on their use should be structured? Should transportation workers, nuclear plant employees, or other categories of workers be forbidden to use them at all times, or just while they are on duty?" This question displays a widely shared lack of knowledge about the effects of illegal drugs on work performance and the dynamics of their use generally. It may help the fearful to think about alcohol, which provides a good model here. It is not illegal to use this powerful drug off-duty but it is a crime to drive a car or an airplane while under the influence of alcohol—or, for that matter, of a mind-altering prescription medicine, such as a tranquilizer. The test should be impairment, whatever the substance. There is no evidence that the currently illegal drugs constituted a different problem or that they now present a major threat to worker performance in the country generally. This is true despite contrary mythology, as reflected in this question.

9. "As is the case with alcohol, will certain establishments be permitted to serve drugs (and which drugs) to their customers? . . . As with coffee and cigarette breaks, should users be permitted pot and coke breaks as part of their union contracts?" Drug bars present many problems, especially that of setting up the conditions for driving while intoxicated on the way home. However, I recommend that states experiment with a variety of plans that would allow private entrepreneurs to set up establishments serving some of the milder drugs in the least harmful fashion. There is room here for many innovative ideas, some of which will shock prohibitionists but which might do a great deal of good. For example, I would like to see smoking parlors where opium and marijuana might be smoked in quiet, peaceful settings at the end of work or on weekends. On the other hand, the idea of pot or coke breaks for workers during the working day is an obviously flawed one. Pot and coke breaks for workers would interfere with performance in the same way that three-martini lunches do. All of these drugs are intoxicants; that is why people like and use them. They make life more pleasant and bearable. Almost all people expect the state of intoxication to pass within a matter of a few hours so that they can get on with their lives. It almost always does. Thus a bottle of wine—or a modest amount of a currently illegal substance—at night may sometimes make sense for a functioning person. Taking the same substance during the

workday does not make sense in practical performance terms, regardless of the legal status of the drugs involved.

10. "[W]hat government bureaucracy should be charged with the enforcement of the legalization statutes? . . . FBI . . . DEA . . . FDA? Going further, what kinds of penalties ought to be established for violation of the legalization restrictions?" The federal government has failed utterly in drug control through the criminal law. Thus, the FBI and the DEA would have very little role in control utilizing the criminal law. Indeed, DEA might well vanish in its current form. Those criminal laws that remain would be enforced primarily by the states. The Food and Drug Administration could continue to have a major role in assuring the safety and effectiveness of the drugs marketed in interstate commerce, which means virtually all of the drugs. Penalties for violations would be primarily civil, as in the case of alcohol enforcement. However, the states would have major responsibility for enforcement of drunk-driving laws and those penalizing sales to minors. These could continue to carry criminal as well as civil penalties.

In a related section of his book Inciardi raises the question as to why the legalizers seem to believe that ineffective criminal drug laws can be replaced by effective regulations. "The point is that there is real naivete to the belief that drug laws are unenforceable but drug regulations are," he observes (254). This statement misses the whole point. The criminal drug laws are ineffective and destructive because they attempt to prohibit activities that cannot be stopped. Civil regulations that sought to prohibit adults from using drugs would fail also. By bringing the primary activities—the production, selling, and personal ingestion of drugs—out of the cold and into legality, it is possible to set up civil and criminal laws and regulations that deal with the secondary and tertiary aspects of the activity. The latter involve controls on such matters as purity, safety, labeling, age limits, advertising, and operating machinery while intoxicated on these substances. While those latter laws and regulations will also be certainly violated, they will not be mass violations on an international scale by armed bands, requiring the unleashing of police SWAT teams and military invasion forces.

In any event, the major controls on the use and abuse of all drugs are not to be found in the laws. Those controls are found primarily in nonlegal forces—personal ethics, family values, social trends, cultural role models, education, and religion. Our major efforts should turn away from the use of the criminal sanction propping up the dying prohibition empire and toward shoring up the institutions that create those positive forces, especially in those minority communities that now seem so riven with hate and despair. Accordingly, even though legalization of drugs is seen by Inciardi as a "nightmare" for ghetto dwellers (1992, 155), it could well herald the dawn of a new day for them.

References

Advisory Committee on Drug Dependence. 1968. *Cannabis*. London: H. M. Stationery Office.

Alexander, Bruce K. 1990. *Peaceful Measures: Canada's Way Out of the "War on Drugs."* Toronto: University of Toronto Press.

Baltimore Police Department. 1890. *Report of the Board of Police Commissioners for the City of Baltimore to the General Assembly of Maryland for 1889 and 1890*. Baltimore: Baltimore Police Department.

————. 1990. *Summary of Index Crimes*. Baltimore: Planning and Research Division.

Benjamin, Daniel K., and Roger Leroy Miller. 1991. *Undoing Drugs: Beyond Legalization*. New York: Basic Books.

Boston Police Department. 1890. *Boston Board of Police Annual Report, December 1889*. Boston: Boston Police Department.

————. 1990. *Annual Report of the Boston Policy Board 1989*. Boston: Boston Police Department.

Brecher, Edward M., and the Editors of Consumer Reports. 1972. *Licit and Illicit Drugs*. New York: Little, Brown.

Bureau of Justice Statistics. 1992a. *National Update*. Washington: U.S. Department of Justice (July).

————. 1992b. *Sourcebook of Criminal Justice Statistics—1991*. Washington: U.S. Department of Justice.

Califano, Joseph A., Jr. 1992. Statement at Columbia University, New York (18 May).

Cauchon, Dennis. 1992. "Government Doesn't Have to Prove Guilt," *USA Today* (18 May): 1A.

Centers for Disease Control. 1991. *Morbidity and Mortality Weekly Report*. Atlanta: Centers for Disease Control (8 November).

―――. 1992. *HIV AIDS Surveillance*. Atlanta: Centers for Disease Control (20 July).

Chicago Police Department. 1890. *Report of the General Superintendent of Police for the City of Chicago*. Chicago: Chicago Police Department.

City of Minneapolis. 1890. *Annual Reports of the Various City Officers of the City of Minneapolis for the Year 1889*. Minneapolis: Harrison and Smith.

Cleveland Police Department. 1890. *Annual Report of Police Commissioners: I. L. Morris, James Macneil, Frank D. Bosworth, E. B. Cornell, Commissioners Year Ending 1889*. Cleveland: Cleveland Police Department.

―――. 1990. *Annual Report of the Police Department, Cleveland, Ohio, 1989*. Cleveland: Cleveland Police Department.

Courtwright, David T. 1982. *Dark Paradise: Opiate Addiction in America Before 1940*. Cambridge, MA: Harvard University Press.

D.C. Commissioners. 1890. "The Report of the Police Commissioner." In *Report of D.C. Commissioners 1890*. Washington: District of Columbia Government Printing Office.

Dennis, Richard J. 1990a. "The American People Are Starting To Question the Drug War." In *The Great Issues in Drug Policy*, edited by Arnold S. Trebach and Kevin B. Zeese. Washington: Drug Policy Foundation.

―――. 1990b. "The Economics of Legalizing Drugs," *The Atlantic* (November): 126.

Detroit Police Department. 1890. *Twenty-fifth Annual Report of the Board of Commissioners of the Metropolitan Police to the Common Council of the City of Detroit*. Detroit: Raynor and Taylor (15 February).

―――. 1990. "Arrests and Disposition, 1989," in *Annual Report*. Detroit: Detroit Police Department.

Drug Policy Foundation. 1992a. "The Bush Drug War Record: The Real Story of a $45 Billion Domestic War" (5 September).

―――. 1992b. "Milton Friedman Talks About Liberty and Drug Policy," *The Drug Policy Letter* (Winter).

Engelsman, Eddy L. 1990. "The Pragmatic Strategies of the Dutch 'Drug Czar.' " In *The Great Issues in Drug Policy*, edited by Arnold S. Trebach and Kevin B. Zeese. Washington: Drug Policy Foundation.

Evans, Richard. 1990. "The Many Forms of Legalization: Beyond 'Whether' to 'How.' " In *The Great Issues in Drug Policy*, edited by Arnold S. Trebach and Kevin B. Zeese. Washington: Drug Policy Foundation.

Federal Bureau of Investigation. 1991. *Uniform Crime Reports for the United States 1990*. Washington: U.S. Government Printing Office.

Forfeiture Endangers American Rights. 1992. *FEAR Chronicles* (May): 1.

Friedman, Milton. 1991. "A War We're Losing." In *New Frontiers in Drug Policy,* edited by Arnold S. Trebach and Kevin B. Zeese. Washington: Drug Policy Foundation.

Gieringer, Dale. 1990. "How Many Crack Babies?" In *The Great Issues in Drug Policy,* edited by Arnold S. Trebach and Kevin B. Zeese. Washington: Drug Policy Foundation.

Goldstein, Paul J., Henry H. Brownstein, Patrick J. Ryan, and Patricia A. Bellucci. 1989. "Prohibition May Be More Toxic Than Crack," *The Lancet* (16 December).

Government of Canada. 1970. *Interim Report of the Commission of Inquiry into the Non-Medical Use of Drugs*. Ottawa: Queen's Printer for Canada.

Inciardi, James A. 1986. *The War on Drugs*. Palo Alto, CA: Mayfield.

———. 1992. *The War on Drugs II*. Palo Alto, CA: Mayfield.

Indian Hemp Drugs Commission. [1894] 1969. *Marijuana: Report of the Indian Hemp Drugs Commission, 1893–94*. Silver Spring, MD: Thomas Jefferson.

Judson, Horace Freeland. 1974. *Heroin Addiction in Britain: What Americans Can Learn from the English Experience*. New York: Harcourt Brace Jovanovich.

Kane, Harry Hubbell. 1882. *Opium-Smoking in America and China*. New York: G. P. Putnam's Sons.

Koren, Gideon, et al. 1989. "Bias Against the Null Hypothesis: The Reproductive Hazards of Cocaine," *The Lancet* (16 December).

Kyvig, David E., ed. 1985. *Law, Alcohol, and Order: Perspectives on National Prohibition*. Westport, CT: Greenwood Press.

Lender, Mark Edward, and James Kirby Martin. 1982. *Drinking in America: A History*. New York: Free Press.

Macguire, Kathleen, and Timothy J. Flanagan, eds. 1991. *Sourcebook of Criminal Justice Statistics 1990*. Washington: U.S. Department of Justice.

Mandel, Jerry. 1989. "The Mythical Roots of U.S. Drug Policy: Soldier's Disease and Addiction in the Civil War." In *Drug Policy 1989–1990: A Reformer's Catalogue,* edited by Arnold S. Trebach and Kevin B. Zeese. Washington: Drug Policy Foundation.

Mauer, Marc. 1991. *Americans Behind Bars*. Washington: The Sentencing Project (January).

Mayes, Linda C., et al. 1992. "The Problem of Prenatal Cocaine Exposure: A Rush to Judgment," *Journal of the American Medical Association* 267:3 (15 January).

Mayor's Committee on Marijuana. 1944. *The Marihuana Problem in the City of New York*. Lancaster, PA: Jacques Cattell Press.

Minneapolis Police Department. 1990. *1989 Annual Report*. Minneapolis: Minneapolis Police Department.

Musto, David F. [1973] 1987. *The American Disease: Origins of Narcotic Control*. New York: Oxford University Press.

———. 1987. "The History of Legislative Control Over Opium, Cocaine, and Their Derivatives." In *Dealing with Drugs,* edited by Ronald Hamowy. Lexington, MA: Lexington Books.

National Center for Health Statistics. 1992. *Health, United States, 1991*. Hyattsville, MD: Public Health Service.

National Commission on AIDS. 1991. *The Twin Epidemics of Substance Use and HIV*. Washington: National Commission on AIDS (July).

National Commission on Marihuana and Drug Abuse. 1973. *Drug Use in America: Problem in Perspective*. Washington: U.S. Government Printing Office.

National Institute on Alcohol Abuse and Alcoholism. 1991. *Surveillance Report #20. Apparent Per Capita Alcohol Consumption: National, State, and Regional Trends, 1977–1989*. Washington: NIAAA.

National Institute on Drug Abuse. 1989. *Annual Data, 1988: Data from the Drug Abuse Warning Network*. Rockville, MD: NIDA.

National Institute on Drug Abuse. 1990. *Annual Medical Examiner Data, 1990*. Rockville, MD: National Institute on Drug Abuse.

National Narcotics Intelligence Consumers Committee. 1992. *The NNICC Report 1991*. Washington: Drug Enforcement Administration.

National Research Council. 1982. *An Analysis of Marijuana Policy*. Washington: National Academy Press.

New York City Police Department. 1890. *Report of the Police Department of the City of New York for the Year Ending December 31, 1889*. New York: Martin B. Brown.

Office of Management Analysis and Planning. 1990. *Complaints and Arrests: Police Department of the City of New York, 1989*. New York: Office of Management Analysis and Planning.

Philadelphia Police Department. 1890. "Third Annual Message of Edwin H. Fiddler, Mayor of Philadelphia." In *Public Safety 1889,* vol. 2. Philadelphia: Philadelphia Police Department.

————. 1990. *Meeting Tomorrow's Challenge: Annual Report.* Philadelphia: Philadelphia Police Department.

Ryan, Michael. 1988. "Give People Hope, Not Drugs," *Parade Magazine* (25 September).

San Francisco Police Department. 1890. *Annual Commissioner's Report—City of San Francisco 1889.* San Francisco: San Francisco Police Department.

————. 1990. *Arrest Report,* cable. San Francisco: San Francisco Police Department.

Schneider, Andrew, and Mary Pat Flaherty. 1991. "Presumed Guilty," *Pittsburgh Press* (11–16 August 1991).

Secretary of Health and Human Services. 1990. *Alcohol and Health: Seventh Special Report to the U.S. Congress.* Washington: Department of Health and Human Services (January).

Siler, J. F., et al. 1933. "Marijuana Smoking in Panama," *The Military Surgeon* 73 (July–December).

Solomon, David, ed. 1966. *The Marihuana Papers.* New York: Bobbs-Merrill.

State of Illinois. 1991. *Crime in Illinois, 1990.* Springfield: Authority of the State of Illinois.

Stinson, Frederick S., and Samar Farha DeBakey. 1992. "Alcohol-Related Mortality in the United States, 1979–1988," *British Journal of Addiction* 87:777.

Sullum, Jacob. 1992. "The Cocaine Kids," *Reason* 24:14 (August/ September).

Szasz, Thomas S. 1974. *Ceremonial Chemistry: The Ritual Persecution of Drugs, Addicts, and Pushers.* Garden City, NY: Doubleday.

Terry, Charles E., and Mildred Pellens. [1928] 1970. *The Opium Problem.* Montclair, NJ: Patterson Smith.

Trebach, Arnold S. 1982. *The Heroin Solution.* New Haven, CT: Yale University Press.

————. 1987. *The Great Drug War.* New York: Macmillan.

————. 1989. "Legalization Versus the Law of the Jungle," Testimony in support of S.1918, New York Senate (16 June).

Trebach, Arnold S., and Kevin B. Zeese, eds. 1989. *Drug Policy 1989–1990: A Reformer's Catalogue.* Washington: Drug Policy Foundation.

————, eds. 1990a. *Drug Prohibition and the Conscience of Nations*. Washington: Drug Policy Foundation.

————, eds. 1990b. *The Great Issues in Drug Policy*. Washington: Drug Policy Foundation.

————, eds. 1991. *New Frontiers in Drug Policy*. Washington: Drug Policy Foundation.

————, eds. 1992. *Strategies for Change*. Washington: Drug Policy Foundation.

U.S. Congress. 1992. House Select Committee on Narcotics Abuse and Control. *Quick Facts on Heroin—Overview*. 100th Cong., 2d Sess. Washington: U.S. Government Printing Office (5 June).

Weil, Andrew. 1983. *Chocolate to Morphine*. Boston: Houghton Mifflin.

————. 1986. *The Natural Mind,* rev. ed. Boston: Houghton Mifflin.

White House Office of National Drug Control Policy. 1989. *National Drug Control Strategy*. Washington: U.S. Government Printing Office.

————. 1992. *National Drug Control Strategy*. Washington: U.S. Government Printing Office.

Wilson, James Q. 1990. "Against the Legalization of Drugs," *Commentary* (February).

Zeese, Kevin B. 1991. "Losing Our Soul," *The Drug Policy Letter* (March–April): 7.

Part Two

Against Legalization of Drugs

James A. Inciardi

Introduction

At a meeting of the U.S. Conference of Mayors in 1988, Baltimore Mayor Kurt L. Schmoke called for a national debate on American drug-control strategies and the potential benefits of legalizing marijuana, heroin, cocaine, crack, and other illicit substances. Schmoke's argument was that for generations, our country has been pursuing policies of prosecution and repression that have resulted in little more than overcrowded courts and prisons, increased profits for drug traffickers, and higher rates of addiction (Schmoke 1989).

Schmoke's comments certainly didn't pass unnoticed. From a broad assortment of metaphorical garrets and cloisters and cellars and towers they came—a highly vocal minority of academicians and attorneys, editors and economists, and liberals and libertarians, capped by a fragmentary sampling of Marxist criminologists, blue-chip conservatives, and marijuana smokers and enthusiasts. There they were, all sharing the same podium. It was a curious mixture, like an odd and mismatched arrangement of roses, dandelions, ornamental grasses, and shaggy weeds crowded into a small rooftop flower garden. And how vocal they were. They captured the attention of the television networks, *Time* and *Newsweek,* the major dailies, House and Senate committees, and the TV talk show circuit, including even Donahue and Geraldo. As a researcher who had been working in the drug field in one capacity or another for almost three decades, I found the spectacle and pageantry of it all rather curious. I reacted to it. I wrote about it. I debated it. I became known as a ''drug warrior'' to some observers, primarily, I guess, because I vehemently opposed the whole notion of legalizing drugs.

The drug legalization debate received considerable attention in 1988 and 1989, but in the years since, interest in the topic (or at least media coverage of it) has dwindled. Nevertheless, a bit more needs to be said. There are additional thoughts to be offered, errors to be corrected, some missing facts and considerations to be added to the annals and archives of the debate, and elements of logic to be introduced. A number of the points made here I have presented elsewhere. They bear repeating and expanding. As such, this essay is a series of reflections on the great drug war and the great drug debate, the history of American drug policy, issues surrounding the drugs-crime connection, the course of the crack epidemic, the treatment of addiction, and the state of American drug policy. Too, it offers both fervent and dispassionate views on individuals and events, resulting in an essay of mixed identity—part history and part biography, presented in a manner that is partly scientific, partly literary, partly philosophical, and partly speculative.

1. The Pro-Legalization Issues and Contenders

The drug legalization debate emerged in both generic and specific configurations. In its most generic adaptation, it went something like this. First, the drug laws have created evils far worse than the drugs themselves—corruption, violence, street crime, and disrespect for the law. Second, legislation passed to control drugs has failed to reduce demand. Third, you should not prohibit that which a major segment of the population is committed to doing; that is, you simply cannot arrest, prosecute, and punish such large numbers of people, particularly in a democracy. And specifically in this behalf, in a liberal democracy the government must not interfere with personal behavior if liberty is to be maintained. And fourth, if marijuana, cocaine, heroin, and other drugs were legalized, a number of very positive things would happen:

- drug prices would fall;
- users could obtain their drugs at low, government-regulated prices and would no longer be forced to engage in prostitution and street crime to support their habits;
- levels of drug-related crime would significantly decline, resulting in less crowded courts, jails, and prisons, and freeing law-enforcement personnel to focus their energies on the "real criminals" in society;
- drug production, distribution, and sale would be removed from the criminal arena; no longer would it be within the province of organized crime, and thus, such criminal syndicates as the Colombian cocaine cartels, the Jamaican posses, and the various "mafias" around the country and the world would be decapital-

143

ized and the violence associated with drug distribution rivalries would be eliminated;

- government corruption and intimidation by traffickers and "narcoterrorists," as well as drug-based foreign policies, would be effectively reduced, if not eliminated entirely; and,
- the often draconian measures undertaken by police to enforce the drug laws would be curtailed, thus restoring to the American public many of its hard-won civil liberties (Inciardi and McBride 1989).

This, then, was the generic case. But as mentioned earlier, the "legalizers" had come from all walks of life. There were (and still are) elite troupers and thespians, as well as many bit players and others in supporting roles; there were those making only cameo appearances, and importantly, there was comic relief. Each had something a little different to assert—specific ideas, points, choices, perspectives. Many of the arguments were insightful and important for the evolution and growth of an informed drug policy, while others were droll, naive, ludicrous, gormless, and potentially destructive. The major theses of a number of these players are outlined in the following pages. First, however, it is important to document that the legalization debate has a history that predates its resurrection by Mayor Kurt Schmoke in 1988.

The Early Protagonists for Legalization

During the early years of this century, two competing models of the drug "problem" emerged that served to shape the nature and direction of federal policy formation. On the one hand, there was the *criminal model of drug abuse*. This posture, actively pursued by the police establishment, held that "addicts" ought to be the objects of vigorous enforcement activity because the great majority of them were members of criminal subcultures, gangs, and organizations. To support this view, law-enforcement groups pointed to the experiences of their officers and agents, and to several studies that demonstrated that most addicts were already criminals before they began using drugs (United States Treasury Department 1939).

The counterpoint to the criminal model was the *medical model of drug abuse,* a notion fostered by the medical community as early as the late nineteenth century. Although physicians had been among the first to contend that "morphinism" and "cocainism" were the result of a moral weakness, they also emphasized that addiction itself was a chronic and relapsing disease. As such, the medical model argued that the addict should be dealt with as any patient suffering from some physiological or medical disorder. At the same time, numerous proponents of this view sought to mitigate addict criminality by putting forth the "enslavement theory" of addiction. The idea there was that the monopolistic controls over the heroin black market forced "sick" and otherwise law-abiding drug users into lives of crime to support their habits.

Influenced more by the criminal than the medical model, the federal approach to drug abuse control evolved a variety of avenues for reducing both the supply of and the demand for illicit drugs. Supply-and-demand-reduction strategies were initially grounded in the classic deterrence model: through legislation and criminal penalties, individuals could be discouraged from using drugs; by making an example of traffickers, the government could force potential dealers to seek other economic pursuits.

Alfred R. Lindesmith and the Lexington Studies During the early years of policy formation, there seemed to be few critics of the emerging drug-control efforts. A conspicuous exception was Alfred R. Lindesmith, who during the 1930s was a graduate student at the University of Chicago and in subsequent years was a member of the sociology faculty at Indiana University. Lindesmith's doctoral dissertation represented the first systematic study of drug addiction in the field of sociology (Inciardi 1990), and much of his early research had been based on interviews with patients at the United States Public Health Service Hospital in Lexington, Kentucky (Lindesmith 1937, 1938, 1940, 1947). There, the addicts being cared for had been dependent primarily on either morphine or paregoric, and their drugs had been obtained from physicians through legal or quasi-legal means. As "patients" under treatment for some illness, they were not members of criminal subcultures. Lindesmith's writings, which held that criminal penalties were inappropriate for "sick" patients, had been heavily influenced by his research at the Lexington hospital. His opinions were almost exclusively in the form of vigorous attacks on federal policy. In a 1956 issue of *The Nation,* for example, Lindesmith argued:

> For 40 years the United States has tried in vain to control the problem of drug addiction by prohibition and police suppression. The disastrous consequences of turning over to the police what is an essentially medical

problem are steadily becoming more apparent as narcotic arrests rise each year to new records and the habit continues to spread, especially among young persons. Control by prohibition has failed; but the proposed remedies for this failure consist mainly of more of the same measures which have already proved futile (Lindesmith 1956).

Although a direct call for a legalization of drugs was not apparent in Lindesmith's early work, it was clearly implied. Moreover, it would appear that he was the first member of the academic community to venture into the political arena of drug-policy debate, and the criticisms of his work were fierce (for example, see Michelsen 1940).

One can hardly argue with Lindesmith's point that arrest and incarceration are inappropriate and inhumane ways of dealing with medical patients. However, there were some problems in his research and conclusions that did not pass unnoticed. First, his central argument for a policy change was based on data from a biased sample. Whereas the Lexington treatment population was indeed composed of medically addicted patients (see Ball 1965; O'Donnell 1967), the criminal subculture of addicts was real, visible, and active, and was having almost daily confrontations with federal law enforcement authorities (see Sharpe 1928; Ingram 1930; Sutherland 1937; Campion 1957; Inciardi and Russe 1977). Second, his arguments offered no policy solutions or alternatives, other than abrupt changes in the law. As such, Lindesmith opinions were not well received, nor was academia's first brush with drug policy-making.

Allen Ginsberg and the Beat Generation "Beat," as a slang term, originated in "Harlem jive," the jargon of the black musician of the 1920s and 1930s. With a meaning of "exhausted and worn out," beat was descriptive of a partly social, partly literary phenomenon of the late 1940s and 1950s initiated by the post–World War II disaffected and a cult of West Coast writers. They were part of a generation that was trying to make sense of a postwar world, a world that seemed to offer no respite, only an eternal state of war and chaos. Reality, as the Beats viewed it, was a state of consciousness where nature, history, and humanity could not be controlled; where the worship of reason had fallen into obscurity; where progress was both a false concept and an illusion; and where the future and the past were of little value (Lipton 1959; McDarrah 1985; Sukenick 1987).

The Beats believed that the path to harmony in a chaotic world could not be found by the more traditional consolations of success and achievement which demanded a feigning of beliefs, feelings, and virtues, and a relentless obligation to the prevailing social forms and customs. Many Beats, in their attempt to more readily attain the realization of setting themselves right with nature, pursued their "true" reality through an effort of the mind and rejected the perceived discontinuities of life in organized society. For most, however, their conceptual reality of the irrational properties of everyday existence was escaped through drug use, and high-frequency, long-duration marijuana and hashish use became a pervasive part of Beat life.

The chief spokespersons of the Beat movement were Allen Ginsberg, Jack Kerouac, William Burroughs, and Lawrence Ferlinghetti (Knight and Knight 1988), but perhaps the most celebrated of these was Ginsberg, whose writings were so charged with obscenity that they were considered by many to be little more than the ravings of a sexually maladjusted literary renegade. The best known of Ginsberg's works, for example, was *Howl,* composed for the most part while he was under the influence of drugs (Miles 1989). Written in 1956, it was a rambling indictment of American materialism. In its 75 lines of rather inelegant poetry, aimed at dismaying the middle class of the 1950s, *Howl* suggested a new set of values that were almost totally antisocial.

By the early 1960s Ginsberg was a guru of the new "hippie" counterculture and an exponent of meditation and "flower power." And it was from this backdrop that he emerged during the cultural revolution of the 1960s, making the rounds on Capitol Hill lobbying for the legalization of marijuana. Ginsberg's argument was that marijuana was a natural agent that offered people the chance to experience a true expansion of consciousness, an increase in awareness, and a general improvement and heightening of perceptions of all kinds (Ginsberg 1966). Quite understandably, legalizing marijuana was viewed as little more than the radical politics of the time. Ginsberg's appearance in the midst of it all seemed to confirm in the minds of the majority that drug legalization was the banner of a collection of what social critic Norman Mailer called "philosophical psychopaths" (Viorst 1979, 57), nonconformists who lived immoderately and for the moment, congregated in communes, spoke a special avant-garde language, experimented with sex, and took drugs.

Thomas S. Szasz and the Control of Conduct Thomas S. Szasz is a Hungarian-born psychiatrist who emigrated to the United States in 1938 and studied medicine at the University of Cincinnati. Trained in psychiatry at the University of Chicago, he became a well-known critic of his profession. Szasz has written that "mental illness" is a mythological concept used by the state to control deviants and thereby limit freedom in American society (Szasz 1961, 1963, 1965, 1970). In his view, the conditions comprising mental illness are social and moral problems, not medical ones. He repeatedly warns against replacing a theological worldview with a therapeutic one. Moreover, he is an uncompromising libertarian and humanist who has argued against involuntary psychiatric examination and hospitalization, and who believes that the psychoanalytic relationship should be free of coercion and control.

Szasz's view of mental illness has been considered by many as inordinately radical in its recommendation of an essentially laissez-faire approach toward schizophrenia and other forms of mental dysfunction. But it is nevertheless a thoughtful and important perspective in that it shifts the focus of inquiry from medicine to the individual and society.

During the 1970s, relying on the postulates and assertions that he had applied to mental illness, Szasz became the most outspoken critic of the medical or "disease" model of addiction (Szasz 1974). His primary concern with the disease model is that it diminishes an individual's responsibility for his or her dysfunctional or antisocial behavior. He also argues that the concept of addiction as a disease places undue emphasis on medical authority in determining how society should manage what is actually an individual violation of legal and social norms.

On the matter of whether society should attempt to control, and hence "prohibit" the use of certain substances, he offers the following:

The plain historical facts are that before 1914 there was no "drug problem" in the United States; nor did we have a name for it. Today there is an immense drug problem in the United States, and we have lots of names for it. Which came first: "the problem of drug abuse" or its name? It is the same as asking which came first: the chicken or the egg? All we can be sure of now is that the more chickens, the more eggs, and vice versa; and similarly, the more problems, the more names for them, and vice versa. My point is simply that our drug abuse experts, legislators, psychiatrists, and other professional guardians of our medical morals have been operating chicken hatcheries: they continue—partly by means of certain characteristic tactical abuses of our language—to manufacture and maintain the "drug problem" they ostensibly try to solve (Szasz 1974, 11–12).

What he was suggesting is something that nominalists have been saying for centuries: that a thing does not exist until it is imagined and given a name. For Szasz, a hopeless believer in this position, the "drug problem" in the United States did not exist before the passage of the Harrison Act in 1914, but became a reality when the behavior under consideration was *labeled* as a problem. Stated differently, he argues that the drug problem in America was created in great part by the very policies designed to control it.

For Szasz, the solution to the drug problem is simple. Ignore it, and it will no longer be a problem. After all, he maintained, there is precedent for it:

> What does this larger view show us? How can it help us? It shows us that our present attitudes toward the whole subject of drug use, drug abuse, and drug control are nothing but the reflections, in the mirror of "social reality," of our own expectations toward drugs and toward those who use them; and that our ideas about and interventions in drug-taking behavior have only the most tenuous connection with the actual pharmacological properties of "dangerous drugs." The "danger" of masturbation disappeared when we ceased to believe in it: when we ceased to attribute danger to the practice and to its practitioners; and ceased to call it "self-abuse" (Szasz 1974, 180).

What Szasz seems to be suggesting is that heroin, cocaine, and other "dangerous drugs" be legalized; hence, the problems associated with their use would disappear. And this is where he runs into difficulty, for his argument is so riddled with faulty scholarship and flagrant errors of fact that he lost credibility with those familiar with the history of the American drug scene.

Szasz's libertarian-laissez-faire position has continued into the 1990s. He perseveres in his argument that people should be allowed to ingest, inhale, or inject whatever substances they wish. And it would appear from his comments that he is opposed to drug regulation of any type, even by prescription. For example:

> The constraints on the power of the federal government, as laid down in the Constitution, have been eroded by a monopolistic medical profession administering a system of prescription laws that have, in effect, removed most of the drugs people want from the free market. . . . It is futile to debate whether the War on Drugs should be escalated or de-escalated, without first coming to grips with the popular, medical, and political mindset concerning the trade in drugs generated by nearly a century of drug prohibitions (Szasz 1992, xvi–xvii).

Legalization's Troupers and Thespians

It would appear that by the onset of the 1980s, the drug legalization debate had little in its formative years that could be built upon. If anything, its progenitors had given the debate an aura of foolishness, absurdity, and extremism. But rationality and scholarship quickly came to the forefront.

Arnold S. Trebach and Harm Reduction Perhaps most respected in the field of drug-policy reform is Arnold S. Trebach, professor of justice at The American University and the coauthor of this book. And since he *is* the coauthor of this book, in which he details his philosophy and proposals for policy reform, my review of his position is in summary form. Moreover, since our knowledge and perspectives on this topic continue to evolve, perhaps segments of Trebach's position have changed in recent months.

Trebach is the founder and president of the Drug Policy Foundation, and what I believe to be his most current ideas are discussed in a recent document from that organization (Drug Policy Foundation 1992). Briefly, his proposals for drug-policy reform are the following:

1. *Reverse drug-policy funding priorities.* The White House should eschew the course set by the previous director of the Office of National Drug Control Policy (ONDCP), the "drug czar," and give highest priority to drug education and treatment. Reversing the current 70 percent–30 percent funding disparity favoring law enforcement over drug prevention is a moral imperative.

2. *Curtail AIDS: Make clean needles available to intravenous drug addicts.* The White House and the ONDCP should heed the advice of the National Commission on AIDS, which urged implementation of clean-needle exchanges and other programs targeting addicts.

3. *Develop a plan for drug treatment on demand, allow Medicaid to pay for treatment for the poor, and expand the variety of treatment options available.* ONDCP should make a comprehensive assessment of drug treatment availability nationwide, then propose a target date and plan of attack for achieving treatment on demand everywhere in the United States. The director of ONDCP should also work with Congress on legislation allowing Medicaid to cover drug treatment expenses for the nation's poor.

4. *Stop prosecutions of pregnant drug users.* ONDCP should use its national pulpit to urge states to cease the counterproductive practice of prosecuting pregnant drug users. Ending such prosecutions, while

expanding drug treatment and prenatal care, will help reduce the problem of drug-exposed infants.

5. *Make medical marijuana available to the seriously ill.* The President should order the Food and Drug Administration and Drug Enforcement Administration to join in making marijuana available, by prescription, to the tens of thousands of seriously ill Americans who could benefit from its use.

6. *Appoint a commission to seriously examine alternatives to prohibition.* The national policy of drug prohibition has not reduced the supply of illegal drugs, but it has bred crime and violence on a massive scale. It is time to look honestly at the experiences of other nations with illegal drugs and at our own experiences with legal drugs to develop new, health-based policies for reducing substance abuse (Drug Policy Foundation 1992, 1).

Many readers may be surprised to know that I have little or no argument with most of these proposals. The extent to which I support these reform possibilities is addressed elsewhere in this essay. The only major departure occurs with Trebach's final reform strategy. Although I have no problems with appointing a commission to *examine* alternatives, I find some of the alternatives he proposes a bit troubling. They include the following:

- A treatment and prevention emphasis aimed at reducing the demand for drugs while imposing less of a burden on the criminal justice system.
- Reduction or elimination of criminal sanctions for drug possession and use, lessening the costs associated with prosecuting individuals who pose no immediate threat to others. Treatment offerings could be combined with civil fines toward this end.
- Eliminating the federal monopoly on drug policy and leaving the states to decide which drugs, if any, to prohibit. States would have maximum choice to tailor drug policy in various cities and counties, as problems warranted. This model is based on the repeal of Prohibition, which returned control over the drug alcohol to state legislatures.
- Allowing some physicians to prescribe currently illegal drugs to their addicted patients as part of a privatized treatment regime. This strategy could ultimately bring more people into treatment at less cost to taxpayers.
- Conversion of the unregulated black market in drugs to a legal free market with moderate government regulation. This would be

part of a strategy to eliminate drug-trade-related crime and thefts related to high prohibition-era drug prices. Such a change would require us to look carefully at our current policies toward legal drugs, such as alcohol and tobacco, where success has been mixed (Drug Policy Foundation 1992, 24).

Although my objections and alternatives are discussed later, let me just say that Trebach has experienced a "conversion" of sorts in recent years. There was a time when he denied endorsing the legalization of drugs. In the closing pages of his book, *The Great Drug War,* he stated:

> Up to now in this book, I have not argued that we should legalize *all* drugs nor that we should give heroin addicts *all* the heroin they want. However, if past experience is a guide, that is precisely how my position in this book will be summarized by scholarly experts and by journalists, friend and foe alike, as has occurred frequently in recent years. *Allow me to state once again that I have never taken that position. Never. And I do not now* (Trebach 1987, 368, emphasis added).

But then in 1989, he recanted:

> . . . I am now convinced that our society would be safer and healthier if all of the illegal drugs were fully removed from the control of the criminal law tomorrow morning at the start of business. I would be very worried about the possibility of future harm if that radical legal change took place but less worried than I am now about the reality of present harm being inflicted every day by our current laws and policies (Trebach 1989, 254).

In 1990, Trebach wrote about his change of heart, commenting that it was brought on by the realization, an "epiphany" as he put it, that full legalization would create order out of chaos (Trebach 1990, 518). Let me make four comments. First, as is discussed later at length, I hold that full legalization would bring even greater chaos and human suffering than exist now. Second, we all experience conversions. In 1986, I urged that interdiction efforts move ahead with the full assistance of the military (Inciardi 1986, 212). I no longer feel that way. Third, I understand how Trebach feels about having his position incorrectly stated. *I* have misstated it. Moreover, my own work has been misinterpreted. Although I have always opposed a legalization of drugs, I have always argued that the thrust of American drug policy should be in the direction of prevention and treatment rather than interdiction and enforcement (Inciardi 1986, 211). And fourth, I was fascinated with Trebach's use of the word "epiphany." It was refreshing. Having spent four years in a Jesuit high school and another four in a Jesuit university, to me the Epiphany was the 6 January festival commemorating the manifestation of Christ to the Gentiles as represented by the Magi (the three wise men who came from the east). But after a brief conference with Noah Webster, I learned that Trebach's epiphany was some intuitive grasp of reality—the "whatness" of it all suddenly became clear to him.

Ethan A. Nadelmann's Case for Legalization Professor Ethan A. Nadelmann of the Woodrow Wilson School of Public and International Affairs at Princeton University has clearly been the most vocal player in the pro-legalization debate (see Nadelmann 1987, 1988a, 1988b, 1988c, 1989). Like others, he argues that America's prohibitions against marijuana, cocaine, heroin, and other drugs impose far too large a cost in terms of tax dollars, crime, and infringements on civil rights and individual liberties.

On the domestic front, the criminalization of the drug market has proven to be as counterproductive as was Prohibition sixty years ago, at costs that have become unsupportable. He documents how drug cases are clogging the criminal justice system, with the expense of processing and incarcerating drug offenders rising at an astronomical rate. Ironically, he adds, the primary beneficiaries of drug laws are the traffickers. The criminalization of the drug market effectively imposes a de facto value-added tax paid to dealers.

Legalization, Nadelmann suggests, would slash the costs to the criminal justice system and reduce the number of crimes committed to buy drugs at artificially high prices. The quality of urban life would rise, the rate of homicide would decline, and American foreign-policy makers would be freed to pursue more realistic goals. The logic of legalization is grounded on two assumptions: that most illegal drugs are not as dangerous as is commonly believed, and that the most risky among them are unlikely to prove widely appealing precisely because of their obvious danger. Legalization would be risky, he adds, but risk is not a certainty. But one thing is certain, Nadelmann concludes: current control policies have produced little progress and have proven highly counterproductive.

The Debate's Supporting Cast and Bit Players

An aspect of the drug-policy debates of the second half of the 1980s was a forum awash with self-defined experts from many walks of life.

All had a point of view and most claimed to have expertise on the subject. Police officers and probation officers claimed expertise; judges and drug agents and magazine editors claimed expertise; plumbers, schoolteachers, deans, carpenters, disabled war veterans, physicians, clinicians, and free-market economists claimed expertise; and legislators and librarians and lawyers claimed expertise. They came in every size, shape, and political hue. But exactly what was their expertise based on? In the main, it was either from some other field, or nothing at all. Only one of these, Steven Wisotsky, played an active role in the debate.

Steven Wisotsky and Breaking the Impasse   Steven Wisotsky, a professor at Nova University Law Center, entered the debate a few years prior to Mayor Schmoke's main event (see Wisotsky 1986, 1987, 1988). He seemed to be the most informed of the "supporting cast," although I don't believe he had any direct contact with the drug scene, other than from a classroom, a courtroom, or a law library.

Wisotsky's argument (like numerous others, and I realize that there is a feeling of *déjà vu* here) is that despite the most recent war on drugs begun in 1982, there has been an increase in drug use, in crime, in police corruption, and in terror and murder, especially in foreign nations. National security has been threatened because there is the incentive to make large amounts of money by breaking the law. All of the tighter laws have led to a repressive type of government that, in order to enforce its laws, has taken away individual rights.

The Crime Control Act of 1984 was a blow to the morale of criminal defendants, he added, and interfered with their ability to prepare defenses. Some citizens are being stopped and searched without probable cause, and the government won almost all the drug cases and seriously punished the first-time offenders.

Wisotsky emphasizes that the war on drugs cannot be won. It is destructive to civil liberties and is encouraging and enriching mobsters. Time has proven its failure; now we need to set realistic priorities based on facts. These facts should be researched by a national study commission of experts and leaders, he believes. The goals of this commission should be to decrease drug use and to decrease the black-market pathologies of drug use. These include the street violence associated with the distribution of currently illegal drugs and the corruption of the police and other public officials. These goals can be accomplished by defining the real causes of drug-use problems, distinguishing between problems that arise from actual drug use and those that emerge from current laws and enforcement practices, and establishing practical goals that are based on scientific truth. Too often research has been funded to support existing drug policy, failing to provide an accurate picture.

In an alternative direction, Wisotsky adds that most drug use does not cause real harm; it is the drug laws that cause the most harm. He sites the Dutch model, which he describes as one in which drug use remains illegal but is ignored, as a good example of a reasonable national policy. If the legal system would ignore the harmless drug use of adults, attention could be focused on the real issues. These include preventing drug use by children, placing a top priority on discouraging the public use of drugs and drug impairment, and treating chronic users who cause harm to themselves and others. In an unoppressive society, drug users would be more likely to accept treatment if they were not afraid of the criminal justice system. Addicts should be treated voluntarily, and treatment budgets should be increased.

Wisotsky's model for dealing with drugs is through regulation. The regulations might include getting tougher on such legal drugs as tobacco and alcohol. Vending machines for cigarettes should be eliminated, and the hours of sale of alcohol and tobacco should be restricted. Taxes should also be raised to reflect the cost of dealing with the consequences of use. While there have been isolated achievements of current drug laws, a cost-benefit analysis would show that current policy and enforcement have a very minimal benefit, yet an extremely high cost in terms of resources, crime, corruption, and the loss of liberty. Cocaine use is down, he argues—not because of law enforcement, but because of education and health concerns. In addition, the heavy drug-using generation is aging and using fewer drugs, while the younger generations are not using as much as their predecessors. It is not the role of government in a free society to tell its adult citizens what risks to take. To do so is totalitarian. Bicycles kill 10,000 people a year, and yet no one proposes making them illegal.

In conclusion, Wisotsky holds that national policy should be to maintain zero tolerance for the use of drugs by children, to relax drug laws for adults, and to initiate more stringent regulations regarding the sale of alcohol and tobacco. Research should focus on the prevalence and frequency of use and on the real consequences of use. This would enable the development of a meaningful index of health and well-being relative to drug use. Such research would also document non-harmful, and even therapeutic, drug use.

The Bit Players The "bit players" were the many who had a lot to say on the debate, but from what I feel were not particularly informed positions. They wrote books, or they published papers, but they remained on the sidelines because either no one took them seriously, their work was carelessly done, or their arguments were just not persuasive. I'll comment on just a few.

In testimony before the House Select Committee on Narcotics Abuse and Control, Professor William J. Chambliss of George Washington University reported that "drugs are already available everywhere" and that "present policy is designed to increase usage" (Chambliss 1988). Since his generalizations were unsupported by data of any kind, his position wasn't pursued further, and he quickly dropped out of the debate.

Then there was Chester Nelson Mitchell (1990), a professor of law at Carleton University in Ottawa, Canada. Nelson discussed the U.S. and Canadian drug scenes and drug wars and called for civil disobedience in both nations, as well as constitutional amendments adding the "right to use drugs" to the list of the nations' hard-won freedoms.

A rather pathetically hatched entry to the debate was Richard Lawrence Miller's book, *The Case for Legalizing Drugs* (1991). Interestingly, in 1990, Miller's publisher sent me a review copy of the manuscript, asking my opinion. After explaining that I was on the opposite side of the debate, it was agreed that I would address the quality of the work. I recommended that the book not be published. I found the work so riddled with errors of fact, leaps of the imagination, unsupported generalizations, misinterpretations of studies, and outright falsehoods I believed it would be an embarrassment to the author and publisher, a disservice to the drug and policy fields, and misleading to readers. It was published, and I know the editor wasn't happy with my review. He was probably looking for a positive testimonial. Perhaps most misleading in the book is the list of "benefits" of using illicit drugs. I'll cite but one example to provide a glimpse of the author's approach:

Heroin can calm rowdy teenagers—reducing aggression, sexual drive, fertility, and teen pregnancy—helping adolescents through that time of life (Miller 1991, 153).

I have a teenage daughter, so I guess I'll have to remember that if she ever gets rowdy. Enough!

Cameos and Comic Relief After the great drug debate reached the United States House of Representatives, the weekly news magazines, television networks, and such well-known personages as conservative pundit William F. Buckley, Jr., Nobel laureate economist Milton Friedman, former Secretary of State George P. Shultz, journalist Anthony Lewis, *Harper's* editor Lewis H. Lapham, and even Washington, D.C., Mayor Marion Barry came forward to endorse legalization. The "legalizers" viewed the support of these notables as a legitimation of their argument, but all had entered the debate from disturbingly uninformed positions. With the exception of Marion Barry, and I say this facetiously, none had any first-hand experience with the issues.[1]

In contrast to the thoughtful proposals put forth by many of the players in the legalization debate, there were also many that were so ludicrous that they could hardly be taken seriously. To cite but one example, consider the suggestion that came from the Washington, D.C.–area journalist Richard B. Karel (1991). He advocated the idea of cocaine chewing gum—available in packages of 20, each piece containing 10 to 20 milligrams of pharmaceutical cocaine, dispensed through vending machines activated by ATM bank cards, with purchases limited to one package every 48 to 72 hours. Karel offered similar proposals for other drugs.

1. For a collection of papers by these and numerous others in "cameo" roles, see Boaz 1990.

2. Arguing Against Legalization

The arguments for legalization seem to boil down to the basic belief that America's prohibitions against marijuana, cocaine, heroin, and other drugs impose far too large a cost in terms of tax dollars, crime, and infringements on civil rights and individual liberties. And while the general argument may be well-intended and appear quite logical, I find it to be highly questionable in its historical, sociocultural, and empirical underpinnings, and demonstrably naive in its understanding of the negative consequences of a legalized drug market. While there are numerous arguments *for* legalization, there are likely an equal or greater number *against*.

Some Public Health Considerations

Tomorrow, like every other average day in the United States, about 11,449.3 babies will be born, 90 acres of pizza will be ordered, almost 600,000 M&M candies will be eaten, and some 95 holes-in-one will be claimed. At the same time, 171 million bottles of beer will be consumed, and almost 1.5 billion cigarettes will be smoked (Ruth 1992). In 1965, the annual death toll from smoking-related diseases was estimated at 188,000. By the close of the 1980s that figure had more than doubled, to 434,000, and it is expected to increase throughout the 1990s (Centers for Disease Control 1990, 1991b). And these figures do not include the almost 40,000 nonsmokers who die each year from ailments associated with the inhalation of passive smoke (*New York Times,* 1 February 1991, A14; *Time,* 11 February 1991, 58).

In addition, for millennia people have turned to alcohol to celebrate

159

life's pleasures and to dull its pains. As a result, it is estimated that there are 10.5 million alcoholics in the United States, and that a total of 73 million adults have been touched by alcoholism (*Alcoholism and Drug Abuse Weekly,* 9 October 1991, 1). Each year there are some 45,000 alcohol-related traffic fatalities in the United States (Centers for Disease Control 1991a), and thousands of women who drink during pregnancy bear children with irreversible alcohol-related defects (Steinmetz 1992). Alcohol use in the past year was reported by 54 percent of the nation's eighth graders, 72 percent of tenth graders, and 78 percent of twelfth graders, and almost a third of high school seniors in 1991 reported "binge drinking" (five or more drinks in a row) at least once during the two-week period prior to being surveyed (University of Michigan 1992). And finally, as illustrated in table 1, the cost of alcohol abuse in the United States for 1990 has been estimated at $136.31 billion (*Substance Abuse Report,* 15 June 1991, 3).

Table 1. Estimated Costs of Alcohol Abuse, 1990

Core Costs	**in $ Billions**
Direct	
Treatment	15.70
Health support services	1.81
Indirect	
Mortality	21.17
Reduced productivity	76.48
Lost employment	6.20
Other Related Costs	
Direct	
Motor vehicle crashes (injuries and damages)	3.15
Crime	3.07
Social welfare	0.06
Other	4.28
Indirect	
Victims of crime	0.23
Incarceration	3.48
Motor vehicle crashes (lost employment)	0.68
TOTAL	**$136.31**

Source   Substance Abuse Report, 15 June 1991, 3.

Sophism, Legalization, and Illicit Drug Use   Keep the above data in mind, and consider that they relate to only two of the *legal* drugs. Now for some reason, numerous members of the pro-legalization lobby argue that if drugs were to be legalized, usage would likely not increase very much, if at all (see, for example, Chambliss 1988; Boaz 1990; Miller 1991). The reasons, they state, are that "drugs are everywhere," and that everyone who wants to use them already does. But the data beg to differ. For example, as indicated in table 2, 56 percent of high school seniors in 1991 had never used an illicit drug in their lifetimes, and 73 percent had never used an illicit drug other than marijuana in their lifetimes. As indicated in table 3, 50 percent of college students in 1991 had never used an illicit drug in their lifetimes, and 74 percent had never used an illicit drug other than marijuana in their lifetimes. True, these surveys did not include "dropout" populations in which usage rates are higher, but nevertheless, the absolute numbers in these age cohorts who have never even *tried* any illicit drugs are in the tens of millions. And most significantly for the argument that "drugs are everywhere," half of all high school students do not feel that drugs are easy to obtain.

Going further, as indicated in figure 1, most people in the general population do not use drugs. Granted, these data are limited to the "general population," which excludes such hard-to-reach populations as members of deviant and exotic subcultures, the homeless, and others living "on the streets," and particularly those in which drug use rates are highest. However, the data do document that the overwhelming majority of Americans do not use illicit drugs. This suggests two things: that the drug prohibitions may be working quite well; and that there is a large population who might, and I emphasize might, use drugs if they were legal and readily available.

This brings us to "sophism." The Sophists were Greek philosophers of the fifth century B.C., masters of the arts of rhetoric and persuasion. They were the first professional teachers of Greece, and the first to give practical help in politics. Since rhetorical training was the key to political power, these teachers emphasized the arts of persuasion.

Originally, *sophist* was the Greek term for any highly skilled craftsman or artist. However, it was later applied to scholars who devoted themselves to wisdom. Because the Sophists were in the service of the rich, a class then inimical to democracy and held in contempt by Plato and Aristotle, the word Sophist was given a pejorative sense by these two philosphers. They felt that the object of the Sophists was not genuine knowledge, and "sophist" in a general sense came to mean

Table 2. Lifetime Prevalence of Various Types of Drugs Among High School Seniors, 1982–1991

	Class of 1982	Class of 1983	Class of 1984	Class of 1985	Class of 1986	Class of 1987	Class of 1988	Class of 1989	Class of 1990	Class of 1991
					Percent Ever Used					
N =	17,700	16,300	15,900	16,000	15,200	16,300	16,300	16,700	15,200	15,000
Any Illicit Drug Use	64.4	62.9	61.6	60.6	57.6	56.6	53.9	50.9	47.9	44.1
Any Illicit Drug Other Than Marijuana	41.1	40.4	40.3	39.7	37.7	35.8	32.5	31.4	29.4	26.9
Marijuana/Hashish	58.7	57.0	54.9	54.2	50.9	50.2	47.2	43.7	40.7	36.7
Inhalants	12.8	13.6	14.4	15.4	15.9	17.0	16.7	17.6	18.0	17.6
Inhalants Adjusted	17.7	18.2	18.0	18.1	20.1	18.6	17.5	18.6	18.5	18.0
Amyl & Butyl Nitrites	9.8	8.4	8.1	7.9	8.6	4.7	3.2	3.3	2.1	1.6
Hallucinogens	12.5	11.9	10.7	10.3	9.7	10.3	8.9	9.4	9.4	9.6
Hallucinogens Adjusted	14.3	13.6	12.3	12.1	11.9	10.6	9.2	9.9	9.7	10.0
LSD	9.6	8.9	8.0	7.5	7.2	8.4	7.7	8.3	8.7	8.8
PCP	6.0	5.6	5.0	4.9	4.8	3.0	2.9	3.9	2.8	2.9
Cocaine	16.0	16.2	16.1	17.3	16.9	15.2	12.1	10.3	9.4	7.8
"Crack"	n.a.	n.a.	n.a.	n.a.	n.a.	5.4	4.8	4.7	3.5	3.1
Other cocaine	n.a.	n.a.	n.a.	n.a.	n.a.	14.0	12.1	8.5	8.6	7.0
Heroin	1.2	1.2	1.3	1.2	1.1	1.2	1.1	1.3	1.3	0.9
Other Opiates	9.6	9.4	9.7	10.2	9.0	9.2	8.6	8.3	8.3	6.6
Stimulants	35.6	35.4	n.a.	n.a.	n.a.	n.a.	n.a.	n.a.	n.a.	n.a.
Stimulants Adjusted	27.9	26.9	27.9	26.2	23.4	21.6	19.8	19.1	17.5	15.4
Crystal Methamphetamine	n.a.	n.a.	n.a.	n.a.	n.a.	n.a.	n.a.	n.a.	2.7	3.3
Sedatives	15.2	14.4	13.3	11.8	10.4	8.7	7.8	7.4	7.5	6.7
Barbiturates	10.3	9.9	9.9	9.2	8.4	7.4	6.7	6.5	6.8	6.2
Methaqualone	10.7	10.1	8.3	6.7	5.2	4.0	3.3	2.7	2.3	1.3
Tranquilizers	14.0	13.3	12.4	11.9	10.9	10.9	9.4	7.6	7.2	7.2
Alcohol	92.8	92.6	92.6	92.2	91.3	92.2	92.0	90.7	89.5	88.0
Cigarettes	70.1	70.6	69.7	68.8	67.6	67.2	66.4	65.7	64.4	63.1
Steroids	n.a.	n.a.	n.a.	n.a.	n.a.	n.a.	n.a.	3.0	2.9	2.1

n.a.   not available

Source   University of Michigan News and Information Services Release, 27 January 1992.

Table 3. Lifetime Prevalence of Various Types of Drugs Among College Students 1 to 4 Years Beyond High School, 1980–1991

	Percent Who Used in Lifetime											
	1980	1981	1982	1983	1984	1985	1986	1987	1988	1989	1990	1991
	1,040	1,130	1,150	1,170	1,110	1,080	1,190	1,220	1,310	1,300	1,400	1,410
Any Illicit Drug	69.4	66.8	64.6	66.9	62.7	65.2	61.8	60.0	58.4	55.6	54.0	50.4
Any Illicit Drug												
Other than Marijuana	42.2	41.3	39.6	41.7	38.6	40.0	37.5	35.7	33.4	30.5	28.4	25.8
Marijuana	65.0	63.3	60.5	63.1	59.0	60.6	57.9	55.8	54.3	51.3	49.1	46.3
Inhalants	10.2	8.8	10.6	11.0	10.4	10.6	11.0	13.2	12.6	15.0	13.9	14.4
Hallucinogens	15.0	12.0	15.0	12.2	12.9	11.4	11.2	10.9	10.2	10.7	11.2	11.3
LSD	10.3	8.5	11.5	8.8	9.4	7.4	7.7	8.0	7.5	7.8	9.1	9.6
Cocaine	22.0	21.5	22.4	23.1	21.7	22.9	23.3	20.6	15.8	14.6	11.4	9.4
Crack	n.a.	n.a.	n.a.	n.a.	n.a.	n.a.	n.a.	3.3	3.4	2.4	1.4	1.5
MDMA ("Ecstasy")	0.9	0.6	0.5	0.3	0.5	0.4	0.4	0.6	0.3	3.8	3.9	2.0
Heroin	0.9	0.6	0.5	0.3	0.5	0.4	0.4	0.6	0.3	0.7	0.3	0.5
Other Opiates	8.9	8.3	8.1	8.4	8.9	6.3	8.8	7.6	6.3	7.6	6.8	7.3
Stimulants	29.5	29.4									n.a.	n.a.
Stimulants, Adjusted	n.a.	n.a.	30.1	27.8	27.8	25.4	22.3	19.8	17.7	14.6	13.2	13.0
Crystal Methamphetamine	n.a.	n.a.	n.a.	n.a.	n.a.	n.a.	n.a.	n.a.	n.a.	n.a.	1.0	1.3
Sedatives	13.7	14.2	14.1	12.2	10.8	9.3	8.0	6.1	4.7	4.1	n.a.	n.a.
Barbiturates	8.1	7.8	8.2	6.6	6.4	4.9	5.4	3.5	3.6	3.2	3.8	3.5
Methaqualone	10.3	10.4	11.1	9.2	9.0	7.2	5.8	4.1	2.2	2.4	n.a.	n.a.
Tranquilizers	15.2	11.4	11.7	10.8	10.8	9.8	10.7	8.7	8.0	8.0	7.1	6.8
Alcohol	94.3	95.2	95.2	95.0	94.2	95.3	94.9	94.1	94.9	93.7	93.1	93.6

n.a. = not available.

Source University of Michigan News and Information Services Release, 27 January 1992.

Figure 1. Drug Use in the General U.S. Population, 1979–1991

Percentage of Americans Who Used an Illicit Drug in the Month Prior to the Survey

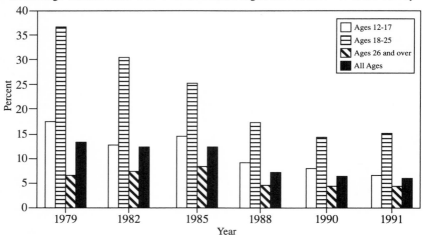

Percentage of Americans Who Used Cocaine in the Month Prior to the Survey

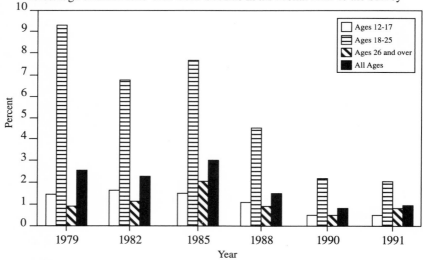

Source National Institute on Drug Abuse. National Household Survey on Drug Abuse
(Rockville, MD: National Institute on Drug Abuse, 1990).

anyone who made the worse reason appear the better, or who used fallacious arguments to prove a point.

An interesting variety of sophist reasoning pervades segments of the pro-legalization thesis. It is argued over and over that drugs should be legalized because they don't really do that much harm. Those making this contention point to the data from the Drug Abuse Warning Network. The Drug Abuse Warning Network, more commonly known as DAWN, is a large-scale data-collection effort designed to monitor changing patterns of drug abuse in the United States. Hundreds of hospital emergency rooms, as well as county medical examiners in 27 metropolitan areas, regularly report to the DAWN system. The result is extensive data on deaths and emergency room episodes associated with illicit drug use. The legalizers use these data to demonstrate that not too many people actually have adverse encounters with heroin, cocaine, and other illicit drugs, as compared with the hundreds of thousands of deaths each year linked to alcohol and tobacco use. This has always been a significant part of Steven Wisotsky's (1986) arguments for legalizing drugs. But interestingly, it is never stated that proportionately few people actually use illicit drugs, and that the segment of the population "at risk" for overdose or other physical complications from illegal drug use is but an insignificant fraction of that at risk for disease and death from alcohol and tobacco use.

The Problems with Illegal Drugs   Considerable evidence exists to suggest that the legalization of drugs could create behavioral and public health problems that would far outweigh the current consequences of drug prohibition. There are some excellent reasons why marijuana, cocaine, heroin, and other drugs are now controlled, and why they ought to remain so. What follows is a brief look at a few of these drugs. I have discussed this subject already on several occasions (see Inciardi and McBride 1989; Inciardi 1992, 244–47), but it warrants repeating in order that this essay stand by itself.

Marijuana. There is considerable misinformation about marijuana. To the millions of adolescents and young adults who were introduced to the drug during the social revolution of the 1960s and early 1970s, marijuana was a harmless herb of ecstasy. As the "new social drug" and a "natural organic product," it was deemed to be far less harmful than either alcohol or tobacco (see Grinspoon 1971; Smith 1970; Sloman 1979). More recent research suggests, however, that marijuana smoking is a practice that combines the hazardous features of both tobacco and alcohol with a number of pitfalls of its own. Moreover, there are many disturbing questions about marijuana's effect on the vital systems of the body, on the brain and mind, on immunity and resistance, and on sex and reproduction (Jones and Lovinger 1985).

One of the more serious difficulties with marijuana use relates to lung damage. The most recent findings in this behalf should put to rest the rather tiresome argument by marijuana devotees that smoking just a few "joints" daily is less harmful than regularly smoking several times as many cigarettes. Researchers at the University of California at Los Angeles reported early in 1988 that the respiratory burden in smoke particulates and absorption of carbon monoxide from smoking just one marijuana "joint" is some *four times greater* than from smoking a single tobacco cigarette (Macdonald 1988; Chaing and Hawks 1990). Specifically, it was found that one "toke" of marijuana delivers three times more tar to the mouth and lungs than one puff of a filter-tipped cigarette; that marijuana deposits four times more tar in the throat and lungs and increases carbon monoxide levels in the blood fourfold to fivefold.

There seem to be three distinct sets of facts about marijuana its apologists tend to downplay, if not totally ignore—those about its chemical structure, its "persistence-of-residue" effect, and its changing potency.

First, the *cannabis sativa* plant from which marijuana comes is a complex chemical factory. Marijuana contains 426 known chemicals which are transformed into 2,000 chemicals when burned during the smoking process. Seventy of these chemicals are *cannabinoids*, substances that are found nowhere else in nature. Since they are fat-soluble, they are immediately deposited in those body tissues that have a high fat content—the brain, lungs, liver, and reproductive organs.

Second, THC (delta-9-tetrahydrocannabinol), the active ingredient and most potent psychoactive chemical in marijuana, is soluble in fat but not in water, which has a significant implication. The human body has a water-based waste disposal system—through blood, urine, sweat, and feces. A chemical such as THC that does not dissolve in water becomes trapped, principally in the brain, lungs, liver, and reproductive organs. This is the "persistence-of-residue" effect. One puff of smoke from a marijuana cigarette delivers a significant amount of THC, half of which remains in the body for several weeks. As such, if a person is smoking marijuana more than once a month, the residue levels of THC are not only retained, but also building up—in the brain, lungs, liver, and reproductive organs.

Third, the potency of marijuana has risen dramatically over the years. During the 1960s the THC content of marijuana was only two-tenths of one percent. By the 1980s the potency of imported marijuana was up to 5 percent, representing a 25-fold increase. Moreover, California *sinsemilla*, a seedless, domestic variety of marijuana, has a THC potency of 14 percent. In fact, so potent is *sinsemilla* that it has become the "pot of choice" both inside and outside the United States. On the streets of Bogota, Colombia, *sinsemilla* has been traded for cocaine on an equal weight basis (*Street Pharmacologist*, May–June 1988, 5).

Finally, aside from the health consequences of marijuana use, recent research on the behavioral aspects of the drug suggests that it severely affects the social perceptions of heavy users. Findings from the Center for Psychological Studies in New York City, for example, report that adults who smoked marijuana daily believed the drug helped them to function better—improving their self-awareness and relationships with others (Hendin et al. 1987). In reality, however, marijuana had acted as a "buffer," enabling users to tolerate problems rather than face them and make changes that might increase the quality of their social functioning and satisfaction with life. The study found that the research subjects used marijuana to avoid dealing with their difficulties, and the avoidance inevitably made their problems worse, on the job, at home, and in family and sexual relationships.

What this research documented was what clinicians had been saying for years. Personal growth evolves from learning to cope with stress, anxiety, frustration, and the many other difficulties that life presents, both small and large. Marijuana use (and the use of other drugs as well, including alcohol), particularly among adolescents and young adults, interferes with this process, and the result is a drug-induced arrested development (see DuPont 1984, 80–83; Spencer and Boren 1990).

Alternatively, it has been argued that for humanitarian reasons, a reclassification of marijuana under the scheduling provisions of the Controlled Substances Act is in order. At present, marijuana is a Schedule I drug, which means that it has no recognized "accepted" medical use.[2] Cocaine, on the other hand, is a Schedule II drug,

2. Under federal regulations, Schedule I drugs are the most strictly controlled, have a high potential for abuse, no currently accepted use in the United States, and no acceptable safe level of use under medical supervision. Many narcotics, such as heroin and other opiates and opium derivatives, fall into this category. In addition, many hallucinogenic drugs that have no recognized medical value in this country, such as mescaline, peyote, and lysergic acid diethylamide (LSD), are listed in Schedule I.

meaning that it can be legally obtained on a prescription basis under special circumstances. As such, with many AIDS patients saying that marijuana alleviates the nausea and vomiting caused by the syndrome and the drugs used to treat it (an argument also made by cancer chemotherapy patients), a reclassification of the drug into Schedule II would make it available for medical purposes (Van Pelt 1991). Moreover, this is one of the explicit positions of Arnold Trebach and the Drug Policy Foundation (1992). It is a position that I fully agree with; it is simply the humanitarian thing to do.

Cocaine. Lured by the Lorelei of orgasmic pleasure, millions of Americans use cocaine each year—a snort in each nostril and the user is up and away for 20 minutes or so. Alert, witty, and with it, the user has no hangover, no lung cancer, and no holes in the arms or burned-out cells in the brain. The cocaine high is an immediate, intensively vivid, and sensation-enhancing experience. Moreover, it has the reputation for being a spectacular aphrodisiac: it is believed to create sexual desire, to heighten it, to increase sexual endurance, and to cure frigidity and impotence.

Given all these positives, it is no wonder that cocaine became an "all-American drug" and a multibillion-dollar-a-year industry. The drug permeates all levels of society, from Park Avenue to the inner city: lawyers and executives use cocaine; baby boomers and yuppies use cocaine; college students and high school drop-outs use cocaine; police officers, prosecutors, and prisoners use cocaine; politicians use cocaine; housewives and pensioners use cocaine; Democrats, Republicans, Independents, and Socialists use cocaine; bartenders and stockbrokers and children and athletes use cocaine; even some priests and members of Congress use cocaine.

Yet, the pleasure and feelings of power that cocaine engenders in actuality make its use an unwise recreational pursuit. In very small and occasional doses it is no more harmful than equally moderate doses of alcohol, but there is a side to cocaine that can be very destructive. That euphoric lift, with its feelings of pleasure, confidence, and being on top of things, that comes from but a few brief snorts is short-lived and invariably followed by a letdown. More specifically, when the elation and grandiose feelings begin to wane, a corresponding deep depression is often felt, which is in such marked contrast to users' previous states that they are strongly motivated to repeat the dose and restore the euphoria. This leads to chronic, compulsive use. And when chronic users try to stop using cocaine, they are typically plunged into a severe depression from which only more cocaine can arouse them. Most clinicians estimate that approximately 10 percent of those who begin to use cocaine "recreationally" will go on to serious, heavy, chronic, compulsive use (Grabowski 1984; Kozel and Adams 1985; Erickson et al. 1987; Spitz and Rosecan 1987; Washton 1989; Washton and Gold 1987).

To this can be added what is known as the "cocaine psychosis" (see Weiss and Mirin 1987, 50–53; Satel et al. 1991). As dose and duration of cocaine use increase, the development of cocaine-related psychopathology is not uncommon. Cocaine psychosis is generally preceded by a transitional period characterized by increased suspiciousness, compulsive behavior, faultfinding, and eventually paranoia. When the psychotic state is reached, individuals may experience visual and/or auditory hallucinations, with persecutory voices commonly heard. Many believe that they are being followed by police or that family, friends, and others are plotting against them. Moreover, everyday events tend to be misinterpreted in a way that supports delusional beliefs. When coupled with the irritability and hyperactivity that the stimulant nature of cocaine tends to generate in almost all of its users, the cocaine-induced paranoia may lead to violent behavior as a means of "self-defense" against imagined persecutors.

Not to be forgotten are the physiological consequences of cocaine use. Since the drug is an extremely potent central-nervous-system stimulant, its physical effects include increased temperature, heart rate, and blood pressure. As table 4 shows, there are tens of thousands of cocaine-related hospital room emergency visits that occur each year.[3] In addition, there has been a gradual increase in the number of cocaine-related deaths in the United States, from only 53 in 1976 to 615 in 1985, to 2,483 in 1990 (National Institute on Drug Abuse 1986, 1991b). And while these numbers may seem infinitesimal when compared with the magnitude of deaths associated with alcohol- and tobacco-related diseases and accidents, it should be remembered that at present only a small segment of the American population uses cocaine. And too, in terms of numbers of overdose deaths, cocaine ranks higher than any other drug—legal or illegal (National Institute on Drug Abuse 1986, 1991b).

3. In 1990, for example, there were more than 80,000 cocaine-related emergencies reported to the Drug Abuse Warning Network system (see National Institute on Drug Abuse 1991a). In 1991, this figure had increased to over 100,000 (see table 4 and *Substance Abuse Report,* 1 September 1992, 5–6).

Table 4. Drug-Related Emergencies Reported by the Drug Abuse Warning Network, 1988–1991*

	1988	1989	1990	1991
Alcohol in combination	120,117	125,861	115,162	123,564
Cocaine	104,731	110,013	80,355	103,890
Heroin/Morphine	39,026	41,656	33,884	37,185
Acetaminophen	24,288	29,667	25,422	30,424
Aspirin	23,570	23,435	19,188	21,896
Ibuprofen	15,425	16,537	16,299	15,529
Alprazolam	16,571	14,946	15,846	16,325
Marijuana	20,708	20,703	15,706	16,370
Diazepam	18,268	17,032	14,836	14,719
Amitriptyline	9,049	10,497	8,642	8,768
Acetaminophen/codeine	8,980	9,981	8,222	6,970
OTC sleep aids	8,362	8,517	7,984	6,300
Lorazepam	4,953	7,056	7,625	6,781
D,Propoxyphene	7,899	7,552	7,417	7,577
Fluoxetine	1,004	3,555	6,917	6,983
Diphenhydramine	6,155	6,787	6,483	6,877
Methamphetamine/speed	9,345	8,722	5,236	4,949
Oxycodone	3,550	3,566	4,526	4,036
PCP/PCP in combination	12,966	8,042	4,408	3,428
Lithium	3,892	3,843	4,402	4,476
Clonazepam	1,456	2,634	4,335	6,399
Hydantoin	3,705	4,193	4,026	3,137
Hydrocodone	2,539	3,679	3,921	5,086
LSD	3,988	3,421	3,869	3,855
Triazolam	6,028	4,381	3,801	3,335
Phenobarbital	3,095	4,395	3,668	2,954
Doxepin	3,789	4,135	3,457	3,772
Cyclobenzaprine	2,311	2,615	3,453	3,074
Haloperidol	2,637	2,944	3,415	3,193
Amphetamine	3,985	3,437	3,362	2,308
Total	416,961	425,904	371,208	398,349

Source Substance Abuse Report, 1 September 1992, 9.
*Drug-related emergencies involve chronic medical conditions, psychiatric or side effects, or a need for detoxification (see Inciardi, McBride et al. 1978).

Finally, what has been said about cocaine also applies to crack, and perhaps more so. Crack's low price (as little as $2 per rock in some locales) has made it an attractive drug of abuse for those with limited funds. Its rapid absorption brings on a faster onset of dependence than is typical with other forms of cocaine, resulting in higher rates of addiction, binge use, and psychoses. The consequences include higher levels of cocaine-related violence and all the same manifestations of personal, familial, and occupational neglect that are associated with other forms of drug dependence. Issues related to crack are addressed in detail in a separate section of this essay.

Heroin. A derivative of morphine, heroin is a highly addictive narcotic, and is the drug historically associated with addiction and street crime. Although heroin overdose is not uncommon, unlike alcohol, cocaine, tobacco, and many prescription drugs, the direct physiological damage caused by heroin use tends to be minimal. And it is for this reason that the protagonists of drug legalization include heroin in their arguments. By making heroin readily available to users, they argue, many problems could be sharply reduced if not totally eliminated, including: the crime associated with supporting a heroin habit; the overdoses resulting from unknown levels of heroin purity and potency; the HIV and hepatitis infections brought about by needle-sharing; and the personal, social, and occupational dislocations resulting from the drug-induced criminal lifestyle.[4]

The belief that the legalization of heroin would eliminate crime, overdose, infections, and life dislocations for its users is for the most part delusional. Instead, it is likely that the heroin-use lifestyle would change little for most addicts regardless of the legal status of the drug, an argument supported by ample evidence in the biographies and autobiographies of narcotics addicts, the clinical assessments of heroin addiction, and the drug abuse treatment literature (for example, see Anonymous 1903; Burroughs 1953; Nyswander 1956; Street 1953; Hirsch 1968; Fiddle 1967; Smith and Gay 1971; Fisher 1972; Gould et al. 1974; Rettig, Torres, and Garrett 1977; Rosenbaum 1981; Peele 1985; Platt 1986). And to this can be added the many thousands of conversations I have had over the past 30 years with heroin users and members of their families.

The point is this. Heroin is a highly addicting drug. For the addict, it becomes life-consuming: it becomes mother, father, spouse, lover,

---

4. This point of view is most thoroughly articulated in Trebach (1982).

counselor, and confessor. Because heroin is a short-acting drug, with its effects lasting at best four to six hours, it must be taken regularly and repeatedly. Because there is a more rapid onset when taken intravenously, most heroin users inject the drug. Because heroin has depressant effects, a portion of the user's day is spent in a semi-stupefied state. Collectively, these attributes result in a user more concerned with drug-taking and drug-seeking than health, family, work, relationships, responsibility, or anything else.

The Pursuit of Pleasure and Escape   Before concluding this discussion of health consequences, there are some additional points. Importantly, recently completed research by professors Michael D. Newcomb and Peter M. Bentler of the University of California at Los Angeles has documented the long-term behavioral effects of drug use on teenagers (Newcomb and Bentler 1988). Beginning in 1976, a total of 654 Los Angeles County youths were tracked for a period of eight years. Most of these youths were only occasional users of drugs, using drugs and alcohol moderately at social gatherings, whereas upwards of 10 percent were frequent, committed users. The impact of drugs on these frequent users was considerable. As teenagers, drug use tended to intensify the typical adolescent problems with family and school. In addition, drugs contributed to such psychological difficulties as loneliness, bizarre and disorganized thinking, and suicidal thoughts. Moreover, frequent drug users left school earlier, started jobs earlier, and formed families earlier, and as such, they moved into adult roles with the maturity levels of adolescents. The consequences of this pattern included rapid family break-ups, job instability, serious crime, and ineffective personal relationships. In short, frequent drug use prevented the acquisition of the coping mechanisms that are part of maturing; it blocked teenagers' learning of interpersonal skills and general emotional development.

At this point in the public health argument I have suggested that although we have no explicit data on whether the numbers of addicts and associated problems would increase if drugs were legalized, there are reasons to believe that they would, and rather dramatically. First, the number of people who actually use drugs is proportionately small. Second, the great majority of people in the United States have never used illicit drugs, and hence, have never been ''at risk'' for addiction. Third, because of the drug prohibition, illicit drugs are *not* ''everywhere,'' and as a result, most people have not had the opportunity to even experiment with them. Fourth, alcohol *is* readily available, and the numbers of people who have been touched by alcoholism are in the dozens of millions.

Given this, let's take the argument one step further. There is extensive physiological, neurological, and anthropological evidence to suggest that we are members of a species that has been honed for pleasure (Black 1969; Tiger 1992; Cohen 1988; Siegel 1989; Peele 1985; Milkman and Sunderwirth 1987). Nearly all people want and enjoy pleasure, and the pursuit of drugs—whether caffeine, nicotine, alcohol, opium, heroin, marijuana, or cocaine—seems to be universal and inescapable. It is found across time and across cultures (and species). The process of evolution has for whatever reasons resulted in a human neurophysiology that responds both vividly and avidly to a variety of common substances. The brain has pleasure centers—receptor sites and cortical cells—that react to "rewarding" dosages of many substances. Or as University of California pharmacologist Larry Stein explained it in 1989:

> The fact that *cells* respond to a reward shows just how deeply embedded in the design of the brain this reinforcement mechanism is. . . . Dopamine and the opioid peptides are transmitters in very powerful control systems based on a certain chemistry. . . . Along come poppy seeds and coca leaves that have chemicals very similar to these central systems. They go right in, do not pass GO. To say that cocaine or amphetamines, or heroin or morphine, should be highly appealing is an understatement (quoted in Tiger 1992, 98).

Some years ago I argued that given the political opposition to the legalization of drugs, what is needed is a controlled legalization experiment to determine if such a model could work (Inciardi 1987). One approach would be to locate and observe a society, isolated from the drug-related cultural influences of the West, where some narcotic is legal, readily available, and cheap. If the legalization model were of value, then in this society the narcotic would just be there—attracting little attention. There would be minimal use, addiction, and the attendant social and public health problems—as long as the drug's availability was not restricted and legislated against.

Although finding such a society is unlikely, consider Poland. For generations, Poles have cultivated home-grown poppies for the use of their seeds as flavoring in breads, stews, pretzel sticks, cookies, cakes, and chocolates. During the early 1970s, many Polish farmers began transforming their poppy straw into what has become known as *jam, compote,* or "Polish heroin." Then, many Poles began using heroin, but the practice was for the most part ignored. By the end of the 1970s heroin use in Poland had escalated significantly, but still the situation was ignored. By late 1985, at a time when the number of heroin users was estimated at 600,000 and the number of heroin-dependent persons was fixed at 200,000, the Polish government could no longer ignore what was happening. The number of overdose deaths was mounting, and the range of psychosocial and public health problems associated with heroin use was beginning to affect the structure of the already troubled country. By 1986, feeling that heroin use had gotten out of hand, the Communist government in Poland placed controls on the cultivation of poppy seeds, and the transformation of poppy straw into heroin was outlawed.

There are no empirical studies of the extent of heroin use in Poland reported in the literature, and estimates as to the prevalence and incidence of heroin use and addiction vary widely. The Polish Ministry of Health and Social Welfare has estimated the number of heroin users to be in the vicinity of 200,000 (Tobolska-Rydz 1986), while international press and wire-service reports place the number at three to four times that level (see Warsaw *Dziennik Ustaw,* 20 September 1985, item 217, 606; Helsinki *Helsingin Sonomat,* 17 December 1985, 2; *Warsaw Domestic Service,* 1800 GMT, 18 November 1985; Warsaw *Trybunda Ludu,* 3 December 1985, 4; *Hamburg ARD Television Network,* 2030 GMT, 14 April 1986; Warsaw *Monitor Polski,* 31 October 1985, item 209, 369–70; Warsaw *Zycie Warszawy,* 19–20 April 1986, 3; Warsaw *Prawo I Zycie,* no. 41, 12 October 1991, 1, 7; Warsaw *TVP Television Network,* 1730 GMT, 9 April 1992).

Although the events in Poland have not been systematically studied, what is known of the experience suggests that introducing potent intoxicants to a population can have problematic consequences. Moreover, the notion that "availability creates demand" has been found in numerous other parts of the world, particularly with cocaine in the Andean regions of South America (see Inciardi 1992, 222).

The Legacy of Crack Cocaine

The great drug wars in the United States have endured now for generations, although the drug legalization debates have less of a history—on again, off again since the 1930s, with a sudden burst of energy at the close of the 1980s. But as the wars linger on and the debates abide, a coda must be added to both of these politically charged topics. It concerns crack cocaine, a drug that has brought about a level of human suffering heretofore unknown in the American drug scene. The problem with crack is not that it is prohibited, but rather, the fact that it exists at all in the pharmacopoeia of intoxicants. The chemistry and psychopharmacology of crack, combined with the tangle of socioeconomic and psychocultural strains that exist in those communities where the drug is concentrated, warrant some consideration of whether further discussion of its legality or illegality serves any purpose. Focusing on crack as an example, my intent here is to argue that both the "drug wars" and "harm reduction effort" are better served by a shifting away from the drug legalization debate.

Crack Cocaine in the United States   Crack is not a particularly new drug to the United States, but goes back several decades, to a time when cocaine was still known as *charlie, corrine, bernice, schoolboy*, and the "rich man's drug." It was first reported in the literature during the early 1970s (Anonymous 1972), but even then it had been known for a number of years. At that time, however, knowledge of crack, known then as "base" or "rock" (not to be confused with "rock cocaine"—a cocaine hydrochloride product for intranasal snorting), seemed to be restricted to segments of cocaine's freebasing subculture. But since the drug contained many impurities, it was often referred to as "garbage freebase" by cocaine aficionados, and was quickly discarded. It was rediscovered at the beginning of the 1980s, and by the middle of the decade it had taken on a life of its own (see Inciardi 1992, 103–32).

For the inner cities across America, the introduction of crack couldn't have happened at a worse time. The economic base of the working poor had been shrinking for years, the result of a number of factors, including the loss of many skilled and unskilled jobs to cheaper labor markets, the movement of many businesses to the surburbs and the Sun Belt, and competition from foreign manufacturers. Standards of living, health, and overall quality of life were also in a downward direction, as consequences of suburbanization and the shrinking tax bases of central cities, combined with changing economic policies at the federal level that shifted the responsibility for many social supports to the local and private sectors. Without question, by the early to mid-1980s there was a growing and pervasive climate of hopelessness in ghetto America. And at the same time, as HIV and AIDS began to spread through inner-city populations of injectable drug users and their sex partners and as funding for drug abuse treatment declined, the production of coca and cocaine in South America reached an all-time high, resulting in high-purity cocaine at a low price on the streets of urban America. As I said, crack couldn't have come to the inner city at a worse time.

The next chapter in the story of crack is pretty well known, having been reported (and perhaps over-reported) in the media since early in 1986—the "highs," binges, and "crashes" that induce addicts to sell their belongings and their bodies in pursuit of more crack; the high addiction liability of the drug that instigates users to commit any manner and variety of crimes to support their habits. Also well known are the rivalries in crack distribution networks that have turned some inner-city communities into urban "dead zones," where homicide rates are so high that police have written them off as anarchic badlands; the involvement of inner-city youths in the crack business, including the "peewees" and "wannabees" (want-to-bes), those street-gang acolytes in grade school and junior high who patrol the streets with walkie-talkies in the vicinity of crack houses, serving in networks of lookouts, spotters, and steerers, and aspiring to be "rollers" (short for high-rollers) in the drug distribution business. Well known as well is the child abuse, child neglect, and child abandonment by crack-addicted mothers; and finally, the growing cohort of "crack babies" that appear troubled not only physically, but emotionally and behaviorally as well.

Drug Policy and the American Crack House Drug policy is typically formulated and established by politicians and other government officials after input from the field, public hearings, various constituencies, and panels of advisers and experts. It is then deliberated and debated, pondered and argued by political and social observers of all types, and researchers and analysts from a variety of academic fields. Much of the deliberation and debate is typically based on what has appeared in the press, in the research literature, and from focused theoretical and empirical study. As such, policy formulation and subsequent discussions generally occur within the safe, secure, and existentially antiseptic confines of legislative chambers, government conference rooms, collegiate study halls, and the highest of academic roosts. It must be that way, for rational and measured thought has difficulty in the face of immediate chaos. But now and then, those who have the most to say about drug affairs ought to visit the mean and despairing streets.

It has been argued that you don't have to be a soldier to understand war, to live in the ghetto to understand poverty and hopelessness, to be a rape victim to understand sexual assault, or be a member of an oppressed minority to understand discrimination. But it sure can help. I know that the perspective and insight are different. Having seen the 1972 Warner Brothers epic *Deliverance* just doesn't convey the same experience as white-water rafting the wild and scenic Chattooga River through Georgia's Chattahoochee National Forest, where much of the movie was filmed. Or similarly, reading about a fatal automobile accident in the newspaper, no matter how vivid the description, is quite different from watching and listening to people burn to death, trapped in their overturned car. The cries of the dying seem to scream into your soul forever. As such, reading about crack houses, seeing pictures of crack houses, or even walking past a few on the street is entirely different from spending time in them. The ambiance is different. In the photo or the street scene, the aura of despair and hopelessness just isn't there, nor is the smell of fear, the constant threat of violence, and the degradation and suffering.

I've been doing street studies in Miami, Florida, for more years than I care to remember, and during that time I've had many an experience in the shooting galleries, base houses, and open-air drug and prostitution markets that populate the local drug scene. None of these prepared me, however, with what I was to encounter in the crack houses. As part of a federally funded street survey and ethnography of cocaine and crack use, my first trip to a crack house came in 1988.[5] I had gained entrée through a local drug dealer who had been a key informant of mine for almost a decade. He introduced me to the crack house "door man" as someone "straight but OK." After the door man checked us for weapons, my guide proceeded to show me around.

Upon entering a room in the rear of the crack house (what I later learned was called a "freak room"), I observed what appeared to be the forcible gang-rape of an unconscious child. Emaciated, seemingly comatose, and likely no older than 14 years of age, she was lying spread-eagled on a filthy mattress while four men in succession had vaginal intercourse with her. Despite what was happening, I was urged not to interfere.[6] After they had finished and left the room, another man came in, and they engaged in oral sex.

Upon leaving the crack house sometime later, the dealer/informant explained that she was a "house girl"—a person in the employ of the

5. This research was supported by Health and Human Services grant # 1-R01-DA04862, "Crack Abuse Patterns and Crime Linkages," James A. Inciardi, Principal Investigator, from the National Institute on Drug Abuse.
6. This incident, as well as a discussion of the methods, dangers, and ethics of crack house research, is examined in detail in Inciardi, Lockwood, and Pottieger (1993).

crack house owner. He gave her food, a place to sleep, some cigarettes and cheap wine, and all the crack she wanted in return for her providing sex—any type and amount of sex—to his crack house customers.

That was my first trip to a crack house. During subsequent trips to this and other crack houses, there were other scenes: a woman purchasing crack, with an infant tucked under her arm—so neglected that she had maggots crawling out of her diaper; a man "skin-popping" his toddler with a small dose of heroin, so the child would remain quietly sedated and not interrupt a crack-smoking session; people in various states of excitement and paranoia, crouching in the corners of smoking rooms inhaling from "the devil's dick" (the stem of the crack pipe); arguments, fist fights, stabbings, and shootings over crack, the price of crack, the quantity and quality of crack, and the use and sharing of crack; any manner and variety of sexual activity—by individuals and/or groups, with members of the opposite sex, the same sex, or both, or with animals, in private or public, in exchange for crack. I also saw "drug hounds" and "rock monsters" (some of the "regulars" in a crack house) crawling on their hands and knees, inspecting the floors for slivers of crack that may have dropped; beatings and gang rapes of small-time drug couriers—women, men, girls, and boys—as punishment for "messing up the money"; people in convulsions and seizures, brought on by crack use, cocaine use, the use of some other drug, or whatever; users of both sexes, so dependent on crack, so desperate for more crack, that they would do anything for another hit, eagerly risking the full array of sexually transmitted diseases, including AIDS; imprisonment and sexual slavery, one of the ultimate results of crack addiction (see Inciardi 1991; Inciardi, Lockwood, and Pottieger 1991, 1993). And then there was the time I was arrested in a Miami crack house.

It should be pointed out that not all of these activities occur all of the time, or even in all crack houses. But they do happen sufficiently often enough to make one wonder about it all.[7] Do these users who frequent crack houses represent some special breed of degenerate rarely seen elsewhere in the drug scene? Or is it something else? What is it about crack that engenders such behavior? To these three questions my answers are "no, not especially"; "yes, definitely"; and "a whole lot of things."

Crack has been called the "fast-food" variety of cocaine. It is cheap

7. For descriptions of other crack houses in other cities, see Ratner (1993).

and easy to conceal, it vaporizes with practically no odor, and the gratification is swift: an intense, almost sexual euphoria that lasts less than five minutes. Smoking cocaine as opposed to snorting it results in more immediate and direct absorption of the drug, producing a quicker and more compelling "high," greatly increasing the dependence potential. Users typically smoke for as long as they have crack or the means to purchase it—money, personal belongings, sexual services, stolen goods, or other drugs. It is rare that smokers have but a single hit. More likely they spend $50 to $500 during a "mission"—a three- or four-day binge, smoking almost constantly, 3 to 50 rocks per day. During these cycles, crack users rarely eat or sleep. And once crack is tried, for many users it is not long before it becomes a daily habit. Many crack users engage in sexual behaviors with extremely high frequency. However, to suggest that crack turns men into "sex-crazed fiends" and women into "sex-crazed whores," as sensationalized media stories imply, is anything but precise. The situation is far more complex than that.

A strong association between crack use and apparent "hypersexual behaviors" is evident in my observations and interviews in Miami, as well as other ethnographic analyses of the crack scene (for example, Bourgois and Dunlap 1991; Koester and Schwartz 1991; Ratner, in press). The crack-sex association has both pharmacological and sociocultural explanations (Inciardi, Lockwood, and Pottieger 1991). The former begins with psychopharmacology: one effect of all forms of cocaine, including crack, is the release of normal inhibitions on behavior, including sexual behavior. The disinhibiting effect of cocaine is markedly stronger than that of depressants such as alcohol, Valium, or heroin. While the latter drugs typically cause a release from worry and an accompanying increase of self-confidence, cocaine typically causes elation and an accompanying gross overestimation of one's own capabilities. Further, since crack effects have a rapid onset, so too does the related release of inhibitions. Medical authorities generally concede that because of the disinhibiting effects of cocaine, its use among new users does indeed enhance sexual enjoyment and improve sexual functioning, including more intense orgasms (Weiss and Mirin 1987; Grinspoon and Bakalar 1985). These same reports maintain, however, that among long-term addicts, cocaine decreases both sexual desire and performance.

Going further, the crack-sex association involves the need of female crack addicts to pay for their drug. Even this connection has a pharmacological component—crack's rapid onset, extremely short duration of effects, and high addiction liability combine to result in compulsive use and a willingness to obtain the drug through any means. Other parts of the economic crack-sex relationship, however, are strictly sociocultural. As in the legal job market, the access of women in the street subcultures to illegal income is typically more limited than that of men. Prostitution has long been the easiest, most lucrative, and most reliable means for women to finance drug use (Goldstein 1979).

The combined pharmacological and sociocultural effects of crack use can put female users in severe jeopardy. Because crack makes its users ecstatic and yet is so short-acting, it has an extremely high addiction potential. Use rapidly becomes compulsive use. Crack acquisition thus becomes enormously more important than family, work, social responsibility, health, values, modesty, morality, or self-respect. This makes sex-for-crack exchanges psychologically tolerable as an economic necessity. Further, the disinhibiting effects of crack enable users to engage in sexual acts they might not otherwise even consider.

And what about the men, are they some special species of libertine, bent on degrading and exploiting women at every turn? Again, likely not. Most of the male crack users that I have interviewed, or observed in crack houses, are as forlorn and pathetic as the women. For some, it is indeed a "macho" thing, for the sake of dominating women, while others view the crack house as a vehicle for satisfying unfulfilled sexual fantasies. But for most, who have spent their lives in poverty or at its edge, attempting to cope with the series of tragedies and misfortunes that characterize existing and passing time in the inner city, trying to make lives for themselves in the cultures of terror and hopelessness that so often typify life in the street, the sex scene seems to provide a measure of influence and status. As one 44-year-old male put it in late 1990:

> I' been a loser all my life, except when I be in the *hut* [crack house] with a few dollars or some *cracks* [more than one rock]. Then I can tell the lady to get on her knees and put her face between my legs. It's the only time in my life I feel like I'm a little in control of things.

But the pathos of it all is that even then, the control is both limited and distorted. Only in the beginnings of a career in cocaine or crack use do men exhibit any sexual vitality, or experience sexual satisfaction. Chronic crack use engenders both impotence and the inability to climax. As such, in those crack houses where public sex is common, a customary sight is the seemingly never-ending oral stimulation of a flaccid penis.

In the final analysis, because of its chemistry, crack is easy to produce—mix a little bit of street cocaine, baking soda, and some additives for bulk with water, heat it in a microwave oven, and you have crack cocaine. It is also rather inexpensive to produce, and will likely remain that way for quite some time, regardless of its legal status. A benefit of its current criminalization is that since it *is* against the law, it doesn't have widespread availability, so proportionately few people use it.

So where does all of this take us? My point is this. Within the context of reversing the human suffering that crack has helped to exacerbate, what purpose is served by arguing for its legalization? Will legalizing crack make it less available, less attractive, less expensive, less addictive, or less troublesome? Nobody really knows for sure, but I doubt it.

Drugs-Crime Connections

For the better part of this century there has been a concerted belief that addicts commit crimes because they are "enslaved" to drugs, that because of the high prices of heroin, cocaine, and other illicit chemicals on the drug black market, users are forced to commit crimes in order to support their drug habits. I have often referred to this as the "enslavement theory" of addiction (Inciardi 1986, 147–49; Inciardi 1992, 263–64). Although the origins of the theory date back to nineteenth-century America with the early clinical writings about morphine dependence, its most complete statement appears in the work of David W. Maurer and Victor H. Vogel. In the third edition of their *Narcotics and Narcotic Addiction,* Maurer and Vogel stated:

> First, the potential addict begins to take very small doses of some addicting drug, let us say morphine, or heroin. He either does not realize what the drug will do to him, or he knows that others have become addicted but believes that it will never happen to him. . . .
> Second, the addict notices that the amount of the drug he has been taking does not "hold" him, and, if he is addiction-prone, he no longer experiences the intense pleasure which he felt in the very early stages of the use of the drug. If he has been "pleasure-shooting" (taking small doses at intervals of several days or several weeks) he notices that he must increase these in size to continue to get any pleasure from the drug;

eventually, of course, he will also increase the frequency until he is taking a shot four to six times daily. . . .

Third, as the habit increases in size over a period of weeks or months, the addict who must buy his drugs from bootleg sources finds that more and more of his wages go for drugs and that he has less and less for the other necessities; in fact, other things come to mean less and less to him, and he becomes heavily preoccupied with simply supporting his habit. . . .

Fourth, it becomes obvious to him that he must have increasing amounts of money on a regular basis, and that legitimate employment is not likely to supply that kind of money. . . . *Therefore, some form of crime is the only alternative* (Maurer and Vogel 1967, 286–87, italics added).

The theory, of course, is not without some logic. During the latter part of the nineteenth century and the early years of the twentieth, the use of narcotics was fairly widespread, and both morphine and heroin were readily available through legal channels. When the Harrison Act was passed in 1914, users had to embrace the black market to obtain their drugs. Since that time, the possession of heroin has remained a crime, and most users seem to have criminal records. But is this really so? Is the drug-crime connection really a legacy of the Harrison Act?

Most supporters of drug legalization argue that if the criminal penalties attached to heroin and cocaine possession and sale were removed, several things would occur: the black market would disappear; the violence associated with drug distribution would cease; the prices of heroin, cocaine, and other drugs would decline significantly; and users would no longer have to engage in street crime in order to support their desired levels of drug intake. Let's consider some of these issues.

The Legacy of the Harrison Act Revisited   As noted earlier in this essay, it would appear that American drug policy originated from two competing models of addiction. In the *medical model,* addiction was considered to be a chronic and relapsing disease that should be addressed in the manner of other physical disorders—by the medical and other healing professions. The *criminal model* viewed addiction as one more of the many antisocial behaviors manifested by the growing classes of predatory and dangerous criminals. Many commentators have viewed the Harrison Act of 1914 as the ultimate triumph of the criminal model over the medical view, and as such, that single piece of legislation served to shape the direction of drug policy for years to come and generations yet unborn (see King 1972, 1974; Trebach 1982;

Lindesmith 1965). Or as Auburn University sociologist Charles E. Faupel recently put it:

> The long-term result of this legislation was dramatic. Narcotics use was transformed from a relatively benign vice practiced by some of society's most respectable citizens to an openly disdained activity prohibited by law, relegating the narcotics user to pariah status in most communities (Faupel 1991, 151).

This, of course, is a considerable overstatement, for history suggests a somewhat alternative story. Briefly, the Harrison Act required all people who imported, manufactured, produced, compounded, sold, dispensed, or otherwise distributed cocaine and opiate drugs to register with the Treasury Department, pay special taxes, and keep records of all transactions (see Walsh 1981). As such, it was a revenue measure designed to exercise some measure of public control over narcotics and other drugs. Certain provisions of the Harrison Act permitted physicians to prescribe, dispense, or administer narcotics to their patients for "legitimate medical purposes" and "in the course of professional practice." But how these two phrases were to be interpreted was another matter entirely.

On the one hand, the medical establishment held that addiction was a disease and that addicts were patients to whom drugs could be prescribed to alleviate the distress of withdrawal. On the other hand, the Treasury Department interpreted the Harrison Act to mean that a doctor's prescription for an addict was unlawful. The United States Supreme Court quickly laid the controversy to rest. In *Webb v. U.S.* (249 U.S. 96 [1919]), the High Court held that it was not legal for a physician to prescribe narcotic drugs to an addict-patient for the purpose of maintaining his or her use and comfort. *U.S. v. Behrman* (258 U.S. 280 [1992]) went one step further by declaring that a *narcotic* prescription for an addict was unlawful, even if the drugs were prescribed as part of a "cure program." The impact of these decisions combined to make it almost impossible for addicts to obtain drugs legally. In 1925 the Supreme Court emphatically reversed itself in *Lindner v. U.S.* (268 U.S. 5 [1925]), disavowing the *Behrman* opinion and holding that addicts were entitled to medical care like other patients, but the ruling had almost no effect. By that time, physicians were unwilling to treat addicts under any circumstances, and well-developed illegal drug markets were catering to the needs of the addict population.

In retrospect, numerous commentators on the history of drug use in the United States have argued that the Harrison Act snatched addicts from legitimate society and forced them into the underworld. As attorney Rufus King (1974), a well-known chronicler of American narcotics legislation, once described it, "Exit the addict-patient, enter the addict-criminal" (22). Or similarly:

> Drug abuse and drug addiction are social problems created largely by unenforceable laws and ineffective political bureaucracies. For example, in 1914 the Harrison Act was promulgated at the insistence of the Federal Narcotics Bureau. This Act, which defined all addicts as criminals and all physicians who prescribed opiates in treatment as law violators, was a significant contribution to making drug abuse and drug addiction socially created evils (Brown, Mazze, and Glaser 1974, xiii).

I just hate gross misstatements and overgeneralizations. First of all, the Federal Bureau of Narcotics had nothing to do with the passage of the Harrison Act of 1914, primarily because the agency wasn't established until 1930 (Anslinger and Tompkins 1953, 117). Second, this cause-and-effect interpretation tends to be a rather extreme misrepresentation of historical fact.

Without question, at the beginning of the twentieth century, most users of narcotics were members of legitimate society. In fact, the majority had first encountered the effects of narcotics through their family physician or local pharmacist or grocer. Over-the-counter patent medicines and "home remedies" containing opium, morphine, and even heroin and cocaine had been available for years, and some even for decades (Inciardi 1992, 2–11). In other words, addiction had been medically induced during the course of treatment for some perceived ailment. Yet long before the Harrison Act had been passed, before it had even been conceived, there were indications that this population of users had begun to shrink (Morgan 1974). Agitation had existed in both the medical and religious communities against the haphazard use of narcotics, defining much of it as a moral disease (see Terry and Pellens 1928). For many, the sheer force of social stigma and pressure served to alter their use of drugs. Similarly, the decline of the patent-medicine industry after the passage of the Pure Food and Drug Act was believed to have substantially reduced the number of narcotics and cocaine users (Courtwright 1982). Moreover, by 1912, most state governments had enacted legislative controls over the dispensing and sales of narcotics. Thus, it is plausible to assert that the size of the drug-using population had started to decline years before the Harrison Act had become the subject of Supreme Court interpretation.

Even more important, however, there are historical indications that a well-developed subculture of criminal addicts had emerged many years before the passage of the Harrison Act. By the 1880s, for example, opium dens had become relatively commonplace in New York and San Francisco, and the police literature of the era indicates that they were populated with not only "hop heads" (addicts), but also smokers who were gamblers, prostitutes, and thieves as well. As New York City Chief of Detectives Thomas Byrnes noted in 1886:

> The people who frequent these places are, with very few exceptions, thieves, sharpers and sporting men, and a few bad actors; the women, without exception, are immoral. No respectable woman ever entered one of these places, notwithstanding the reports to the contrary. The language used is of the coarsest kind, full of profanity and obscenity (Byrnes 1886, 385).

Importantly, the opium den, "dive," or "joint" was not only a place for smoking, but a meeting place, a sanctuary. For members of the underworld it was a place to gather in relative safety, to enjoy a smoke (of opium, hashish, or tobacco) with friends and associates. The autobiographies of pickpockets and other professional thieves from generations ago note that by the turn of the twentieth century, opium, morphine, heroin, and cocaine were in widespread use by all manner of criminals (Hapgood 1903; White 1907; Irwin 1909; Scott 1916; Anonymous 1922; Black 1927). And it might also be pointed out here that the first jail-based program for the treatment of heroin addiction was established in the infamous New York Tombs (Manhattan City Prison) two years before the Harrison Act went into effect (Lichtenstein 1914). At the time, it was estimated that some 5 percent of the city's arrestees were addicted to narcotics. And finally, the involvement of criminal groups in subcultures of opiate and cocaine use went beyond the major urban areas, to include numerous small cities as well (see Muth 1902; Werner 1909).

Thus, while the Harrison Act *contributed* to the criminalization of addiction, subcultures of criminal addicts had been accumulating for decades before its passage.

Drug Use and Street Crime   Despite the contentions of the enslavement theory, there has never been any solid empirical evidence to support it. From the 1920s through the close of the 1960s, hundreds of studies of the relationship between crime and addiction were conducted.[8] Invariably, when one analysis would support enslavement theory, the next would affirm the view that addicts were criminals first, and that their drug use was but one more manifestation of their deviant life-styles. In retrospect, the difficulty lay in the way the studies had been conducted, with biases and deficiencies in research designs that rendered their findings nearly useless.

Research since the middle of the 1970s with active drug users in the streets of New York, Miami, Baltimore, and elsewhere has demonstrated that enslavement theory has little basis in reality, and that the contentions of the legalization proponents in this behalf are mistaken (see Inciardi 1986, 115–43; Johnson et al. 1985; Nurco et al. 1985; Stephens and McBride 1976; McBride and McCoy 1982). All of these studies of the criminal careers of heroin and other drug users have convincingly documented that while drug use tends to intensify and perpetuate criminal behavior, it usually does not initiate criminal careers. In fact, the evidence suggests that among the majority of street drug users who are involved in crime, their criminal careers were well established prior to the onset of either narcotics or cocaine use.

To briefly highlight segments of the research studies that I conducted in Miami (Dade County), Florida, over the years, consider the following. First, as indicated in table 5, among 239 male and 117 female

Table 5. Drugs-Crime Sequence Among 239 Male and 117 Female Heroin Users, Miami, 1978

	Median Age of Onset	
Drug/Crime Event	Males	Females
first alcohol use	12.8	13.8
first alcohol high	13.3	13.9
first crime committed	**15.1**	**15.9**
first marijuana use	15.5	15.4
first barbiturate use	17.5	17.0
first heroin use	18.7	18.2
first cocaine use	19.7	18.7

Source   James A. Inciardi. 1979. "Heroin Use and Street Crime," *Crime and Delinquency* 25 (July): 335–46.

8. For bibliographies and analyses of the literature on drugs and crime, see Austin and Lettieri (1976); Greenberg and Adler (1974).

heroin users contacted during 1978, criminal activity typically preceded the onset of any use of expensive drugs (Inciardi 1979). For
example, crime began at a median age of 15.1 for the males and 15.9
for the females, yet heroin didn't occur until ages 18.7 and 18.2,
respectively, and cocaine did not occur until ages 19.7 and 18.7,
respectively.

Second, among 70 youthful heroin users and 96 non-heroin drug
users drawn from the streets of Miami during the same year, crime
again preceded expensive drug use (Inciardi 1980). For example, as
indicated in table 6, using median ages, for the heroin group crime
preceded all but alcohol and marijuana use. For the youths not using
heroin, criminal activity preceded all drug use.

Third, as indicated in table 7, among 133 narcotics-using women
studied during 1983–84, the same sequential pattern emerged once
again (Inciardi and Pottieger 1986). For example, focusing on median
age of onset, criminal activity began at age 15.7, followed by heroin
and cocaine use two and three years later.

Fourth, and most recently, among 387 primary crack users drawn
from street and treatment settings at the close of the 1980s and the
beginning of 1990, the onset of criminal activity preceded expensive
drug use in almost every case (table 8).

Based on these data and the findings of numerous other studies, it
would appear that the inference of causality, that the high price of
drugs on the black market per se causes crime, is simply not supported.
On the other hand, these same data also suggest that *drugs drive crime*
in that careers in drugs tend to intensify and perpetuate criminal

**Table 6. Drugs-Crime Sequence of 70 Adolescent Heroin Users and 96
Adolescent Non-Heroin Users, Miami, 1978**

	Median Age of Onset	
Drug/Crime Event	Heroin Users	Non-Heroin Users
first crime	**14.2**	**13.0**
first marijuana use	13.3	14.4
first alcohol use	13.5	14.3
first barbiturate use	15.3	15.8
first heroin use	16.8	—
first cocaine use	17.0	16.8

Source   James A. Inciardi. 1980. "Youth, Drugs, and Street Crime." In *Drugs and the Youth Culture,* edited by Frank R. Scarpitti and Susan K. Datesman. Beverly Hills: Sage, 175–203.

Table 7. Drugs-Crime Sequence among 133 Narcotics-Using Women, Miami, 1983–1984

Drug/Crime Event	Median Age of Onset
first alcohol use	13.8
first solvent/inhalant use	13.9
first hallucinogen use	14.9
first marijuana use	15.0
first crime committed	**15.7**
first heroin use	17.5
first cocaine use	18.1

Source James A. Inciardi and Anne E. Pottieger. 1986. "Drug Use and Crime Among Two Cohorts of Women Narcotic Users: An Empirical Assessment," *Journal of Drug Issues* 19 (Winter): 91–106.

careers. One might argue that little can be generalized from a few Miami studies. However, as noted earlier, the same basic conclusions have been drawn from similar studies conducted by other researchers in different locales (Johnson et al. 1985; Nurco et al. 1985; Stephens and McBride 1976; McBride and McCoy 1982; Anglin and Speckart 1986; Ball 1986; Ball et al. 1982; Ball, Shaffer, and Nurco 1983).

Drugs, Crime, and the Urban Killing Fields There seems to be three models of drug-related violence: the psychopharmacologic, the economically compulsive, and the systemic (Goldstein, 1985, 1986). The *psychopharmacological model* of violence suggests that some individuals, as the result of short-term or long-term ingestion of specific substances, may become excitable and irrational and exhibit violent behavior. The paranoia and aggression associated with the cocaine psychosis fit into the psychopharmacological model, as does most alcohol-related violence. The *economically compulsive model* of violence holds that some drug users engage in economically oriented violent crime to support drug use. This model is illustrated in the many studies of drug use and criminal behavior which have demonstrated that while drug sales, property crimes, and prostitution are the primary economic offenses committed by users, armed robberies and muggings do indeed occur. The *systemic model* of violence maintains that violent crime is intrinsic to the very involvement with illicit substances. As such, systemic violence refers to the traditionally aggressive patterns of interaction within systems of illegal drug trafficking and distribution.

It is the systemic violence associated with trafficking in cocaine and crack in the inner cities that has brought the most attention to drug-

Table 8. Drugs-Crime Sequence among Adult Male and Female Primary Crack Users Drawn from Street and Treatment Settings, Miami, 1988–1990

| | Median Age of Onset | | | |
| | Street | | Treatment | |
Drug/Crime Event	Male (N = 114)	Female (N = 84)	Male (N = 116)	Female (N = 73)
first alcohol use	10.0	10.0	14.0	14.0
first illicit drug use	14.0	14.0	14.0	15.0
first marijuana use	14.0	14.0	14.5	15.0
first crime committed	**14.0**	**14.0**	**16.0**	**18.5**
first pill use	15.0	15.0	17.0	17.0
first cocaine use	16.0	16.0	17.0	18.0
first heroin use	17.0	16.5	19.0	19.5

Source "Crack Abuse Patterns and Crime Linkages," U.S. Department of Health and Human Services, Grant no. R01-DA04862 from the National Institute on Drug Abuse, James A. Inciardi, Principal Investigator.

related violence in recent years. Moreover, it is concerns with this same violence that focused the current interest on the possibility of legalizing drugs (see *Time*, 30 May 1988, 12–19; *USA Today*, 18 May 1988, 10A; *Drug Abuse Report*, 6 April 1988, 7–8; Wilmington (Delaware) *News-Journal*, 3 April 1988, E2; *Newsweek*, 30 May 1988, 36–38; *Fortune*, 20 June 1988, 39–41; *New York Times*, 2 June 1988, A26). And it is certainly logical to assume that if heroin and cocaine were legal substances, systemic drug-related violence would indeed decline significantly. But too, there are some very troubling considerations.

First, achieving the desired declines in systemic violence would require that crack be legalized as well. For after all, it is in the crack distribution system that much of the violence is occurring. Second, it is already clear that there is considerable psychopharmacologic violence associated with the cocaine psychosis. Moreover, research has demonstrated that there is far more psychopharmacologic violence connected with heroin use than is generally believed (see Goldstein 1979, 126; McBride 1981; Inciardi 1986, 135). Given that drug use would probably increase significantly with legalization, in all likelihood any declines in systemic violence would be accompanied by increases in psychopharmacologic violence. The country already pays a high price for alcohol-related violence, a phenomenon well documented by empirical research (see Collins 1981). Why compound the problem with the legalization of additional violence-producing substances?

Finally, although it cannot be denied that there is indeed considerable violence associated with illegal drug markets and distribution systems, does anyone really have a concrete understanding or measure of the extent to which drugs impact rates of violent crime? If I had a giant vacuum and could suck all of the heroin, cocaine, crack, and PCP out of Washington, D.C., New York City, Miami, or Los Angeles this evening, would the predatory crime and violence be gone from the streets of those cities when we all wake up tomorrow morning? The drive-by shootings that are occurring in the nation's inner cities have little, if anything, to do with drugs. The convulsion of rage and incendiary violence that occurred in Los Angeles and other cities after the acquittal of four white police officers in the beating of motorist Rodney King had nothing to do with drugs. The stabbings and shootings perpetrated by so many elementary-school and high-school youths have nothing to do with drugs. All of these are connected with a wide spectrum of social ills that are unrelated to the legal status of drugs.

3. Altering the Course of the War on Drugs

When I was in the sixth grade, I remember having had a "civics" teacher—"Brother John" is what we called him—who spent an inordinate amount of time providing the class with cross-cultural perspectives on such diverse topics as electing leaders, marriage ceremonies, male rites of passage, symbols of power, and the like. One of his more esoteric presentations had to do with differences in diet and food production around the world. We heard about everything from the harvesting of flax and millet in the dry uplands of southwest Asia, to the cultivation of tubers and taro in the tropical wetlands of South America, to horticulture and pig feasts among the Gururumba of New Guinea.

During this lecture on food Brother John talked about dietary preferences, and to our horror, we were told that small dogs were considered a delicacy in China. Just as he finished his sentence, one of my schoolmates raised his hand. To protect his name and shield his infamy and humiliation, I'll simply call him "Edward H." I remember that he was a good student, an excellent cartoonist, and an outstanding stickball player. But too, he was a "bullshit artist," to use one of the more consecrated elementary school terms of the 1950s. He was that person—and every class likely had one—who always came up with a story intended to outdo what someone else had to say. Edward H. proceeded to reveal how during a hunting trip with his uncle the previous year, they became lost, stranded, snowed in, and I don't remember what else. But to shorten the story, he related how they ran out of food and were forced to kill and eat "Molly," his uncle's champion hunting dog.

191

Well, the class had heard his stories before, but that one really got to us. From that day forward, through the balance of elementary school and all of high school (Catholic schools in Brooklyn back in those days didn't have middle school and junior high), Edward H. was known as "the dog eater." That became his epithet, designation, and master status. Henceforth, it was "where's the dog eater?" or "the dog eater forgot his lunch today," or "I went to the movies with Chris and the dog eater." The label followed him everywhere. Even when choosing up sides for an after-school game of stickball, my team would be Chris, Fred, Frank, Jim, Teddy, and "the dog eater."

Why am I resurrecting this story from my childhood? Well, like Edward H., who for generations to come will be known as "the dog eater" because of one small indiscretion, people tend to be labeled on the basis of a single piece of information, while the balance of their lives and work are set aside and forgotten. When it comes to talking about American drug policy, time and again I seem to have this way of being misconstrued. If I were to actually walk on water some day, people will probably say "Inciardi can't swim!" So be it. But at any rate, I am hoping that readers would reflect on *all* of what I have to say in this section and not come away with the simplistic conclusion that "Inciardi wants to lock up all druggies and junkies!"

Psychopathology and Addiction

Anyone who has spent any length of time in drug-abuse treatment facilities, the court system, and the corrections industry, or has had extensive contact with street-drug users in some capacity, has recognized that there is something "different" about most heroin and cocaine addicts. Sometimes it is referred to as the "addiction-prone personality." As elucidated by Dr. Kenneth Chapman of the United States Public Health Service more than four decades ago:

> ... the typical addict is emotionally unstable and immature, often seeking pleasure and excitement outside of the conventional realms. Unable to adapt comfortably to the pressures and tensions in today's speedy world, he may become either an extremely dependent individual or turn into a hostile "lone wolf" incapable of attaching deep feelings toward anyone. In his discomfort, he may suffer pain—real or imaginary. The ordinary human being has normal defense machinery with which to meet life's disappointments, frustrations, and conflicts. But the potential addict lacks enough of this inner strength to conquer his emotional problems and the

anxiety they create. In a moment of stress, he may be introduced to narcotics as a "sure-fire" answer to his needs. Experiencing relief from his pain, or an unreal flight from his problems, or a puffed-up sense of power and control regarding them, he is well on the road toward making narcotics his way of life (Chapman 1957).

Stated differently, when "stable" people are introduced to drugs, they will discard them spontaneously before becoming dependent. Those who have "addiction-prone personalities," because of psychoses, psychopathic or psychoneurotic disorders, or predispositons toward mental dysfunctioning, "become transformed into the typical addict" (Yost 1964, 68–69, 82).

I have always been critical of the theory of the addiction-prone personality. It evolved from studies of addicts in psychiatric facilities during the early years of addiction treatment, and it seemed to be applied universally and uncritically, and continues to be accepted by many. Yet as researchers, who have gone beyond the confines of their laboratories, hospitals, and university campuses to study addicts in their natural environment understand, the problem of "addiction" is far more complex than personality characteristics.

Those of us who have worked with the legions of addicts who come in contact with the criminal justice system have found repeatedly that "drug abuse" and "criminality" are but symptoms of a complex behavioral disorder that cannot be properly addressed through legalizing drugs, chemical detoxification, public assistance, vocational rehabilitation, a war on poverty, imprisonment, or even drug-abuse counseling. Dr. Douglas S. Lipton of New York's National Development and Research Institute has conveniently listed and explained the aspects of this disorder, referring to them as crime-related "impedimenta" to social functioning. The major ones are as follows (Lipton 1989):

Inadequacy, characterized by a pervasive feeling of inability to cope with needs; a generalized feeling of helplessness; the inability to plan ahead; frequent feelings of despair, negativism, and cynicism; diffuse anxiety, not seen as related to a specific cause; the perception of tasks as likely to lead to failure rather than success; and a disproportionate fear (and anticipation) of rejection.

Immaturity, characterized by the inability to postpone gratification; a general attitude of irresponsibility; a preoccupation with concrete and immediate objects, wishes, and needs; an orientation of the individual as "receiver" and a tendency to view others as "givers"; manipulativeness; selfishness; and petulance.

Dependency, characterized by difficulty in coping with unstructured or complex environments; anxiety in situations requiring independent action; feelings of guilt with respect to the above elements of dependency; and, feelings of resentment toward what is believed to be the source of dependency.

Ill-equipped in social skills, characterized by a lack of ability to articulate feelings and ideas, and a resulting inability to communicate meaningfully with others except at superficial levels; lack of ability to function in subordinate-superordinate roles (e.g., inability to take orders from a superior in a work situation); inability to "take the role of the other," (i.e., empathize with others); and inadvertent, socially disapproved behavior (e.g., use of language inappropriate to various social situations, dress inappropriate for job interviews, failure to conform to norms of personal hygiene).

Ill-equipped in education, characterized by functional illiteracy or a conspicuous disproportion between the individual's level of education and his or her potential level, or both.

Vocational maladjustment, characterized by a lack of appropriate technical skills for employment that would be meaningful to the individual, or a conspicuous disproportion between the attitudes of the individual and realistic opportunities, or both.

Cognitive deficiency, characterized by a state of mental retardation, restricted mental potentiality, or incomplete development existing from birth or early infancy, as a result of which the individual is confused and bewildered by any complexity of life, overly suggestible and easily exploited, and able to achieve a mental age within a range of only 8 to 12 years.

Compulsive pathology, characterized by a sense that criminal behavior is forced upon the individual against his or her will; inability to obtain any lasting satisfaction from the act committed (e.g., no apparent gain to the individual from act or any reason for injury to another); and repetition of such acts.

Organic pathology, involving such things as glandular and neurological anomalies (e.g., brain damage, organic brain disease). Conduct stemming from organic pathology is not usually typified by any single behavioral pattern.

Antisocial attitudes, consisting of a configuration of values and viewpoints which are defined by society as delinquent, criminal, and antisocial. An individual who possesses antisocial attitudes demonstrates positive affective responses toward trouble, toughness, smartness, excitement, fate, autonomy, and short-run hedonism.

Catalytic impulsivity, a characteristic that requires the presence of a catalyst for it to appear (i.e., criminal acts only occur while the normally over-controlled person is affected by the catalyst). The catalyst may take the form of alcohol or an overwhelming need stemming from psychic or physical dependence (e.g., narcotics) or a specific emotional stimulus (e.g., cursing one's mother). The central concept of catalytic impulsivity is the impulsive, spontaneous, unplanned nature of the criminal act while the offender is under the influence of, or is affected by, the catalyst. Under normal circumstances the catalytic impulsive individual is not antisocial and possesses adequate and even excessive self-control. Under the influence of the catalyst, however, there is first a recognition of the imminence of the criminal act, then the criminal act almost invariably precipitates, and there is total disregard for the consequences of such acts.

Habitual impulsivity, a characteristic that differs from catalytic impulsivity by the absence of the need for a catalyst as a trigger. An habitually impulsive individual may use alcohol or drugs, but the crucial aspect is that these substances are neither necessary nor sufficient for the criminal act to occur. The act itself is always spontaneous and unplanned, and the individual who possesses this characteristic is temperamental and exhibits a low frustration tolerance and high reactivity. His or her volatile temperament typically demonstrates rapid mood swings. The triggering source for impulsive criminal acts cannot be definitely indicated. Such a characteristic may be seen in individuals who react variously to situations of temptation, slight provocation, and frustration. Rages may be a typical reaction for one offender, while another may react by random shoplifting or driving dangerously.

Substance dependency, including alcoholism or drug addiction, or both. Offenders with this characteristic typically (1) have several years' experience as a street-drug addict or alcoholic, (2) have many failed treatment experiences, (3) are driven to use their chosen substance regardless of consequences while on the street, (4) are preoccupied with thoughts about their substance of choice while institutionalized, and (5) intend to use the preferred substance upon discharge.

These characteristics may appear singly, or in combinations of two, three, four, or more in any individual at any given time. And the drug-abuse treatment and psychiatric literatures have documented the presence of "impedimenta" among substance abusers through literally hundreds of studies (for example, see Ball and Ross 1991; Platt, Kaplan, and Mc Kim 1990; Blume 1989; Stoffelmayr et al. 1989; Meek et al. 1989; Wallen and Weiner 1989; Wolfe and Sorenson 1989; De Leon 1989; Chatlos 1989; Gorney 1989; Clark and Zwerben; Schlenger, Kroutil, and Roland 1992; Regier et al. 1990; Weiss and Collins 1992; Bachman et al. 1992; Bauer et al. 1992; McLellan et al. 1981; Turner and Tofler 1986; Hanson 1990; Goodwin, Cheeves, and Connell 1990; Winfield et al. 1990; Cloninger and Guze 1970; Brown and Anderson 1991; Christie et al. 1988; Washton 1989; Washton and Gold 1987; Gerstein and Harwood 1990; Onken and Blaine 1990; Spotts and Schontz 1980; Wallace 1991; Simpson and Sells 1990; Nowinski 1990).

To reiterate, drug addiction is typically but one symptom of a complex of problems that cannot be addressed by legalizing drugs and making them even more available than they are now. Moreover, there is a whole literature which suggests that drug abuse is *overdetermined behavior*. That is, physical dependence is secondary to the wide range of influences that instigate and regulate drug-taking and drug-seeking behaviors. Drug abuse is a disorder of the whole person, affecting some or all areas of functioning. In the vast majority of drug offenders, there are cognitive problems, psychological dysfunction is common, thinking may be unrealistic or disorganized, values are misshapen, and frequently there are deficits in educational and employment skills. As such, drug abuse is a response to a series of social and psychological disturbances. Thus, the goal of treatment should be "habilitation" rather than "rehabilitation." Whereas *rehabilitation* emphasizes the return to a way of life previously known and perhaps forgotten or rejected, *habilitation* involves the client's initial socialization into a productive and responsible way of life (Inciardi and Scarpitti 1992). What the large drug offender population needs is not freely available drugs, but habilitation in long-term residential treatment.

Treatment on Demand versus Compulsory Treatment

I am at the point in this essay where I want to recommend a new paradigm, a new way of looking at drugs, addiction, drug-related crime, treatment, and policy. What I have to say is not particularly new to drug-abuse clinicians, but to many others it might well be. For starters, there's the story of a young male urbanite on a Sunday drive through a quiet stretch of mountainside. Up ahead, he sees a young woman, coming around a curve, her vehicle out of control, headed straight for him. He leans on his horn several times and slams on his brakes, and at the last minute, she gets her car under some measure of control. As she passes him, she looks his way and shouts through her window, "Pig!" As he retorts with vituperative invectives denigrating her ancestry, her profession, and her driving ability, he pops his clutch, races off, and continues his journey. And as he rounds the curve from whence the woman driver had come, he crashes, head on, into a stray quarter-ton hog that stood in the middle of the road, minding its own business. This was a man who needed a new paradigm of response when called "Pig." And so it goes with drug-abuse treatment.

Treatment on Demand   "Treatment on demand," that is, having drug-abuse treatment available to whoever wants it, whenever they want it, certainly sounds humane and logical. Yet the Office of National Drug Control Policy (ONDCP) has ardently opposed the idea, on the grounds that:

> . . . treatment on demand . . . ignores the more immediate and fundamental problems that confront the treatment system. While it is certainly true that there are addicts who do seek treatment voluntarily, many of these volunteers repeatedly enter and impulsively drop out of treatment. Their goal, unlike the goals of their treatment providers, is to return to "controlled use" or to "stay clean" for a few days to reduce their tolerance so the same high can be achieved from lower and cheaper doses. Others who seek treatment on their own do so only after they have "bottomed out"; they have reached a point where their addiction has so consumed them and devastated their lives that they can no longer function; they cannot care for their children, show up for work, or even associate with people who don't use drugs.
>
> For addicts like these, simply providing additional treatment slots does nothing by itself to ensure that treatment generally is made more effective and provided in a more rational way. A policy designed primarily to provide treatment on demand would create a costly, unbalanced system that brings no guarantee of higher treatment success rates. Moreover, the call for such a system obscures the far more pressing and practical needs of drug treatment. Addressing those needs requires us to come to grips with the fact that while the need for treatment is high, the actual demand for it is relatively low.
>
> The overwhelming majority of addicts must be "jolted" into drug treatment and induced to stay there by some external force: the criminal justice system, employers who have discovered drug use, spouses who threaten to leave, or the death of a fellow addict (Office of National Drug Control Policy 1990b).

Without question, there is some truth to the ONDCP remarks. Most addicts *do not* volunteer for treatment; many who do are indeed attempting to reduce the sizes of their habits, and remain for too short a period of time for it to have any long-term impact; and coerced treatment—discussed next—does seem to have better program retention and success rates. Nevertheless, the ONDCP position opposing "treatment on demand" is a bit rigid, particularly since extensive data have demonstrated that reduced drug intake is typically accompanied by reduced criminality (see Nurco et al. 1990; Chaiken and Chaiken 1990). Undoubtedly, there is a need for dialogue and compromise.

Compulsory Treatment of Addiction   The "war on drugs" will persist. Regardless of how many books, articles, and conference presentations argue that "war is not the answer," the war will nevertheless persevere. Political polls repeatedly show that this is what the American people want, and politicians and legislators typically react to the wishes of their constituencies. But *the focus of the war can be shifted*, and this is essentially where I stand. I agree with Dr. Arnold Trebach that the apportionment of anti-drug funding is lopsided. Historically, about three-fourths has been earmarked for supply reduction (enforcement, interdiction, and foreign assistance initiatives), with only one-fourth for demand reduction (prevention and treatment). I believe that we do indeed need drug enforcement, but it is stressed far too much in current policy. Cut it in half, and shift those funds to criminal justice–based treatment programs. This is where a new paradigm and compulsory treatment come into play.

The argument has been made over the years that drug dependence is a medical problem, not a criminal problem, and hence, drug control should be taken out of the hands of the criminal justice system and put into those of the public health and human service delivery networks. But in counterpoint, drug control must remain within the criminal justice sector for some very good reasons! The Drug Use Forecasting (DUF) program clearly demonstrates that the majority of arrestees in urban areas throughout the United States are drug-involved.[9] At the

9. The Drug Use Forecasting program (DUF) was established by the National Institute of Justice to measure the prevalence of drug use among those arrested for serious crimes. Since 1986, the DUF program has used urinalysis to test a sample of arrestees in selected major cities across the United States to determine recent drug use. Urine specimens are collected from arrestees anonymously and voluntarily, and tested so as to detect the use of ten different drugs, including cocaine, marijuana, PCP, methamphetamine, and heroin. What the DUF data have consistently demonstrated is that drug use is pervasive among those coming to the attention of the criminal justice system (Office of National Drug Control Policy 1990a; National Institute of Justice 1989, 1990).

same time, recent research has demonstrated not only that drug abuse treatment works (Hubbard et al. 1989; Platt, Kaplan, and Mc Kim 1990), but that coerced treatment works best! Although logic would dictate that voluntary treatment might have more beneficial effects than mandatory treatment, it would appear that the opposite is the case. What the research demonstrates is that the key variable most related to success in treatment is "length of stay in treatment," and that those who are forced into treatment remain longer than those who volunteer (see Leukefeld and Tims 1988; Hubbard et al. 1989). By remaining longer, they benefit more. As such, compulsory treatment efforts should be expanded for those who are dependent on drugs and are involved in drug-related crime.

Treatment and Criminal Justice

What I am arguing for here is a more humane use of the criminal justice system. Attempting to legislate one's way out of a drug problem through increased penalties for possession of drugs is neither effective nor humane. Attempting to build one's way out of a drug problem by increasing prison capacity is neither effective nor humane. Prosecuting pregnant addicts is certainly not humane. But since street-drug users do indeed commit crimes and eventually get arrested, and since compulsory treatment has a documented record of effectiveness, then coerced treatment after a user has come to the attention of the criminal justice system would appear to be practical.

Treatment Alternatives to Street Crime   Perhaps the most humane and effective use of criminal justice in drug-control activities is its linkage with the treatment system through the Treatment Alternatives to Street Crime (TASC) initiative. TASC represents an efficient and humane use of the criminal justice system, for it acts as an objective bridge between two separate institutions: justice and the drug treatment community. The justice system's legal sanctions reflect concerns for public safety and punishment, whereas treatment emphasizes therapeutic intervention as a means for altering drug-taking and drug-seeking behaviors.

Under TASC, community-based supervision is made available to drug-involved individuals who would otherwise burden the justice system with their persistent drug-associated criminality. More specifically, TASC identifies, assesses, and refers drug-involved offenders to community treatment services as an *alternative* or *supplement* to existing justice system sanctions and procedures. In the more than 100 jurisdictions where TASC currently operates, it serves as a court-diversion mechanism or a supplement to probation or parole supervision. After referral to community-based treatment, TASC monitors the client's progress and compliance, including expectations for abstinence, employment, and improved personal and social functioning. It then reports treatment results back to the referring justice system agency. Clients who violate the conditions of their justice mandate (diversion, deferred sentencing, pretrial intervention, probation, or parole), their TASC contract, or their treatment agreement are typically returned to the justice system for continued processing or sanctions (Bureau of Justice Assistance 1988; Inciardi and McBride 1991).

Although there has not been a national evaluation of the entire TASC effort, more than 40 local programs were assessed from 1972 through 1982 (see Toborg et al. 1976; System Sciences 1979; McBride and Bennett 1978; Collins et al. 1982a, 1982b). In general, it was found that the majority effectively linked criminal justice and treatment systems, identified previously untreated drug-involved offenders, and intervened with clients to reduce drug abuse and criminal activity. Two more recent examinations, one in 1986 and the second in 1988, suggested that the TASC initiative continued to meet its intended operational goals (Tyon 1988; National Association of State Alcohol and Drug Abuse Directors 1989). In short, the TASC experience has been a positive one. TASC has been demonstrated to be highly productive in 1) identifying populations of drug-involved offenders in need of treatment; 2) assessing the nature and extent of their drug-use patterns and specific treatment needs; 3) effectively referring drug-involved offenders to treatment; 4) serving as a linkage between the criminal justice and treatment systems; and 5) providing constructive client identification and monitoring services for the courts, probation, and other segments of the criminal justice system. Perhaps most important, evaluation data indicate that TASC–referred clients remain longer in treatment than non–TASC clients, and as a result, have better post-treatment success.

As such, it is important that TASC be expanded because of the role it can play in reducing the growing rates of violent, drug-related street crime; alleviating court backlogs; and easing crowded prison conditions.

Therapeutic Communities in Corrections In addition to TASC, there should be an expansion of therapeutic community treatment in jails and prisons. The therapeutic community, better known as the "TC" by practitioners in the drug field, is unquestionably the most appropriate form of drug abuse treatment in correctional settings because of the many phenomena in the prison environment that make rehabilitation difficult. Not surprisingly, the availability of drugs in jails and prisons is a pervasive problem. In addition, there is the violence associated with inmate gangs, often formed along racial lines for the purposes of establishing and maintaining status, "turf," and unofficial control over sectors of the penitentiary for distributing contraband and providing "protection" for other inmates (Fleisher 1989; Johnson 1987; Bowker 1980). And finally, there is the prison subculture, a system of norms and values that, among other things, holds that "people in treatment are faggots," as one Delaware inmate put it in 1988.

In contrast, the therapeutic community is a total treatment environment isolated from the rest of the prison population—separated from the drugs, the violence, and the norms and values that militate against treatment and rehabilitation. The primary clinical staff of the TC are typically former substance abusers—"recovering addicts"—who themselves were rehabilitated in therapeutic communities. The treatment perspective of the TC is that drug abuse is a disorder of the whole person—that the problem is the *person* and not the drug, that addiction is a *symptom* and not the essence of the disorder. In the TC's view of recovery, the primary goal is to change the negative patterns of behavior, thinking, and feeling that predispose drug use. As such, the overall goal is a responsible drug-free lifestyle (see De Leon and Ziegenfuss 1986; Yablonsky 1989).

Recovery through the TC process depends on positive and negative pressures to change, and this is brought about through a self-help process in which relationships of mutual responsibility to every resident in the program are built. Or as the noted TC researcher, Dr. George De Leon, once described it:

> The essential dynamic in the TC is mutual self-help. Thus, the day-to-day activities are conducted by the residents themselves. In their jobs, groups, meetings, recreation, personal, and social time, it is residents who continually transmit to each other the main messages and expectations of the community (De Leon 1985).

In addition to individual and group counseling, the TC process has a system of explicit rewards that reinforce the value of earned achievement. As such, privileges are *earned*. Moreover, TCs have their own specific rules and regulations that guide the behavior of residents and the management of their facilities. Their purposes are to maintain the safety and health of the community and to train and teach residents through the use of discipline. TC rules and regulations are numerous, the most conspicuous of which are total prohibitions against violence, theft, and drug use. Violation of these cardinal rules typically results in immediate expulsion from a TC.

Therapeutic communities have been in existence for decades, and their successes have been well documented (see De Leon 190). Yet few exist in jail and prison settings. It has been demonstrated, however, that prison-based TCs are effective not only in addressing the problems of drug dependence, but also in dealing with issues of prison management. On this latter point, prison TCs have been found to be the cleanest and most trouble-free sectors of the institutions in which they are housed (Toch 1980; Wexler and Williams 1986; Lipton and Wexler 1988; Inciardi, Martin, et al. 1990).

Finally, expansions in drug-abuse treatment services, increases in the number of TASC programs, and development of additional prison-based therapeutic communities should represent only the beginning of the extended treatment initiative. Funding is also needed for establishing new and innovative treatment approaches, for researching treatment effectiveness, and for the recruitment and training of those who will staff the new programs.

4. Postscript

Before commenting on where I feel the legalization debate ought to go from here, let me reiterate the major points I have been trying to make.

The arguments *for* legalization are seemingly based on the fervent belief that America's prohibitions against marijuana, cocaine, heroin, and other drugs impose far too large a cost in terms of tax dollars, crime, and infringements on civil rights and individual liberties. And while the overall argument may be well-intended and appear quite logical, I find it to be highly questionable in its historical, sociocultural, and empirical underpinnings, and demonstrably naive in its understanding of the negative consequences of a legalized drug market. In counterpoint:

1. Although drug-prohibition policies have been problematic, it would appear that they have managed to keep drugs away from most people. High school and general population surveys indicate that most Americans don't use drugs, have never even tried them, and don't know where to get them. Thus, the numbers "at risk" are dramatically fewer than is the case with the legal drugs. Or stated differently, there is a rather large population who might be at risk if illicit drugs were suddenly available.

2. Marijuana, heroin, cocaine, crack, and the rest are not "benign" substances. Their health consequences, addiction liability, and/or abuse potential are considerable.

3. There is extensive physiological, neurological, and anthropological evidence to suggest that people are of a species that has been honed for pleasure. Nearly all people want and enjoy pleasure, and the pursuit of drugs—whether caffeine, nicotine, alcohol, opium, heroin, marijuana, or cocaine—seems to be universal and inescapable. It is

found across time and across cultures. Moreover, history and research has demonstrated that "availability creates demand."

4. Crack cocaine is especially problematic because of its pharmacological and sociocultural effects. Because crack makes its users ecstatic and yet is so short-acting, it has an extremely high addiction potential. *Use* rapidly becomes *compulsive use*. Crack acquisition thus becomes enormously more important than family, work, social responsibility, health, values, modesty, morality, or self respect. Because of its chemistry, crack is easy to produce. Moreover, crack is inexpensive to produce, and that will likely remain so regardless of its legal status. A benefit of its current criminalization is that since it is against the law, it doesn't have widespread availability, and proportionately few people use it. Within the context of reversing the human suffering that crack has helped to exacerbate, what purpose is served by arguing for its legalization? Will legalizing crack make it less available, less attractive, less expensive, less addictive, or less troublesome?

5. The research literature on the criminal careers of heroin and other drug users have convincingly documented that while drug use tends to intensify and perpetuate criminal behavior, it usually does not initiate criminal careers. In fact, the evidence suggests that among the majority of street-drug users who are involved in crime, their criminal careers were well established prior to the onset of either narcotics or cocaine use.

6. There is also a large body of work suggesting that drug abuse is overdetermined behavior. That is, physical dependence is secondary to the wide range of influences that instigate and regulate drug-taking and drug-seeking. Drug abuse is a disorder of the whole person, affecting some or all areas of functioning. In the vast majority of drug offenders, there are cognitive problems, psychological dysfunction is common, thinking may be unrealistic or disorganized, values are misshapen, and frequently there are deficits in educational and employment skills. As such, drug abuse is a response to a series of social and psychological disturbances. Thus, the goal of treatment should be "habilitation" rather than "rehabilitation." Whereas *rehabilitation* emphasizes the return to a way of life previously known and perhaps forgotten or rejected, *habilitation* involves the client's initial socialization into a productive and responsible way of life.

7. The focus on the war on drugs can be shifted. I believe that we do indeed need drug enforcement, but it is stressed far too much in current policy. Cut it in half, and shift those funds to criminal justice–based treatment programs.

8. Drug control should remain within the criminal justice sector for some very good reasons. The Drug Use Forecasting (DUF) program clearly demonstrates that the majority of arrestees in urban areas are drug-involved. Moreover, recent research has demonstrated not only that drug abuse treatment works, but also that coerced treatment works best. The key variable most related to success in treatment is "length of stay in treatment," and those who are forced into treatment remain longer than volunteers. By remaining longer, they benefit more. As such, compulsory treatment efforts should be expanded for those who are dependent on drugs and are involved in drug-related crime.

9. Since the "war on drugs" will continue, then a more humane use of the criminal justice system should be structured. This is best done through treatment in lieu of incarceration, and corrections-based treatment for those who do end up in jails and prisons.

Having said all of this, where do we go from here? Is any purpose served by further debating the legalization of drugs? People on both sides of the discussion seem to be galvanized, unwilling to make substantial concessions to one another. The government of the United States is not going to legalize drugs anytime soon, if ever, and certainly not in this century. So why spend so much time, expense, and intellectual and emotional effort on a quixotic undertaking? And aside from the positive or negative merits of the legalization thesis, it represents a problematic approach to a very complex predicament. It is surprising that social and behavioral scientists, more than any other group, would pose such a radical policy. As students of human behavior and social change, conscious of the fact that change is a slow process, we should know by now that neither politicians nor the polity respond positively to abrupt and drastic strategy alterations.

American drug policy as it exists today is not likely to change drastically anytime soon. Given that, something needs to be kept in mind. While the First Amendment and academic freedom enable the scholarly community to continue its attack on American drug policy, verbal assault and vilification will serve no significant purpose in effecting change. Calls for the legalization or decriminalization of marijuana, heroin, cocaine, and other illicit drugs accomplish little more than to further isolate the legalizers from the policy-making enterprise.

Finally, there is far too much suffering as the result of drug abuse that is not being addressed. Many things warrant discussion, debate, and prodding on the steps of Capitol Hill and the White House lawn. More drug abuse treatment slots, a repeal of the statutes designed to prosecute pregnant addicts and prohibit needle-exchange programs, the wider use of treatment as an alternative to incarceration—all of these are worthy of vigorous consideration and lobbying. But not legalizing drugs. It is an argument that is going nowhere.

References

Anglin, M. Douglas, and George Speckart. 1986. "Narcotics Use, Property Crime, and Dealing: Structural Dynamics across the Addiction Career," *Journal of Quantitative Criminology* 2: 355–75.

Anonymous. 1903. *Twenty Years in Hell, or the Life, Experience, Trials, and Tribulations of a Morphine Fiend.* Kansas City, MO: Author's Edition.

Anonymous. 1922. *In the Clutch of Circumstance: My Own Story.* New York: D. Appleton.

Anonymous. 1972. *The Gourmet Cokebook: A Complete Guide to Cocaine.* White Mountain Press.

Anslinger, Harry J., and William F. Tompkins. 1953. *The Traffic in Narcotics.* New York: Funk & Wagnalls.

Austin, Gregory A., and Dan J. Lettieri. 1976. *Drugs and Crime: The Relationship of Drug Use and Concomitant Criminal Behavior.* Rockville, MD: National Institute on Drug Abuse.

Bachman, Sara S., Helen Levine Batten, Kenneth Minkoff, Richard Higgens, Nancy Manzik, and Diane Mahoney. 1992. "Predicting Success in a Community Treatment Program for Substance Abusers," *American Journal of Addictions* 1 (Spring): 155–67.

Ball, John C. 1965. "Two Patterns of Narcotic Addiction in the United States," *Journal of Criminal Law, Criminology, and Police Science* 52: 203–11.

―――. 1986. "The Hyper-Criminal Opiate Addict." In *Crime Rates and Drug Abusing Offenders*, edited by Bruce D. Johnson and Eric Wish. New York: Narcotic and Drug Research, Inc.

Ball, John C., Lawrence Rosen, John A. Flueck, and David N. Nurco. 1982. "Lifetime Criminality of Heroin Addicts in the United States," *Journal of Drug Issues* 12: 225–39.

Ball, John C., John W. Shaffer, and David N. Nurco. 1983. "The Day-to-Day Criminality of Heroin Addicts in Baltimore: A Study in the Continuity of Offense Rates," *Drug and Alcohol Dependence* 12: 119–42.

Ball, John C., and Alan Ross. 1991. *The Effectiveness of Methadone Maintenance Treatment*. New York: Springer-Verlag.

Bauer, Lance O., Rachel Yehuda, Roger E. Meyer, and Earl Giller. 1992. "Effects of a Family History of Alcoholism on Autonomic, Neuroendocrine, and Subjective Reactions to Alcohol," *American Journal of Addictions* 1 (Spring): 168–76.

Black, Jack. 1927. *You Can't Win*. New York: Macmillan.

Black, Perry, ed. 1969. *Drugs and the Brain: Papers on the Action, Use, and Abuse of Psychotropic Agents*. Baltimore: Johns Hopkins Press.

Blume, Sheila B. 1989. "Dual Diagnosis: Psychoactive Substance Abuse and Personality Disorders," *Journal of Psychoactive Drugs* 21 (April–June): 135–38.

Boaz, David, ed. 1990. *The Crisis in Prohibition*. Washington: Cato Institute.

Bourgois, Phillipe, and Eloise Dunlap. 1991. "Sex-for-Crack in Harlem, New York." Paper presented at the Annual Meeting of the Society for Applied Anthropology, Charleston, South Carolina, 13–17 March.

Bowker, Lee. 1980. *Prison Victimization*. New York: Elsevier.

Brown, George R., and Bradley Anderson. 1991. "Psychiatric Morbidity in Assault Inpatients with Childhood Histories of Sexual and Physical Abuse," *American Journal of Psychiatry* 148 (January): 55–61.

Brown, James W., Roger Mazze, and Daniel Glaser. 1974. *Narcotics Knowledge and Nonsense: Program Disaster Versus A Scientific Model*. Cambridge, MA: Ballinger.

Bureau of Justice Assistance. *Treatment Alternatives to Street Crime*. Washington: U.S. Department of Justice, Office of Justice Programs.

Burroughs, William. 1953. *Junkie*. New York: Ace.

Byrnes, Thomas. 1886. *Professional Criminals of America*. New York: G.W. Dillingham.

Campion, Daniel. 1957. *Crooks Are Human Too*. Englewood Cliffs, NJ: Prentice-Hall.

Centers for Disease Control. 1990. "Trends in Lung Cancer Incidence and Mortality," *Morbidity and Mortality Weekly Report* 39 (December 7): 875–83.

———. 1991a. "Annual and New Year's Day Alcohol-Related Traffic Fatalities: United States, 1982–1990," *Morbidity and Mortality Weekly Report* 40 (December 6): 821–25.

———. 1991b. "Cigarette Smoking Among Reproductive-Aged Women," *Morbidity and Mortality Weekly Report* 40 (October 25): 719–23.

Chaiken, Jan M., and Marcia R. Chaiken. 1990. "Drugs and Predatory Crime." In *Drugs and Crime,* edited by Michael Tonry and James Q. Wilson. Chicago: University of Chicago Press, 203–39.

Chaing, C. Nora, and Richard L. Hawks, eds. 1990. *Research Findings on Smoking of Abused Substances.* Rockville, MD: National Institute on Drug Abuse.

Chambliss, William J. 1988. "Testimony." In U.S. Congress. House. Select Committee on Narcotics Abuse and Control. *Hearings on Legalization of Illicit Drugs: Impact and Feasibility.* 100th Cong., 2d sess., 29 September.

Chapman, Kenneth W. 1957. "Narcotic Addiction," *Modern Medicine* 25: 192–214.

Chatlos, J. Calvin. 1989. "Adolescent Dual Diagnosis: A 12-Step Transformational Model," *Journal of Psychoactive Drugs* 21 (April–June): 189–202.

Christie, Kimberly A., Jack D. Burke, Darrel A. Regier, Donald S. Rae, Jeffrey H. Boyd, and Ben Z. Locke. 1988. "Epidemiologic Evidence for Early Onset of Mental Disorders and Higher Risk of Drug Abuse in Young Adults," *American Journal of Psychiatry* 145 (August): 971–75.

Clark, H. Westley, and Joan Ellen Zwerben. 1989. "Legal Vulnerabilities in the Treatment of Chemically Dependent Dual Diagnosis Patients," *Journal of Psychoactive Drugs* 21 (April–June): 251–58.

Cloninger, Robert, and Samuel B. Guze. 1970. "Psychiatric Illness and Female Criminality: The Role of Sociopathy and Hysteria in Antisocial Women," *American Journal of Psychiatry* 127 (September): 79–87.

Cohen, Stanley. 1988. *The Chemical Brain: The Neurochemistry of Addictive Disorders.* Irvine, CA: Care Institute.

Collins, James J., ed. 1981. *Drinking and Crime: Perspectives on the Relationships Between Alcohol Consumption and Criminal Behavior.* New York: Guilford Press.

Collins, James J., Robert L. Hubbard, J. Valley Raschal, E. R. Cavanaugh, and S. G. Craddock. 1982a. *Criminal Justice Clients in Drug Treatment*. Research Triangle Park, NC: Research Triangle Institute.

———. 1982b. *Client Characteristics, Behaviors and Intreatment Outcomes: 1980 TOPS Admission Cohort*. Research Triangle Park, NC: Research Triangle Institute.

Courtwright, David T. 1982. *Dark Paradise: Opiate Addiction in America before 1940*. Cambridge: Harvard University Press.

De Leon, George. 1985. "The Therapeutic Community: Status and Evolution," *International Journal of the Addictions* 20: 823–44.

———. 1989. "Psychopathology and Substance Abuse: What Is Being Learned in Therapeutic Communities," *Journal of Psychoactive Drugs* 21 (April–June): 177–88.

———. 1990. "Treatment Strategies." In *Handbook of Drug Control in the United States*, edited by James A. Inciardi. Westport, CT: Greenwood Press, 115–38.

De Leon, George, and James T. Ziegenfuss. 1986. *Therapeutic Communities for the Addictions*. Springfield, IL: Charles C. Thomas.

Drug Policy Foundation. 1992. *National Drug Reform Strategy*. Washington: Drug Policy Foundation.

DuPont, Robert L. 1984. *Getting Tough on Gateway Drugs*. Washington: American Psychiatric Press.

Erickson, Patricia G., Edward M. Adlaf, Glenn F. Murray, and Reginald G. Smart. 1987. *The Steel Drug: Cocaine in Perspective*. Lexington, MA: Lexington Books.

Faupel, Charles E. 1991. *Shooting Dope: Career Patterns of Hard-Core Heroin Users*. Gainesville: University of Florida Press.

Fiddle, Seymour. 1967. *Portraits from a Shooting Gallery*. New York: Harper & Row.

Fisher, Florrie. 1972. *The Lonely Trip Back*. New York: Bantam.

Fleisher, Mark S. 1989. *Warehousing Violence*. Newbury Park, CA: Sage.

Gerstein, Dean R., and Henrick J. Harwood, eds. 1990. *Treating Drug Problems*. Washington: National Academy Press.

Ginsberg, Allen. 1966. "The Great Marihuana Hoax: First Manifesto to End the Bringdown," *The Atlantic* (November): 107–12.

Goldstein, Paul J. 1979. *Prostitution and Drugs*. Lexington, MA: D.C. Heath.

———. 1985. "Drugs and Violent Behavior," *Journal of Drug Issues* 15: 493–506.

———. 1986. "Homicide Related to Drug Traffic," *Bulletin of the New York Academy of Medicine* 62 (June): 509–16.

Goodwin, Jean M., Katherine Cheeves, and Virginia Connell. 1990. "Borderline and Other Severe Symptoms in Adult Survivors of Incestuous Abuse," *Psychiatric Annals* 20 (January): 22–32.

Gorney, Beth. 1989. "Domestic Violence and Chemical Dependency: Dual Problems, Dual Interventions," *Journal of Psychoactive Drugs* 21 (April–June): 229–38.

Gould, Leroy, Andrew L. Walker, Lansing E. Crane, and Charles W. Litz. 1974. *Connections: Notes from the Heroin World.* New Haven, CT: Yale University Press.

Grabowski, John, ed. 1984. *Cocaine: Pharmacology, Effects, and Treatment of Abuse.* Rockville, MD: National Institute on Drug Abuse.

Greenberg, Stephanie W., and Freda Adler. 1974. "Crime and Addiction: An Empirical Analysis of the Literature, 1920–1973," *Contemporary Drug Problems* 3: 221–70.

Grinspoon, Lester. 1971. *Marihuana Reconsidered.* Cambridge: Harvard University Press.

Grinspoon, Lester, and James B. Bakalar. 1985. *Cocaine: A Drug and Its Social Evolution.* New York: Basic Books.

Hanson, R. Karl. 1990. "The Psychological Impact of Sexual Assault on Women and Children: A Review," *Annals of Sex Research* 3: 187–232.

Hapgood, Hutchins. 1903. *The Autobiography of a Thief.* New York: Fox, Duffield.

Hendin, Herbert, Ann Pollinger Haas, Paul Singer, Melvin Ellner, and Richard Ulman. 1987. *Living High: Daily Marijuana Use Among Adults.* New York: Human Sciences Press.

Hirsch, Phil. 1968. *Hooked.* New York: Pyramid.

Hubbard, Robert L., Mary Ellen Marsden, J. Valley Rachal, Henrick J. Harwood, Elizabeth R. Cavanaugh, and Harold M. Ginzburg. 1989. *Drug Abuse Treatment: A National Study of Effectiveness.* Chapel Hill: University of North Carolina Press.

Inciardi, James A. 1979. "Heroin Use and Street Crime," *Crime and Delinquency* 25 (July): 335–46.

———. 1980. "Youth, Drugs, and Street Crime." In *Drugs and the Youth Culture,* edited by Frank R. Scarpitti and Susan K. Datesman. Beverly Hills, CA: Sage, 175–203.

———. 1986. *The War on Drugs: Heroin, Cocaine, Crime, and Public Policy.* Palo Alto, CA: Mayfield.

———. 1987. "Sociology and American Drug Policy," *American Sociologist* 18 (Summer): 179–88.

————. 1990. "Sociology and the Legalization of Drugs: Some Considerations for the Continuing Policy Debate." Paper presented at the 85th Annual Meeting of the American Sociological Association, 11–15 August, Washington, D.C.

————. 1991. "Kingrats, Chicken Heads, Slow Necks, Freaks, and Blood Suckers: A Glimpse at the Miami Sex for Crack Market." Paper presented at the Annual Meeting of the Society for Applied Anthropology, Charleston, South Carolina, 13–17 March.

————. 1992. *The War on Drugs II: The Continuing Epic of Heroin, Cocaine, Crack, Crime, AIDS, and Public Policy.* Mountain View, CA: Mayfield.

Inciardi, James A., Dorothy Lockwood, and Anne E. Pottieger. 1991. "Crack Dependent Women and Sexuality," *Addiction and Recovery* 11 (July–August): 25–28.

————. 1993. *Women and Crack-Cocaine.* New York: Macmillan.

Inciardi, James A., Steven S. Martin, Dorothy Lockwood, Robert M. Hooper, and Bruce M. Wald. 1990. "Obstacles to the Implementation of Drug Treatment Programs in Correctional Settings," National Institute on Drug Abuse Technical Review on Drug Abuse Treatment in Prisons and Jails, Rockville, Maryland, 24–25.

Inciardi, James A., and Duane C. McBride. 1989. "Legalization: A High Risk Alternative in the War on Drugs," *American Behavioral Scientist* 32 (January–February): 259–89.

————. 1991. *Treatment Alternatives to Street Crime (TASC): History, Experiences, and Issues.* Rockville, MD: National Institute on Drug Abuse.

Inciardi, James A., Duane C. McBride, Anne E. Pottieger, Brian R. Russe, and Harvey A. Siegal. 1978. *Legal and Illicit Drugs: Acute Reactions of Emergency Room Populations.* New York: Praeger.

Inciardi, James A., and Anne E. Pottieger. 1986. "Drug Use and Crime Among Two Cohorts of Women Narcotics Users: An Empirical Assessment," *Journal of Drug Issues* 16 (Winter): 91–106.

Inciardi, James A., and Brian R. Russe. 1977. "Professional Thieves and Drugs," *International Journal of the Addictions* 12: 1087–95.

Inciardi, James A., and Frank R. Scarpitti. 1992. "Therapeutic Communities in Corrections: An Overview." Paper presented at the Annual Meeting of the Academy of Criminal Justice Sciences, Pittsburgh, 10–14 March.

Ingram, George. 1930. *Hell's Kitchen.* London: Jenkins.

Irwin, Will. 1909. *The Confessions of a Con Man.* New York: B.W. Huebsch.

Johnson, Bruce D., Paul J. Goldstein, Edward Preble, James Schmeidler, Douglas S. Lipton, Barry Spunt, and Thomas Miller. 1985. *Taking Care of Business: The Economics of Crime by Heroin Users.* Lexington, MA: Lexington Books.

Johnson, Robert. 1987. *Hard Time: Understanding and Reforming the Prison.* Monterey, CA: Brooks/Cole.

Jones, Helen C., and Paul W. Lovinger. 1985. *The Marijuana Question.* New York: Dodd, Mead.

Karel, Richard B. 1991. "A Model Legalization Proposal." In *The Drug Legalization Debate*, edited by James A. Inciardi. Newbury Park, CA: Sage, 80–102.

King, Rufus. 1972. *The Drug Hang-Up: America's Fifty Year Folly.* New York: W. W. Norton.

———. 1974. "The American System: Legal Sanctions to Repress Drug Abuse." In *Drugs and the Criminal Justice System*, edited by James A. Inciardi and Carl D. Chambers. Beverly Hills, CA: Sage, 22.

Knight, Arthur, and Kim Knight, eds. 1988. *Kerouac and the Beats: A Primary Sourcebook.* New York: Paragon House.

Koester, Stephen, and Judith Schwartz. 1991. "Crack Cocaine and Sex." *Paper presented at the Annual Meeting of the Society for Applied Anthropology*, Charleston, South Carolina, 13–17 March.

Kozel, Nicholas J., and Edgar H. Adams, eds. 1985. *Cocaine Use in America: Epidemiologic and Clinical Perspectives.* Rockville, MD: National Institute on Drug Abuse.

Leukefeld, Carl G., and Frank M. Tims, eds. 1988. *Compulsory Treatment of Drug Abuse: Research and Clinical Practice.* Rockville, MD: National Institute on Drug Abuse.

Lichtenstein, Perry M. 1914. "Narcotic Addiction," *New York Medical Journal* 100 (November 14): 962–66.

Lindesmith, Alfred R. 1937. *The Nature of Opiate Addiction.* Unpublished Ph.D. dissertation, University of Chicago.

———. 1938. "A Sociological Theory of Drug Addiction," *American Journal of Sociology* 43: 593–613.

———. 1940. " 'Dope Fiend' Mythology," *Journal of Criminal Law and Criminology* 31: 199–208.

———. 1947. *Opiate Addiction.* Evanston, IL: Principia Press.

———. 1956. "Editorial," *The Nation* 21 (April): 337.

———. 1965. *The Addict and the Law.* Bloomington: Indiana University Press.

Lipton, Douglas S. 1989. "The Theory of Rehabilitation as Applied to

Addict Offenders." (New York: Narcotic and Drug Research, Inc., unpublished.)

Lipton, Douglas S., and Harry K. Wexler. 1988. "Breaking the Drugs-Crime Connection," *Corrections Today* (August): 144, 146, 155.

Lipton, Lawrence. 1959. *The Holy Barbarians.* New York: Julian Messner.

Macdonald, Donald Ian. 1988. "Marijuana Smoking Worse for Lungs," *Journal of the American Medical Association* 259 (17 June): 3384.

Maurer, David W., and Victor H. Vogel. 1967. *Narcotics and Narcotic Addiction*, 3rd ed. Springfield, IL: Charles C. Thomas.

McBride, Duane C. 1981. "Drugs and Violence." In *The Drugs-Crime Connection*, edited by James A. Inciardi. Beverly Hills, CA: Sage, 105–23.

McBride, Duane C., and A. L. Bennett. 1978. "The Impact of Criminal Justice Diversion on a Community Drug Treatment Structure," *Drug Forum* 8: 8–18.

McBride, Duane C., and Clyde B. McCoy. 1982. "Crime and Drugs: The Issues and the Literature," *Journal of Drug Issues* 12 (Spring): 137–52.

McDarrah, Fred W. 1985. *Kerouac & Friends: A Beat Generation Album.* New York: William Morrow.

McLellan, A. Thomas, Lester Luborsky, George E. Woody, Charles P. O'Brien, and Ruben Kron. 1981. "Are the 'Addiction-Related' Problems of Substance Abusers Really Related?" *Journal of Nervous and Mental Disease* 169: 232–39.

Meek, Patricia S., H. Westley Clark, and Virginia L. Solana. 1989. "Neurocognitive Impairment: An Unrecognized Component of Dual Diagnosis in Substance Abuse Treatment," *Journal of Psychoactive Drugs* 21 (April–June): 153–60.

Michelsen, Twain. 1940. "Lindesmith's Mythology," *Journal of Criminal Law and Criminology* 31: 373–400.

Miles, Barry. 1989. *Ginsberg: A Biography.* New York: Simon and Schuster.

Milkman, Harvey, and Stanley Sunderwirth. 1987. *Craving for Ecstasy: The Consciousness and Chemistry of Escape.* Lexington, MA: Lexington Books.

Miller, Richard Lawrence. 1991. *The Case for Legalizing Drugs.* Westport, CT: Praeger.

Mitchell, Chester Nelson. 1990. *The Drug Solution.* Ottawa: Carleton University Press.

Morgan, H. Wayne. 1974. *Yesterday's Addicts: American Society and Drug Abuse, 1865–1929.* Norman: University of Oklahoma Press.

Muth, Henry. 1902. "Drug Abuse." Proceedings of the 9th Annual Meeting of the International Association of Chiefs of Police, 7–10 May.

Nadelmann, Ethan A. 1987. "The Real International Drug Problem." Paper presented at the Defense Academic Research Support Conference, "International Drugs: Threat and Response," National Defense College, Defense Intelligence Analysis Center, Washington, D.C., 2–3 June.

———. 1988a. "The Case for Legalization," *The Public Interest* 92 (Summer): 3–31.

———. 1988b. "U.S. Drug Policy: A Bad Export," *Foreign Policy* 70 (Spring): 83–108.

———. 1988c. "Testimony." In U.S. Congress. House. Select Committee on Narcotics Abuse and Control. *Hearings on Legalization of Illicit Drugs: Impact and Feasibility.* 100th Cong., 2d sess. 29 September.

———. 1989. "Drug Prohibition in the United States, Costs, Consequences, and Alternatives," *Science* 245 (1 September): 939–47.

National Association of State Alcohol and Drug Abuse Directors. 1989. *Measuring TASC Program Compliance with Established TASC Critical Elements and Performance Standards.* Washington: National Association of State Alcohol and Drug Abuse Directors.

National Institute on Drug Abuse. 1986. *Drug Abuse Warning Network Facility History File.* Rockville, MD: National Institute on Drug Abuse.

———. 1991a. *Annual Emergency Room Data From the Drug Abuse Warning Network.* Rockville, MD: National Institute on Drug Abuse.

———. 1991b. *Annual Medical Examiner Data From the Drug Abuse Warning Network.* Rockville, MD: National Institute on Drug Abuse.

National Institute of Justice. 1989. *Drug Use Forecasting.* Washington: National Institute of Justice.

———. 1990. *DUF: Drug Use Forecasting Annual Report.* Washington: National Institute of Justice.

Newcomb, Michael D., and Peter M. Bentler. 1988. *Consequences of Adolescent Drug Use: Impact on the Lives of Young Adults.* Newbury Park, CA: Sage.

Nowinski, Joseph. 1990. *Substance Abuse in Adolescents and Young Adults: A Guide to Treatment*. New York: W. W. Norton.

Nurco, David N., John C. Ball, John W. Shaffer, and Thomas F. Hanlon. 1985. "The Criminality of Narcotic Addicts," *Journal of Nervous and Mental Disease* 173: 94–102.

Nurco, David N., Timothy W. Kinlock, and Thomas E. Hanlon. 1990. "The Drugs-Crime Connection." In *Handbook of Drug Control in the United States*, edited by James A. Inciardi. Westport, CT: Greenwood Press, 71–90.

Nyswander, Marie. 1956. *The Drug Addict as a Patient*. New York: Grune & Stratton.

O'Donnell, John A. 1967. "The Rise and Decline of a Subculture," *Social Problems* 14: 73–84.

Office of National Drug Control Policy. 1990a. *Leading Drug Indicators*. ONDCP White Paper. Washington: The White House.

————. 1990b. *Understanding Drug Treatment*. Washington: The White House.

Onken, Lisa Simon, and Jack D. Blaine, eds. 1990. *Psychotherapy and Counseling in the Treatment of Drug Abuse*. Rockville, MD: National Institute on Drug Abuse.

Peele, Stanton. 1985. *The Meaning of Addiction*. Lexington, MA: Lexington Books.

Platt, Jerome J. 1986. *Heroin Addiction*. Malabar, FL: Robert E. Krieger.

Platt, Jerome J., Charles D. Kaplan, and Patricia Mc Kim, eds. 1990. *The Effectiveness of Drug Abuse Treatment: Dutch and American Perspectives*. Malabar, FL: Robert E. Krieger.

Ratner, Mitchell. 1993. *Crack Pipe as Pimp: An Ethnographic Investigation of Sex-for-Crack Exchanges*. New York: Lexington Books.

Regier, Darrel A., Mary E. Farmer, Donald S. Rae, Ben Z. Locke, Samuel J. Keith, Lewis L. Judd, and Frederick K. Goodwin. 1990. "Comorbidity of Mental Disorders with Alcohol and Other Drug Abuse: Results from the Epidemiologic Catchment Area (ECA) Study," *Journal of the American Medical Association* 264 (November 21): 2511–18.

Rettig, Richard P., Manual J. Torres, and Gerald R. Garrett. 1977. *Manny: A Criminal-Addict's Story*. Boston: Houghton Mifflin.

Rosenbaum, Marsha. 1981. *Women on Heroin*. New Brunswick, NJ: Rutgers University Press.

Ruth, Eric. 1992. "Leap Day: It's All in the Timing," Wilmington (Delaware) *News-Journal*, 29 February, 1A.

Satel, Sally L., Lawrence H. Price, Joseph M. Palumbo, Christopher J. McDougle, John H. Krystal, Frank Gawin, Dennis S. Charney, George R. Heninger, and Herbert D. Kleber. 1991. "Clinical Phenomenology and Neurobiology of Cocaine Abstinence: A Prospective Inpatient Study," *American Journal of Psychiatry* 148 (December): 1712–16.

Schlenger, William E., Larry A. Kroutil, and E. Joyce Roland. 1992. "Case Management as a Mechanism for Linking Drug Abuse Treatment and Primary Care: Preliminary Evidence from the ADAMHA/HRSA Linkage Demonstration," National Institute on Drug Abuse Technical Review Meeting on Case Management, 4–5 February, Bethesda, Maryland.

Schmoke, Kurt L. 1989. "Forward," *American Behavioral Scientist* 32 (January–February): 231–32.

Scott, Wellington. 1916. *Seventeen Years in the Underworld*. New York: Abingdon Press.

Sharpe, May. 1928. *Chicago May*. New York: Macaulay.

Siegel, Ronald K. 1989. *Intoxication: Life in Pursuit of Artificial Paradise*. New York: E.P. Dutton.

Simpson, D. Dwayne, and Saul B. Sells, eds. 1990. *Opioid Addiction and Treatment: A 12-Year Follow-Up*. Malabar, FL: Robert E. Krieger.

Sloman, Larry. 1979. *Reefer Madness: The History of Marijuana in America*. Indianapolis: Bobbs-Merrill.

Smith, David E., ed. 1970. *The New Social Drug: Cultural, Medical, and Legal Perspectives on Marijuana*. Englewood Cliffs, NJ: Prentice-Hall.

Smith, David E., and George R. Gay, eds. 1971. *"It's So Good, Don't Even Try It Once."* Englewood Cliffs, NJ: Prentice-Hall.

Spencer, John W., and John J. Boren, eds. 1990. *Residual Effects of Abused Drugs on Behavior*. Rockville, MD: National Institute on Drug Abuse.

Spitz, Henry I., and Jeffrey S. Rosecan. 1987. *Cocaine Abuse: New Directions in Treatment and Research*. New York: Brunner/Mazel.

Spotts, James V., and Franklin C. Shontz. 1980. *Cocaine Users: A Representative Case Approach*. New York: Free Press.

Steinmetz, George. 1992. "Fetal Alcohol Syndrome," *National Geographic* 181 (February): 36–39.

Stephens, Richard C., and Duane C. McBride. 1976. "Becoming a Street Addict," *Human Organization* 35: 87–93.

Stoffelmayr, Bertram E., Lois A. Benishek, and Keith Humphreys.

1989. "Substance Abuse Prognosis With an Additional Psychiatric Diagnosis: Understanding the Relationship," *Journal of Psychoactive Drugs* 21 (April–June): 145–52.

Street, Leroy. 1953. *I Was a Drug Addict*. New York: Random House.

Sukenick, Ronald. 1987. *Down and In: Life in the Underground*. New York: William Morrow.

Sutherland, Edwin H. 1937. *The Professional Thief*. Chicago: University Press.

System Sciences. 1979. *Evaluation of Treatment Alternatives to Street Crime: National Evaluation Program, Phase II Report*. Washington: National Institute of Law Enforcement and Criminal Justice.

Szasz, Thomas S. 1961. *The Myth of Mental Illness: Foundations of a Theory of Personal Conduct*. New York: Hoeber-Harper.

———. 1963. *Law, Liberty, and Psychiatry: An Inquiry into the Social Uses of Mental Health Practices*. New York: Macmillan.

———. 1965. *Psychiatric Justice*. New York: Macmillan.

———. 1970. *The Manufacture of Madness: A Comparative Study of the Inquisition and the Mental Health Movement*. New York: Harper & Row.

———. 1974. *Ceremonial Chemistry: The Ritual Persecution of Drugs, Addicts, and Pushers*. Garden City, NY: Doubleday.

———. 1992. *Our Right to Drugs: The Case for a Free Market*. Westport, CT: Praeger.

Terry, Charles E., and Mildred Pellens. 1928. *The Opium Problem*. New York: Bureau of Social Hygiene.

Tiger, Lionel. 1992. *The Pursuit of Pleasure*. Boston: Little, Brown.

Tobolska-Rydz, H. 1986. "Problems of Drug Abuse and Prevention Measures in Poland," *Bulletin on Narcotics* 38: 99–104.

Toborg, Mary A., D. R. Levin, Robert H. Milkman, and L. J. Center. 1976. *Treatment Alternatives to Street Crime (TASC) Projects: National Evaluation Program, Phase I Summary Report*. Washington: National Institute of Law Enforcement and Criminal Justice.

Toch, Hans, ed. 1980. *Therapeutic Communities in Corrections*. New York: Praeger.

Trebach, Arnold S. 1982. *The Heroin Solution*. New Haven, CT: Yale University Press.

———. 1987. *The Great Drug War*. New York: Macmillan.

———. 1989. "Tough Choices: The Practical Politics of Drug Policy Reform," *American Behavioral Scientist* 32 (January–February): 249–58.

References 219

———. 1990. "A Bundle of Peaceful Compromises," *Journal of Drug Issues* 20 (Fall): 515–31.

Turner, T. H., and David S. Tofler. 1986. "Indicators of Psychiatric Disorder Among Women Admitted to Prison," *British Medical Journal* 292 (March): 651–53.

Tyon, Linda P. 1988. *Final Report: Baseline Management and Assessment Data Project.* Portland, OR: National Consortium of TASC Programs.

United States Treasury Department. 1939. *The Traffic in Opium and Other Dangerous Drugs.* Washington: U.S. Government Printing Office.

Van Pelt, Dina. 1991. "AIDS Patients Seek a Legal High," *Insight* 14 (January): 50–51.

Viorst, Milton. 1979. *Fire in the Streets: America in the 1960s.* New York: Simon and Schuster.

Wallace, Barbara C. 1991. *Crack Cocaine: A Practical Treatment Approach for the Chemically Dependent.* New York: Brunner/Mazel.

Wallen, Mark C., and Harvey D. Weiner. 1989. "Impediments to Effective Treatment of the Dually Diagnosed Patient," *Journal of Psychoactive Drugs* 21 (April–June): 161–68.

Walsh, Gerard P. 1981. *Opium and Narcotic Laws.* Washington: United States Government Printing Office.

Washton, Arnold W. 1989. *Cocaine Addiction: Treatment, Recovery, and Relapse Prevention.* New York: W. W. Norton.

Washton, Arnold W., and Mark S. Gold, eds. 1987. *Cocaine: A Clinician's Handbook.* New York: Guilford Press.

Weiss, Roger D., and Daniel A. Collins. 1992. "Substance Abuse and Psychiatric Illness: The Dually Diagnosed Patient," *American Journal on Addictions* 1 (Spring): 93–99.

Weiss, Roger D., and Steven M. Mirin. 1987. *Cocaine.* Washington: American Psychiatric Press.

Werner, J. 1909. "The Illegal Sale of Cocaine." Proceedings of the 16th Annual Meeting of the International Association of Chiefs of Police, 15–18 June.

Wexler, Harry K., and Ronald Williams. 1986. "The Stay 'N Out Therapeutic Community: Prison Treatment for Substance Abusers," *Journal of Psychoactive Drugs* 18 (July–September): 221–30.

White, George M. 1907. *From Boniface to Bank Burglar.* New York: Seaboard.

Winfield, Idee, Linda K. George, Marvin Swartz, and Dan G. Blazer.

1990. "Sexual Assault and Psychiatric Disorders Among A Community Sample of Women," *American Journal of Psychiatry* 147 (March): 335–41.

Wisotsky, Steven. 1986. *Breaking the Impasse in the War on Drugs.* Westport, CT: Greenwood Press.

————. 1987. "Crackdown: The Emerging 'Drug Exception' to the Bill of Rights," *Hastings Law Journal* 38 (July): 889–926.

————. 1988. "Testimony." In U.S. Congress. House. Select Committee on Narcotics Abuse and Control. *Hearings on Legalization of Illicit Drugs: Impact and Feasibility.* 100th Cong., 2d Sess., 29 September.

Wolfe, Harriet L., and James L. Sorensen. 1989. "Dual Diagnosis Patients in the Urban Psychiatric Emergency Room," *Journal of Psychoactive Drugs* 21 (April–June): 169–76.

Yablonsky, Lewis. 1989. *The Therapeutic Community: A Successful Approach for Treating Substance Abusers.* New York: Gardner Press.

Yost, Orin Ross. 1964. *The Bane of Drug Addiction.* New York: Macmillan.

Index of Names

Index of Subjects

University of Delaware. *See* Center
for Drug and Alcohol Studies
USA Today, 32, 189

Valium, 76, 179
Violence, 111, 188–90. *See also* Alcohol; Crime

War on drugs, *x*, 7, 9, 14, 16, 23, 31,
33–37, 75–76, 78, 99, 107, 149,

154, 175, 198, 204. *See also* Drug
enforcement
Washington, D.C.: crime in, 70, 72,
190
Webb v. U.S., 183
"Weed and Seed" program, 36, 39
White House Office of National Drug
Control Policy, 15–16, 33, 52,
100, 150, 197–98
Women: drug use and, 50, 55–56, 58,
61, 65, 117–18, 150–51, 177–80,
185–87. *See also* Prostitution